HUMANITARIAN INTERVENTION AND INTERNATIONAL RELATIONS

Humanitarian Intervention and International Relations

Edited by

Jennifer M. Welsh

OXFORD

UNIVERSITY PRESS

OXFORD
UNIVERSITY PRESS

Great Clarendon Street, Oxford OX2 6DP

Oxford University Press is a department of the University of Oxford.

It furthers the University's objective of excellence in research, scholarship,
and education by publishing worldwide in

Oxford New York

Auckland Bangkok Buenos Aires Cape Town Chennai
Dar es Salaam Delhi Hong Kong Istanbul Karachi Kolkata
Kuala Lumpur Madrid Melbourne Mexico City Mumbai Nairobi
São Paulo Shanghai Taipei Tokyo Toronto

Oxford is a registered trade mark of Oxford University Press
in the UK and in certain other countries

Published in the United States
by Oxford University Press Inc., New York

British Library Cataloguing in publication Data

Data available

Library of Congress Cataloging in Publication Data

Data available

ISBN 0-19-926721-9

3 5 7 9 10 8 6 4 2

Typeset by Newgen Imaging Systems (P) Ltd., Chennai, India
Printed in Great Britain
on acid-free paper by
Biddles Ltd., King's Lynn, Norfolk

CONTENTS

Contents

NOTES ON CONTRIBUTORS

Dr Simon Chesterman is a Senior Associate at the International Peace Academy in New York, where he directs a research project on international administrations. He is the author of *Just War? Just Peace? Humanitarian Intervention and International Law* (Oxford University Press, 2001) and the editor of *Civilians in War* (Lynne Rienner, 2001).

Ian Martin was Special Representative of the United Nations Secretary-General for the East Timor Popular Consultation, May–November 1999, and head of the UN Mission in East Timor (UNAMET).

Prof. James Mayall FBA is Professor of International Relations at Cambridge University, and author of *World Politics: Progress and its Limits* (Polity Press, 2001). He is the author of several works on international relations theory, and editor of *The New Interventionism 1991–1994: United Nations Experience in Cambodia, Former Yugoslavia and Somalia* (Cambridge University Press, 1996). A new co-edited book has just been published—*International Human Rights in the Twenty-First Century: Protecting the Rights of Groups*, ed. with Gene Lyons (Rowman and Littlefield, 2003).

Nicholas Morris is a former Inspector General of the UN High Commissioner for Refugees and was the UNHCR's Special Envoy in the former Yugoslavia in 1993–4 and 1998–9.

Sir Adam Roberts is the Montague Burton Professor of International Relations at Oxford University, and a Fellow of Balliol College. He is co-editor, with Benedict Kingsbury, of *United Nations, Divided World: The UN's Roles in International Relations*, rev. edition (Oxford University Press, 1993). He is the author of several articles on international humanitarian law, and the co-editor, with Richard Guelff, of *Documents on the Laws of War*, 3rd edn (Oxford University Press, 2000).

Prof. Henry Shue is Professor of Politics and International Relations at the University of Oxford and Senior Research Fellow in Philosophy at Merton College, Oxford. Best known for *Basic Rights* (Princeton University Press, 2nd edn, 1996/1980), he is currently writing primarily about ethical issues in the conduct of contemporary warfare and about international justice as it arises within international cooperation to slow climate change.

Dr Jennifer Welsh is University Lecturer in International Relations at Oxford University, and a Fellow of Somerville College, Oxford. She is the author of

Edmund Burke and International Relations (Macmillan, 1995). She has also written on various aspects of international relations theory and European security.

Dr Nicholas J. Wheeler is Reader in the Department of International Politics at the University of Wales, Aberystwyth. He is the author of *Saving Strangers: Humanitarian Intervention and International Society* (Oxford University Press, 2000). Dr Wheeler has written widely on normative questions in international society, and is co-editor, with Timothy Dunne, of *Human Rights in Global Politics* (Cambridge University Press, 1999).

ACKNOWLEDGEMENTS

The idea for this project on humanitarian intervention emerged during a conversation in an Oxford pub with two of my colleagues, David Williams and Neil MacFarlane. I am grateful to both of them for helping me to see that the most interesting issues surrounding humanitarian intervention are not questions of 'right', but rather the agonizing moral and political trade-offs that states make in contemporary world politics.

Neil MacFarlane also supported me as co-chair in the seminar series from which these chapters draw. True to form, his comments and questions in the chair were sceptical and penetrating, and helped to put the process of paper revision on the right track. I would also like to thank all those who acted as discussants for the papers in their earlier renditions: Andrew Hurrell, Richard Crampton, Sir Marrack Goulding, Timothy Garton Ash, Peter Carey, Richard Caplan, Jane Boulden, and Michael Byers.

The Centre for International Studies and the Cyril Foster Fund generously supported both the seminar series and edited book. Mark Philp, Department Head for Politics and International Relations, encouraged my research and facilitated some much-needed sabbatical leave.

In the book preparation phase, I relied heavily on the expertise, efficiency, and good humour of my research assistant—and friend—Carolin Thielking. Her knowledge of the broad subject area of human rights and humanitarian intervention proved invaluable to the overall project, and particularly to my own chapter.

I must also thank the Politics Editor at Oxford University Press, Dominic Byatt, who was enthusiastic from the outset and nudged me very gently toward completion. Desmond King, of Nuffield College, was a quiet supporter in the background and no doubt helped to forge my new relationship with OUP.

Finally, I express my gratitude to all those in the Oxford community who, in one form or another, have supported me in my work over the past four years. Aside from those I list above, I would like to single out Anne Deighton, Rosemary Foot, Eddie Keene, Kalypso Nicolaidis, Avi Shlaim, and Ngaire Woods. Special thanks go to my PPE colleagues at Somerville College, who have done so much to make me feel welcome in my new home: Lesley Brown, Judith Heyer, James Logue, and most of all Lois McNay.

Oxford
March 2003

1

Introduction

Jennifer M. Welsh

The issue of humanitarian intervention has generated one of the most heated discussions in international relations over the past decade—among both theorists and practitioners. At the heart of the debate is the alleged tension between the principle of state sovereignty, a defining pillar of the United Nations (UN) system and international law, and the evolving international norms related to human rights and the use of force.

This edited collection investigates the controversial place of humanitarian intervention in international society through the lenses of theory and practice. Although the subject has gained greater prominence, it continues to have an uneasy relationship with both the major schools of thought in the discipline of IR, and the behaviour of states, international organizations, and non-governmental actors.[1] Many academic discussions focus on the question of whether there is a legal right of humanitarian intervention,[2] giving insufficient attention to the underlying ethical issues, the politics within international organizations and coalitions, and the practical dilemmas faced by international actors—before, during, and after intervention.

The book is the culmination of a series of seminars that were held at the University of Oxford in October–December 2001, and reflects subsequent revisions by and discussion among the contributing authors. It includes chapters by well-known academics from the disciplines of law, philosophy, and international relations, as well as those who have been actively engaged in instances of intervention during the past decade. The cases covered include those which took place in the early years of the post cold war period, such as Somalia and Bosnia, as well as the intervention in 2001 to root out terrorists in Afghanistan. Indeed, as our series began, the world was still reeling from the horrific terrorist attacks on New York and Washington and preparing for the military campaign against the Taliban. The final product here analyses how the issue of humanitarian intervention is evolving in a post-11 September world.

Three main themes unify the book. The first is the expansion of intervention. While very few interventions for humanitarian purposes occurred during the cold war, the 1990s witnessed a series of military actions explicitly supported by humanitarian rationale. In these cases, the apparent conflict between sovereignty and human rights has been addressed in two ways: through an evolution in the notion of sovereignty, from 'sovereignty as authority' (control over territory) to 'sovereignty as responsibility' (respect for a minimum standard of human rights); and through an expanded definition of what constitutes a 'threat to international peace and security' under chapter VII of the United Nations Charter. As a result of the first move, massive violations of human rights inside the domestic jurisdiction of a state have been transformed into a matter of international concern; as a result of the second, the UN can legitimately authorize international action to address security threats that emerge from humanitarian crises.

Several features of contemporary international relations provide added impetus to those calling for more interventionism: the weakness (or complete failure) of state structures in many conflict-ridden societies, which provides opportunity for criminal activity, arms proliferation, and terrorism; the increased vulnerability of civilians in the context of civil conflict, and the intensification of refugee flows; the 'CNN effect', in which global and instantaneous access to information heightens popular awareness of human suffering; the strengthening of human rights norms and proliferation of human rights organizations; the strengthening of international institutions, regional and global, which increases the possibility of states acting on a multilateral basis; and the search by Western governments for new forms of political legitimacy and 'moral authority' to replace the ideologically driven agenda of the cold war. In short, today's debate about the legitimacy of intervention is being conducted in a climate of heightened expectations for action.

Second, despite this new climate of permissiveness, humanitarian intervention remains a controversial norm in international relations—largely because of continued opposition from certain members of international society, and concerns about its potentially negative consequences. These consequences include the impact on the norms of territorial integrity and non-intervention, the creation of unrealistic expectations on the part of oppressed peoples, the negative side effects arising from the use of force, and the potential for long-term 'occupation' by the intervening power. The ambiguous status of the norm is reflected in the cases examined in this book, and the varying degrees to which they conform to a 'classic' understanding of humanitarian intervention.

The third theme is that humanitarian interventions are plagued by problems of will and capacity. While the 1990s saw some successful cases of intervention to address humanitarian catastrophes (such as East Timor), the current capability of international organizations to undertake humanitarian interventions remains limited. In fact, as the book demonstrates, the issue of humanitarian intervention has the potential to divide international institutions such as the UN and damage their credibility. It has also posed new challenges for humanitarian organizations, whose neutrality has been compromised in cases such as Kosovo and Afghanistan. This mixed record of success has, in turn, led to caution on the part of international actors about engaging in military action for humanitarian purposes. As a result, humanitarian intervention is likely to remain an exceptional practice in international society in the coming decades.

1.1   The terms of debate

One of the greatest analytical challenges posed by humanitarian intervention is the variation in how it is defined. Indeed, the field of the analyst (law, ethics, or politics) can often influence the definition that is chosen. The most contentious areas of debate are whether humanitarian intervention is limited to instances where there is an absence of consent from the host state; whether humanitarian intervention is limited to punishment actions—as opposed to actions designed to facilitate the delivery of humanitarian assistance; and whether humanitarian intervention is limited to instances where there has been explicit Security Council authorization for action.

From the standpoint of international law, narrowing the discussion of humanitarian intervention has proven essential to establishing the status of the 'right'.[3] For our purposes, however, it is important to consider the range of actions and cases that have been motivated by humanitarian concerns, even if some do not fully respect the legal definition of humanitarian intervention. What the cases from the 1990s demonstrate is that the legal requirement of 'non-consent' is in practice very difficult to maintain—particularly when consent is ambiguous or coerced. Consequently, our definition will encompass certain interventions for humanitarian purposes that had, at least for some part of their duration, a degree of consent from the host state's government, if not necessarily from all parties and factions. On the other hand, while the term 'humanitarian intervention' has sometimes been used, especially by relief agencies, to refer to any major humanitarian action in an emergency situation, our definition will restrict its meaning to cases where military force is involved. Finally, on the question of authorization, this volume will look at both UN-sanctioned and so-called unilateral humanitarian interventions. Though the latter type has driven much of the controversy over humanitarian intervention,[4] we believe there are important theoretical and practical issues associated with those military actions that received Security Council endorsement.

In subsequent chapters, the following definition of humanitarian intervention will be used: *coercive interference in the internal affairs of a state, involving the use of armed force, with the purposes of addressing massive human rights violations or preventing widespread human suffering.*

1.2   IR theory and humanitarian intervention

A variety of normative IR theorists have addressed the ethical dilemmas related to humanitarian intervention. Part One engages this literature, but also penetrates more deeply into how the various schools of thought in IR (particularly realism, constructivism, and international society) treat the issue of humanitarian intervention, and whether/how recent practice supports these approaches.

In Chapter 2, Henry Shue presents a passionate case for limiting the notion of sovereignty, drawing on both philosophical and historical arguments. His position rests on understanding how rights *necessarily* imply duties. For Shue, sovereignty is limited because the duties that are constitutive of the right—and without which there can be no right—constrain the activity of every sovereign belonging to international society. From this foundation, he demonstrates that one surprising limit on state sovereignty is dictated by the nature of fundamental individual rights.

Chapter 3, by Nicholas Wheeler, confronts two central issues in contemporary IR theory: the relationship between power and norms in international society, and changing conceptions of sovereignty since the end of the cold war. After demonstrating how norms constrain the behaviour of states, he goes on to assess the status of the norm of 'sovereignty as responsibility'. Wheeler argues that this norm has taken firm root in international society—evidenced by the language that states have used to justify humanitarian intervention. Nonetheless, he concludes that states are unlikely to translate the norm into codified criteria for a legitimate humanitarian intervention.

In Chapter 4, I evaluate the legal and ethical objections to humanitarian intervention, and argue that those focused on the consequences for international order are the most compelling. In so doing, I pay particular attention to the arguments of non-Western states and their concerns about 'neo-imperialism'. I conclude by supporting Shue's and Wheeler's contention that despite powerful objections, humanitarian intervention can be legitimized in extreme cases.

1.3   The politics and practice of humanitarian intervention

Part Two of the book looks at the practice of humanitarian intervention, first with respect to the UN system, and then through a series of examples from the last decade. A series of issues emerge from the case treatment.

1.3.1   Ends and rationale for action

First the cases illustrate the two main 'routes' to humanitarian intervention that have been taken since the end of the cold war: one through international human rights and the other through expanded notions of security. But they also demonstrate that, contrary to conventional wisdom, the conflict between sovereignty and individual rights is not clear-cut. As Nicholas Morris notes in Chapter 6, the Bosnian regime did consent to the original placement of UN forces, although they were designed for impartial peacekeeping. Similarly, as Ian Martin's discussion of East Timor shows, the Habibie government's consent was taken as a necessary condition before an international mission could proceed. Moreover, most instances of intervention in the post-cold war period have involved chapter VII Security Council resolutions that refer to the transborder effects of humanitarian crises. This suggests that states remain reluctant to assert that a human rights violation by a government against its own people is, *in itself*, a sufficient justification for the use of force.

The examples in this book also indicate that the rationale for intervention can shift during the course of military action. This was particularly evident in Somalia and Kosovo, where unanticipated consequences led the intervening states to change the objectives of the military mission—even to the point of obtaining additional Security Council resolutions. Such changes in ends and rationale pose challenges for intervening states in operational terms, but also require complex strategies for communicating with their domestic constituencies.

1.3.2   The politics of intervening

Understanding the political motivations behind humanitarian intervention is another important objective of this book. In some instances, key regional powers have taken the lead in lobbying the Security Council for action, as Australia did in the case of East Timor. In other situations, most notably Kosovo, humanitarian organizations such as UNHCR have performed a crucial role in providing evidence for Security Council discussions—leading some to question their independence and impartiality.[5] In at least two of the cases, East Timor and Somalia, strong domestic pressure and media attention played a critical part in convincing Western governments to act. As James Mayall describes in Chapter 7, all of these catalysts for action were absent in the biggest case of 'non-intervention' in the 1990s: Rwanda in 1994. Many of the book's contributors highlight this problem of selectivity in humanitarian intervention, and how it damages the credibility not only of the UN, but also of Western states.

The cases also demonstrate that limited capacity—in terms of personnel, finances, and political commitment—affects the likelihood and shape of interventions. This issue has become even more problematic as several of the interventions evolve into sustained peace-building efforts. The long-term presence of security forces, as well as the significant commitment of civilian expertise, have led some in the West to conclude that a non-interventionist posture is the right one.

Finally, 11 September and its aftermath has had a significant impact on the politics of humanitarian intervention. Afghanistan prior to 11 September could be regarded as another case of 'non-intervention'; despite the significant abuses of human rights (particularly the rights of women), the punitive measures taken by the West were confined to sanctions. The terrorist attacks on New York and Washington, however, changed the equation. As Simon Chesterman argues, while the bombing campaign was an act of self-defence—not a humanitarian intervention—it also sparked debate as to whether preventative actions should be taken to address the root causes of terrorism. Above all, the situation in Afghanistan demonstrated that state failure might have consequences wider than poverty and lawlessness for a state's own population. Addressing those consequences may, in the future, require a combined strategy of military action and civilian reconstruction.

1.3.3   Authorization

The question of who should, or who can, engage in humanitarian intervention has gained greater prominence in the aftermath of the NATO-led action in Kosovo. While international law on the use of force sanctions unilateral action for the purposes of self-defence, Security Council authorization (as outlined in Article 24 of the Charter) is legally required for other kinds of military action. *Ad hoc* 'coalitions of the willing', acting without UN endorsement, have dubious legal status. Furthermore, such efforts threaten to erode an important source of legitimacy in international society.

Nonetheless, as Adam Roberts shows in Chapter 5, the practice of intervention suggests that complete reliance on the Security Council could prove problematic for moral and practical reasons. First, as Kosovo illustrates, claims of illegality do not necessarily absolve those who have the power to act from their moral responsibilities. Second, today's UN is not yet a world government and has only rudimentary competence (legally and practically) to intervene in domestic crises. Indeed, the Security Council still lacks any clear set of criteria for deciding on humanitarian intervention—despite several attempts to try to develop them. Third, while one of the original purposes of the Security Council was to act as a guardian for international order, the behaviour of individual members of the Council is not always encouraging. This problem is exacerbated by the fact that the Security Council is viewed by some states as unrepresentative and a poor proxy for 'international will'. Finally, as James Mayall suggests in his Chapter, policymakers need to confront the possibility that unilateral action can be more timely and effective, especially if undertaken by regional powers with the right mix of knowledge and capability.

1.3.4 Consequences

The legitimacy of an intervention is often judged with reference to its consequences rather than its intentions. In short, there is nothing like success to silence one's critics. The cases reviewed in this book present a mixed story, leading the contributors toward some interesting conclusions. Nicholas Morris, for example, argues that a response whose primary purpose is to relieve human suffering may not be sustainable in conflicts involving serious violations of human rights: It will lose legitimacy the longer it continues without effective action to *prevent* suffering. Loss of legitimacy is likely to be most marked in situations where the creation of such suffering is a war aim, as it was in the Balkans, rather than a consequence of conflict. If the will for coercive military threats or action exists, Morris argues, a humanitarian intervention should have prevention and an end to the causes of suffering as its primary purpose. Civilian humanitarian relief may even need to be suspended during such an intervention. Otherwise, he suggests, the day-to-day activities of organizations such as UNHCR will be hampered by the international community's ambiguous intentions.

This book also addresses longer-term consequences. One of the notable features of humanitarian interventions in the post cold war era is the continued presence of international forces and administrators once the immediate crisis is over. As I suggest in Chapter 4, the real conflict between the imperative to intervene and the norm of state sovereignty comes not at the moment of coercive action, but rather in the aftermath, when the international community takes the target state into trusteeship. A recurring theme of our seminar series was that humanitarian interventions contain within them imperialist implications. A sustained international presence, while crucial to creating lasting stability, raises thorny questions not only about self-determination, but also about the accountability of Western-sponsored transitional authorities. If empire really is back, then decisions about whether to intervene in humanitarian crises will need to incorporate solutions to these new challenges.

PART ONE

International Relations Theory and
Humanitarian Intervention

2

Limiting Sovereignty

Henry Shue

2.1 Introduction

This chapter defends the thesis that if limits on how states may treat their own residents on their own territory are to be effective, states must also be limited, in specific ways, concerning which ill-treatment of residents within the territories of other states they are free to ignore. This relatively controversial burden on the external sovereignty of states follows, I will suggest, from a *relatively* uncontroversial feature of individual rights.

For discussions of military intervention, the sovereign state is still the salient unit, in spite of the fact that states are by no means the only important agents in international affairs.[1] The sovereign state is a historically recent and contingent form of human organization, invented in modern Europe and largely imposed by Europeans upon the remainder of the modern world; other civilizations have been organized in other ways, and even in the West sovereignty has served other purposes from the purposes it serves now (see Reus-Smit 1999). But contemporary sovereign states constitute a single, now-universal system. The good news, from my point of view, is that in principle the purposes of states, and the extent of their sovereignty, could be reformulated; other options are not simply conceivable but have actually functioned for long periods. The bad news is that, in fact, the current system has immense inertia and is supported by entrenched interests, many of which, including the attachments of individual persons I shall discuss in the final section of the chapter, it has itself deeply shaped. Still, it does not seem completely quixotic to articulate the moral case for partially modifying our understanding of the prerogatives of states; and the moral case is, I shall try

The original draft of this chapter was a paper entitled 'Conditional Sovereignty' written for the Working Group on Armed Intervention, convened by the Centre for Philosophy and Public Issues, University of Melbourne. I am grateful to Professor C. A. J. Coady for the invitation to participate and to both Tony Coady and Bruce Langtry for valuable suggestions regarding the original draft, as well as to Jennifer Welsh for her civilizing influence on the more unruly tendencies of the final draft.

to show, ready to be articulated. Consider, first, a prominent political theorist's warning against (what he thinks is) moralism.

2.2 Sovereignty as a right to do wrong

Writing about sovereignty and intervention with his customary provocativeness, Friedrich Kratochwil has remarked:

One of the most important implications of conceptualizing sovereignty as an analogon to dominium is that the exercise of this right is no longer easily defeasible by moral considerations of right and wrong...Having a 'right' conceived along the lines of Roman property rights simply entitled the holder of that right to 'do the wrong thing' as long as he was within his territorially limited domain...Although moral considerations are not irrelevant to an appraisal [of actions possibly targeted for intervention], the relevance of such considerations is clearly bounded by the *institutional* constraints imposed by the notion of an exclusive right [emphasis in original]   (Kratochwil 1995: 26, 33).

I take the gist of Kratochwil's thesis—credited by him to Grotius—to be that sovereignty is the kind of right that creates a space within which the bearer of the right is *sometimes* [my emphasis] free to do what is morally wrong. This seems correct and important, yet misleading if overemphasized. In the case of individual persons it is a well-known, although not entirely uncontroversial, position that a right to liberty includes being guaranteed liberty, for example, to be unkind to animals, insulting to colleagues, and unfaithful to friends, even in circumstances in which all these actions are clearly morally wrong. It is never right to do wrong, but one has a right to do it, sometimes.[2]

While the exercise of sovereignty is certainly not 'easily defeasible' by direct appeals to morality, the proper scope of sovereignty's exercise does change; and it could change partly in response to moral appeals. Kratochwil is correct to imply that the change may require two steps: one cannot merely say, 'this is wrong, so sovereigns are not allowed to do it', since sovereigns are understood to be free to do much that is wrong (as are individual persons). But one can say, (1) this (e.g. the extirpation of minorities) is so very wrong that even sovereigns should be understood in future not to be free to get away with it; and (2) once this is generally understood among sovereigns to be outside the scope of sovereignty, sovereigns ought not, according to the now-tightened rules of sovereignty, to do it in future. In other words, this action has now been removed from the list of wrongs that even they are free to commit.

A rule change *may* have to precede, in order to be the basis for, a demand for a behaviour change, but there is no reason why the rule change cannot be based, at least in part, on moral considerations.[3] Morality can require a change in the specification of a role, and the change in the specification of the role can then require a change in behaviour. The moral considerations influence behaviour indirectly by way of their effect on the role. Morality's work is indirect but not irrelevant. This does not contradict anything Kratochwil says, but it reverses what I take to be his emphases.

2.3   Sovereignty as limited

The content of sovereignty blinds us to its form, but its form imposes unseen limits on its content. I will begin by trying to explain, justify, and spell out practical implications of the obscure thesis just stated.

According to some heads of state, sovereignty is about each state's doing entirely as its current government pleases, at least within what it itself defines as its own territory. In their view, not only may the state sometimes do wrong, it may decide for itself what wrong it may do, without restriction. Yet not even the patron saints of this (distinctly Western) doctrine formulated it in such unqualified terms, even in its 'absolutist' forms. Moreover, attempts to state a doctrine of sovereignty without limits turn out to be quite literally incoherent. I shall look briefly at these two separate kinds of grounds, historical and conceptual, for judging that sovereignty was not originally intended to be, and indeed cannot be, unlimited, before turning at somewhat greater length to an exploration of one surprising kind of limit that minimal morality requires of it.

If we examine some of the classical theorists, we see that aspirations to sovereignty and non-intervention are tempered by considerations above and beyond the state. Hedley Bull, commenting on the approach of Christian Wolff, noted:

The reasons why collective intervention is preferable to unilateral take us back to the contention of Christian Wolff that intervention is acceptable when it is carried out by the *civitas maxima*. Ultimately, we have a rule of non-intervention because unilateral intervention threatens the harmony and concord of the society of sovereign states. If, however, an intervention itself expresses the collective will of the society of states, it may be carried out without bringing that harmony and concord into jeopardy.[4]

Nicholas Onuf finds the same recognition of limits in the writings of the Dutch international lawyer, Emmerich de Vattel:

Nonintervention is Vattel's second general law. 'The first general law, which is to be found in the very end of the society of nations, is that each Nation should contribute as far as it can to the happiness and advancement of other Nations.' By implication, Vattel's first general law expresses a positive duty of mutual aid, limited only by duties to one's own people, and not by the possibility that such assistance may be construed as intervention   (Onuf 1995: 43).

Thus, even for Wolff and Vattel, whose theoretical objective was to establish sovereign states as moral and legal entities, sovereignty was by no means a matter of each state's having some indefeasible and total discretion. In short, it is not unheard of—and, to the contrary, was the original idea—that sovereignty has limits.

Consider an even more abstract point, which has significant practical implications. In his imposing study John Vincent emphasized 'the function of the non-intervention principle as protector of state sovereignty' (Vincent 1974: 15). The connection was explained as follows:

> If a state has a right to sovereignty, this implies that other states have a duty to respect that right by, among other things, refraining from intervention in its domestic affairs...The function of the principle of nonintervention in international relations might be said, then, to be one of protecting the principle of state sovereignty (Vincent 1974: 14).

Vincent was utterly correct: non-intervention does protect sovereignty. However, the story contains more twists than this part of it alone might suggest.

The principle of non-intervention protects the principle of sovereignty, but at the same time the principle of non-intervention limits the principle of sovereignty. In an imaginative recent work that valuably integrates empirical and conceptual considerations, Oliver Ramsbotham and Tom Woodhouse first portray the external sovereignty of any one state being limited by the internal sovereignty of every other state:

> The non-intervention norm...is often described as the other side of the coin of sovereignty. This is somewhat misleading, as can be seen by comparing the right to wage war, long regarded as constitutive of sovereignty (its outward manifestation) with the principle of non-intervention, also seen as constitutive of sovereignty, only this time a manifestation of its inner integrity...The non-intervention norm is in this sense a *constraint on* sovereignty [emphasis in original] (1996: 34–5).

Ramsbotham and Woodhouse go on to suggest that the norm of non-intervention that protects the internal sovereignty of one state by limiting the external sovereignty of all other states has a fundamentally different character from the norm of [external] sovereignty that it constrains. 'The essential point', they write, 'is that whereas the right to wage war *inheres in each state individually* within the international anarchy, the non-intervention norm is *constitutive of the collectivity* of the international society of states' [emphasis in original].[5] The difficulty is that the suggestion of a right within an anarchy is incoherent. Rights rest upon limiting rules, and where rules function, there is less than full anarchy. States might wage war within a genuine anarchy, but if states enjoy a right to do anything, including a right to wage war, they are in a partially rule-governed situation, not a complete anarchy.

The fundamental point is not, as Ramsbotham and Woodhouse have it, that there is a putative difference between sovereignty and non-intervention, or between external and internal sovereignty, but quite simply a point about the concept of a right. Within an anarchical structure states might be at liberty to wage war, but merely being at liberty is distinctly not the same as having a right to a liberty. A right to a liberty holds only where others are bound, at a minimum, by a duty not to interfere forcibly with the exercise of the liberty—by, in Vincent's words, 'a duty to respect that right'. Thus, it cannot be that initially states have some effective right to (external) sovereignty, like a right to wage war, that mysteriously 'inheres in each state individually', and only later do they gain an effective right to non-intervention when a transition occurs from system of states to society of states and collective understandings emerge. Until shared rules emerge, no rights hold.

Being at liberty to wage war is indeed routinely but mistakenly referred to as having a right, but it would be far more accurately called something like having an 'unqualified prerogative' (Bull 1966: 55). Merely being at liberty to wage war is an instance of no-duty-not-to on the part of the state with the prerogative, which is entirely compatible with the total absence of all duties on all sides simply because there are no rules, and thus no society among the states. A right to wage war, by contrast, is a case of duty-not-to-interfere on the part of all others (in whatever the rule specifies as the appropriate circumstances for waging war). As soon as, and to the extent that, any state has a right to anything—either to wage war or to be free of intervention—there is a society among the states in the sense that their relations are to this degree rule-governed. Consequently, either, as Bull and the English school have maintained, there was for some centuries a right to wage war within a society of states or, if there was no society, there was no right, only a prerogative. Without a partially rule-governed society, there are no duties; and with no duties, there are no effective rights. This is nothing specifically to do with sovereignty but is a matter of what a right is.

Thus, if sovereignty is a right, sovereignty is limited. Sovereignty is limited because the duties that are constitutive of the right, and without which there can be no right, constrain the activity of every sovereign belonging to international society. The deeper reason why the principle of non-intervention protects the principle of sovereignty, as Vincent said, is that non-intervention imposes duties that also constrain the sovereignty of the states that bear the duty. It protects mine by constraining everyone else's and protects everyone else's by constraining mine. This is what rights do. Where there are rights, there are duty-imposing rules.[6]

In this respect, what Ramsbotham and Woodhouse rightly sense as important, and wrongly diagnose as a difference in kind between two components of sovereignty, is the *form* of sovereignty—namely, its being a right—dictating a feature of its content—namely, its being limited. An agent's right must have the form of limits on the behaviour of other agents. Where every agent has a right, every other agent's conduct is limited. If all have the right, the conduct of all has limits. Therefore, it is nonsense to describe the international arena, as some self-styled realists do, as anarchical, and mean thereby a complete free-for-all in which outcomes are determined entirely by the distribution of power, while attributing a right to sovereignty to any of the players in the arena. This is not an empirical finding; it is a conceptual requirement on any findings that are to be coherently described using the concept of a right.[7]

2.4 Sovereign limits and default duties

What has been done so far is the easy—perhaps, indeed, the obvious—part: establishing that sovereignty (conceptually) must be limited (if it is to be a right). The hard part is actually specifying some concrete limits. We began with the thesis that the form of sovereignty imposes limits on its content. In explaining why a right to sovereignty must have limits we have also indicated some crucial bits about its form. None of this is to deny Kratochwil's thesis that the right to sovereignty is a right to do wrong (as any right to genuine liberty must be). However, it is a constrained right to do wrong: a right to commit some wrongs but not others. All the interesting questions are about which wrongs come to be prohibited and which do not, and why. Recall Kratochwil's comment:

Although moral considerations are not irrelevant to an appraisal [of actions possibly targeted for intervention], the relevance of such considerations is clearly bounded by the *institutional* constraints imposed by the notion of an exclusive right.

This, while not untrue, requires careful reading. It is, indeed, the case that one cannot *always* argue: this action is wrong, and therefore, no state may be allowed to do it. For, the wrong in question may be a kind of wrong that states have a right to commit—they ought not to commit the wrong, of course, but they have a right to commit it. So the potential relevance of the moral consideration—to the question what the state may be required to do—is blocked, and any action by outsiders to prevent the wrongful action is also blocked. Nevertheless, one can *sometimes* argue: this is wrong, and therefore, no state may be allowed to do it. Everything depends on what specifically 'this' is—on whether it is a wrong that states are at liberty to commit or a wrong that is prohibited even to states, for example, genocide. In order to decide, we need concrete moral and legal arguments.

Now I want to argue that one surprising specific limit on state sovereignty is dictated by the nature of fundamental individual rights. Every effective system of rights needs to include some default, or backup, duties—that is, duties that constitute a second-line of defence requiring someone to step into the breach when those with the primary duty that is the first-line of defence fail to perform it. To ignore default duties is to engage in ideal theory with a vengeance, since it is effectively to assume that everything works as it is supposed to. (It does not.) In some respects ordinary police work is an instance of the performance of default duties. A primary duty not to assault other people falls upon all of us, but not all fulfil this (purely negative) duty all the time. When one of us fails in her duty not to attack someone else, the police have the default duties of, preferably, preventing the assault or, more realistically, apprehending the guilty party, and thereby, perhaps deterring her and others from potential future assaults, that is, providing an incentive (fear of punishment) for the performance of the primary duty. The criminal justice system could be viewed either as carrying out other duties at the first default level or as operating at a third (second default) level.

There is nothing automatic about there being default duties, in spite of the fact that many of the duties that we take to be most obvious—like most police duties—are default duties in the sense that they do not come into play until some more fundamental duty has not been honoured. Yet, surely there are cases in which some interest is important enough that everyone should have a duty not to deprive anyone of it, but not important enough that when someone violates his duty not to deprive, some other category of person should have a default duty to step in either to prevent or to punish the duty-violating deprivation. To put it simply, some matters are presumably worth one whack but not worth two whacks. Naturally, which matters these are must be argued out—I am still offering only an entirely abstract observation.

Other matters, by contrast, may be worth however many whacks they take. Presumably part of what we intend when we solemnly declare some interest to be the protected subject of a fundamental or basic right is that the interest in question is so vital or valuable, or both, that considerable resources ought to be devoted to guaranteeing, insofar as is humanly possible, that people are, at worst, only rarely deprived of it. I take this to entail, at the very least, that if the primary duty regarding the vital interest at the core of a basic right is not performed, a secondary, or default, duty must immediately take hold. Often the ideal content for the secondary duty is simply the enforcement of the primary duty: the default duty falls upon someone who can make the bearer of the primary duty do it. But the nature of any secondary duty, like the nature of any primary duty, will depend on the nature of the interest to be protected, the most effective means for protecting it, and so on, and cannot be specified purely in the abstract; and if, at a particular time, the identity of the bearers of the default duties has not been specified, then the account of rights is simply unfinished. Providing adequately for rights includes spelling out the allocation of default duties as well as of primary duties.

While it might be suspected that acknowledgement of default duties depends upon an embrace of ethical universalism, even paradigm particularist David Miller embraces:

an appealing compromise between ethical universalism and ethical particularism which holds that it is justifiable to act on special loyalties and recognize special obligations to compatriots *provided* that this does not involve violating the basic rights of outsiders... We need to draw a distinction between violating basic rights by one's own actions, and allowing them to be violated by others... If we take nationality seriously, then we must also accept that positive obligations to protect basic rights (e.g. to relieve hunger) fall in the first place on co-nationals, so that outsiders would have strong obligations in this respect only where it was strictly impossible for the rights to be protected within the national community   (Miller 1995: 78–9).

Miller, subsequently, reaffirms the critical point on which I want to focus: 'International obligations should be seen as humanitarian except in cases where people's basic rights were put at risk and it was not feasible for their own national state to protect them.'[8]

How much is already compatible with the distinction around which Miller's view about transnational duties pivots: the distinction between what is and is not 'feasible for their own national state', what is and is not 'strictly impossible... within the national community'?

Default duties are in no way a challenge to Miller's proposed compromise view. Indeed, without using the argot of 'default duties', he has explicitly reserved a place for them by referring to instances in which persons' own state cannot protect their basic rights. Reference to such cases would be pointless unless, in at least some of these cases—not, of course, necessarily all—someone or something other than the unprotected parties' own state inherited responsibility for protecting the unprotected rights. Miller is at a minimum leaving conceptual space for the bearers of the default responsibility to turn out to be the members of a different national community from those whose basic rights are going unprovided for.[9]

Consider a concrete case—a right so basic that we ought surely not simply choose to throw up our hands when people violate it: the right not to be subjected to genocidal assault. I take the right not to be murdered, taken as one component of the more general right to physical security, to be as basic as it gets. The commission of genocidal massacre seems more heinous than the commission of the same number of random killings because, perhaps, of the diabolically evil character of systematic, calculated murders combined with a conviction of one's own superiority to other human beings so strong as to permit one to adopt a conscious policy of exterminating them.[10] Thus, in my view, it would be preposterous to suggest that there is a universal negative duty not to commit genocide but that there is no positive duty to protect intended victims. The twentieth century made it clear that significant numbers of people are perfectly willing to violate their negative duty not to commit genocide, and to do so with unyielding determination. We consequently have as great a need here for a workable allocation of default duties as is imaginable.

In theory nothing is wrong with next saying that the second line of defence—the first level of default duties—should fall upon the state in control over any people threatened with genocide.[11] We do normally consider provisions for physical security generally to be among the absolutely minimum duties of the state. Nevertheless, this would be a largely perfunctory step, since genocide is usually orchestrated by the state. The first non-academic issue, then, is: what next? What is to be done when the state in control of a territory and the people within it is orchestrating genocide? What provisions should the rest of humanity make for dealing with the genocidal state?

It is important to realize that at present we have no effective provisions. The *Convention on Genocide* is very weak, first enforced for the purpose of punishment in September 1998.[12] Some international lawyers contend that if it had been intended to do any serious work for the purpose of prevention, it would have included language authorizing someone to 'use all necessary means', namely military force.[13] As it is, it is strictly permissive concerning implementation, merely inviting any state that should take a notion to do something in order to prevent or punish genocide to approach the International Court of Justice, but binding no one to anything. States routinely ignore it in fact. Similarly, if all five permanent members of the Security Council took the notion at the same time, they could indeed authorize 'all necessary means', although they would, of course, need in the process to declare the genocide a threat to international peace and security in order to bring the case within the scope of chapter VII of the UN Charter. In April 1994 with regard to Rwanda, the Security Council demonstrated that it is perfectly willing, under USA (and Belgian) pressure, to abandon a population to a long-expected genocide in progress even when starting with a small but expandable UN peacekeeping force already in place (with a willing and capable commander).[14] In this case the five permanent members were unanimous in their willingness to desert the Tutsi; ordinarily, of course, any one of the five can block effective Council action with a veto. Basically, at present under international law and United Nations practice, opposition to a genocidal state during a genocide is strictly optional. The Genocide Convention can be used as a basis for criminal trials after the fact, as it finally was in Arusha. The International Criminal Court, which the United States aggressively opposes, includes genocide within its jurisdiction but, of course, only for punishment after the fact.[15] Thus, genocide is in theory punishable but in practice usually unchallenged while underway by anyone who could stop it.

Morally this is intolerable. It is no way to run a 'civilization'. The only clear bearer of a default duty to protect people against genocide is the one organization most likely, judging from historical experience, to have orchestrated the genocide, the victim's own state. Worse than putting the fox to guard the chicken coop, this is putting the fox in charge of apprehending and punishing chicken-killing foxes. These circumstances certainly meet Miller's test: 'strictly impossible for the rights to be protected within the national community'. Yet, intervention is made difficult by the understanding of sovereignty that leaves the permanent members of the Security Council free to abstain from acting.

This supposed total freedom of the permanent members to do nothing is crucial. This is a putative right, not to do wrong, but to permit wrong—to allow the commission of genocide. The claimed freedom of these powerful and privileged (veto-wielding) states to turn their backs on the massacres and walk away is, in my judgement, a pivotal fault in their conception of sovereignty. Sovereignty, as they understand and practise it, provides unlimited indulgence by permanent members of the Security Council for genocidal states. Consequently, no one outside what Miller calls 'the national community' seems to be generally thought under any obligation to rescue the victims within; the Genocide Convention requires no one to take any action; the UN Charter permits but does not require action; and Security Council practice is not to send troops or, if as in Rwanda troops are already there, to yank them out in order to avoid danger to them and embarrassment to the Council.[16] Yet even on Miller's respectful view of national autonomy, it is unacceptable for others with wealth and power simply to allow one community within a state to annihilate another community.

The critical international institution is the institution of the sovereign state, which specifies what the national state may and may not do. But while the states are national, the rules about states are international.[17] Sovereignty provides for a certain range of unilateral decision, a range that, as Kratochwil emphasizes, includes the right to do some wrongs, as any liberty does. Yet, the range of sovereignty is not itself subject to unilateral decision. The content of the rules that specify what may be unilaterally decided may not itself be unilaterally decided. To put it another way, the rules are not 'private'-by-nationality. It is international laws, practices, and norms that specify how states may properly behave. One of our current norms, which is understandably not stated explicitly, appears to be that while no state ought to commit genocide within its territory, no other state and no international organization—most notably, not the Security Council—is *bound* to do anything about genocide. Miller has eloquently defended a far-reaching form of national autonomy, but he stops well short of the implosively inwardly focused autonomy currently practiced by the permanent members of the Security Council, who did nothing to stop genocide in Rwanda, nothing to stop genocide in Burundi, nothing effective for years to stop 'ethnic cleansing' in Bosnia, and nothing to stop 'auto-genocide' in the 1970s in Kampuchea.[18] In every case, aid was provided afterwards to whoever survived, but usually nothing was done to affect how many survived.

We have no decent choice but to accept the thesis that David Miller accepts: that the rest of us are not free merely to leave human beings to their fates when it is impossible for their basic rights to be protected by national institutions. Miller argues not only (a) that the rest of us are obligated to act *only if* it is impossible for national institutions to protect basic rights, but also (b) that *if* it is impossible, then the rest of us are obligated to act, somehow—at least, sometimes. One can, of course, accept (a) and reject (b): the leadership of the five permanent members of the Security Council have evidently done so in the past.[19]

To reject (b), however, is to assign extraordinarily little significance to even the basic rights of non-compatriots—so little that one is virtually writing them off. It is one thing to give non-compatriots significantly less weight—it is quite another to give them virtually none. Obviously 'the rest of us', as in 'the rest of us are obligated to act, somehow', are large numbers of people differently placed from each other; and the spectrum between 'significantly less weight' and 'virtually none' is quite wide. The fundamental point is: if all the rest of us (still undifferentiated) actually do nothing to define and assign default duties for the case in which a state does not protect its own people against genocide—even for the most common case in which the state is the orchestrator of the genocide—then we genuinely are assigning the vital interests and basic rights of non-compatriots zero weight in our calculations about how to organize the planet, specifically how to understand sovereignty.

Consequently, to claim, on the one hand, that one believes that Hutu and Tutsi alike, like all persons, have a basic right not to be killed arbitrarily (genocidally or otherwise), but to claim, on the other hand, that it is the job of 'their' state to protect them, in accord with the customary international division of labour—each state, its own police—is not to be serious about implementing rights in the real world. If we do not believe that anyone beyond their own state can reasonably be asked to bear the responsibility of protecting these people against the single most serious threat to their lives—their own state—we do not believe in any practically meaningful way that they have a basic right not to be killed. We simply have not yet admitted to ourselves that these people, at least, we have written off. They must face their own particular terrors without any protection from the rest of us. Even the most basic 'human' rights are not yet quite universal. Humans divide into two groups, those able to protect themselves, who do not have genocidal states, and the unprotected, who do have genocidal states.

Now, if it could indeed be established that all assignments of default duties to protect Rwandans against the Rwandan state, and—the following naturally is a large part of the rub—similarly placed others against their respective states, would impose burdens or dangers on the duty-bearers that are unreasonably great, then we could, and presumably should, conclude that we are not yet in a position to extend human rights to the Rwandans and other non-compatriots. They would be outside the pale because, in a sense, we did not have enough room for them inside. We would have discovered that in reality in a concrete case it is impossible to combine 'institutional adequacy' from the point of view of some potential right-bearers with 'individual fairness' from the point of view of any available duty-bearers (Shue 1996: 166). The tunnel dug under the channel from the rights side and the tunnel dug from the duties side do not meet under the channel; our social world has turned out to be profoundly perverse. In that case, of course, we should not mislead people like the Tutsi by telling them we believe they have rights and leading them to count on implied assistance that they are not, in fact, going to receive.

Even thesis (b), which I am attributing to Miller—that *if* it is impossible for national institutions to protect basic rights, then the rest of us are obligated to act, somehow—presumably carries the usual tacit condition: provided that the performance of the obligations entailed would not be unreasonably burdensome or dangerous. Yet, certainly before we embrace any wild conclusions about human rights not yet being actually universal, we ought imaginatively to explore quite a few alternative social arrangements for providing default protection in order to be quite sure that we cannot invent one that is not unreasonably burdensome or dangerous.

I want, in summary, to highlight some general features of the type of argument I have been trying to formulate. It is forward-looking (or 'goal-oriented', except that the 'goals' are not goods to be maximized or optimized but rights to be secured), not backward-looking. Backward-looking arguments, about corrective justice and compensation for wrongs committed, are clearly available, but I simply want to leave them to one side.[20] With the securing of at least the basic rights for everyone as the goal sought, a full treatment would investigate alternative institutional structures, not behind a veil of ignorance but with as much information relevant to the comparative feasibility of the various structures as can be pulled together, and in light of considered but defeasible judgements about fairness in the assignment of duties grounded in basic rights. I am not trying to squeeze social structures out of bare 'rationality' or mere 'reasonableness'. At heart the question is whether basic rights can be secured for everyone without imposing unfair levels or types of duties on anyone. Here, I discuss only one of the least controversial of all rights, namely, the right not to be killed. The issues ultimately involve some 'balancing' of fewer rights for some against more duties for others, but by starting with the right not to be killed I attempt to consider whether any right at all can be guaranteed against the most serious threats to it for everyone. If some people must be left without protection against genocidal massacre, the basic right not to be killed is not universally effective. Some people do not enjoy an effective right not to be killed; this would constitute, among other things, a profound inequality. By 'universally effective' I do not, of course, mean infallibly guaranteed; I mean merely secure to some reasonable level for everyone.

2.5 The chicken, the egg, and the argument from insufficient motive

One of the most admirable features, by my lights, of Miller's argumentation is that, far from trying to squeeze conclusions out of rationality or reasonableness in the abstract, he asks what seems feasible on the part of ordinary, non-demonic but non-angelic human beings with the loves and hates, and capacities and limits that, in fact, go with the territory, for the foreseeable future. This is embedded, not detached, reasoning and, in my judgement, all the better for it. Yet, it clearly involves delicate judgements about what is and is not changeable, over what period of time. One is trying not to ignore realities, while trying as well not to accept evils that could be modified if resisted with adequate determination. It is not easy to tell the difference, and those theorists who, unlike Miller, content themselves with 'ideal theory' are not even trying.

Miller offers, on a different issue, a type of argument, which I shall call 'the argument from insufficient motive', that could take the wind out of the sails of my project here before it really gets started. In discussing distributions and redistributions of wealth and income, Miller argues that one cannot expect levels of international transfers to approximate the levels of domestic transfers entailed by a meaningful welfare state because, to sum it up with crude brevity, a meaningful welfare system involves sacrifices on the part of the 'losers' that those who can foresee that they will, in fact, be the losers—the sources of the transfers to others—will, nevertheless, make willingly. They will choose to incur such losses only if they identify strongly with the 'winners' by seeing them as fellow members of some highly significant community involving certain expectations of long-run reciprocity (Miller 1995: chapter 3). Naturally, if widespread willing cooperation is not forthcoming, the system of welfare can be maintained only through considerable coercion, perhaps even authoritarianism. It is important not to demand greater sacrifice than available motivation can sustain, then, on pain of a rapid slide into reliance on coercion, a backlash against the system, or both. If one thought the unwillingness to sacrifice was 'selfish' or small-minded to the point of vice, one could suggest that these are dwarf-souled people whose moral horizons need stretching. Miller's contentions, by contrast, are (empirically) that this is at worst human psychology as one generally finds it, and (normatively) that this is mostly admirable insofar as it makes possible loyalties and communities that, while limited in geographical scope, deepen and enrich life beyond anything sustainable on the thin gruel of cosmopolitanism.

Now one can imagine a variant of the argument from insufficient motive directed against an assignment of backup duties to protect even victims of genocide, without any attempt being made to diminish the horror of genocide. Of course, it can be entirely conceded, a slaughter of all the members of a group from the aged to the infant for no other reason than their being whatever kind of people they were born is an unimaginably terrible crime and ought never to be allowed to continue if it is humanly possible to stop it. Yet, if an attempted genocide is to be stopped, it must be stopped by some people in particular. Any given population ought to be protected by its own state, but the more typical cases admittedly are the less tractable ones in which the state is conducting the genocide. Who, then, are to be the particular people who interpose themselves in harm's way and block the killers? Which other people from which other country could have the duty, and could find in themselves the motivation, to stand between a fanatic, murderous government and its defenceless people (Where did you say Rwanda is?).

Actually, it is not the reluctance but the readiness of idealistic youth to sacrifice on behalf of noble causes that is the more striking. So the difficulty is not precisely finding young and able fighters willing to do battle, but more likely finding parents willing to allow them to go to the other side of the earth and risk dismemberment and death in an effort to sort out other people's problems, and neighbours willing to pay the taxes to equip and maintain them.

One need only reflect on the mythic proportions rapidly assumed in the minds of US citizens by the deaths of eighteen US Army Rangers, some of whose corpses were immediately seen on television being dragged through the streets by joyful and triumphant Somalis, and the capture of a wounded pilot, soon to be viewed in close-ups as a bloodied and terrified hostage, in the daylight helicopter raid on 3 October 1993 on the Olympic Hotel in Mogadishu (Lyons and Samatar 1995: 59; Bowden 1999). The public shock was compounded by the Clinton Administration's failure to explain to the public what the country's military was actually doing in Somalia prior to 3 October, not to mention its duty to pay enough attention to have a sensible policy. As *New York Times* columnist Thomas L. Friedman noted: 'Americans were told that their soldiers were being sent to work in a soup kitchen and they were understandably shocked to find them in house-to-house combat' (Thomas L. Friedman, 'Harm's Way: U.S. Pays Dearly for an Education in Somalia', *New York Times*, 10 October 1993, p. E1, quoted in Lyons and Samatar 1995: 59). The mindlessness of the 'mission creep' that led to these truly unnecessary deaths (and far larger numbers of pointless Somali civilian casualties—hundreds in the ferocious urban firefight on 3 October) added to the fury of the minority of US citizens who were paying attention to the details.

If anything, the argument from insufficient motive is much clearer in cases involving the expenditure of lives than in cases involving the expenditure of money. While it is important to acknowledge that US policy in Somalia in 1993 was, in fact, out of control and that the casualties inflicted on and by the US peacekeepers were largely avoidable and pointless, I believe that there could have been a policy that would have justified eighteen unavoidable American deaths in Somalia or, to return to our main case, in Rwanda. Suppose eighteen Americans had been lost in Rwanda in April 1994, along with the ten Belgians who were tortured to death the first night, while suppressing the genocide in time to save 500,000 Rwandans.

Miller is surely correct—obviously his is an empirical hypothesis—that the average citizen is far more willing to see her own income reduced for the sake of alleviating poverty among compatriots than for alleviating it among non-compatriots, even when the poverty among the non-compatriots is more severe and the same expenditure would accomplish much more abroad than at home. I have no doubt that it is even more apparent that she would rather see her daughter die defending a compatriot than a stranger, although this too is an empirical, not a conceptual, thesis. So, who bears the default duty to protect strangers against a genocidal state? Who could summon up the motivation to do it? And if the answer to that is, 'many idealistic young people', the key question becomes: 'what could motivate the parents and neighbours to let them go?—and pay their way?'

It is here that one seems to face a chicken-and-egg problem. Walzer has written: 'There cannot be a just society until there is a society; and the adjective *just* doesn't determine, it only modifies, the substantive life of the societies it describes' (Walzer 1983: 313). This is exactly wrong, it seems to me. Understandings of justice *do* constitute—or determine—societies. It is profoundly inaccurate to suggest that only after a society has formed can 'it' begin to shape shared understandings of justice (and other normative matters).[21] On the contrary, the coming together around shared convictions— often, convictions about what the main issues are, not agreement about the answers—*is* a major element in the formation of a society at any level. Walzer is quite right that shared understandings are at the heart of what makes a society one society, but the understandings and the society take shape together. Even that puts it too weakly, as if the conjunction were a coincidence. The agreements about what is just, fair, important, and so on constitute the fabric of the society—the shared beliefs (and aspirations and fears) are the skeleton around which the society forms. It is impossible that the society should take shape first and only then the skeleton be added. To the extent that the skeleton of 'values' is unified and tightly articulated, so is the society; to the extent not, it is not. Such oneness and integrity as a society has—some skeletons are loosely articulated—depends heavily (not entirely) on shared understandings of history, of the permissible and the outrageous, of the trivial and the significant, of the fair division of labour, and of the other matters taken to be important.

I have introduced Walzer's thesis—society first, shared norms later— because it expresses a natural-seeming explanation of why the mothers of Western sons and daughters would not accept their children dying to save Tutsi. The so-called international society, a somewhat Walzerian explanation might run, is too 'thin'; it lacks the richness and robustness essential to the kind of community whose members will willingly die for each other, or even—Miller's point—be taxed for each other. We are all human, but 'human' does not cut it. What humans all share is not enough. Humans are not to die for; fellow Americans, British, Japanese—fellow nationals—are to die for. Fellow humans must not be sold as slaves, and they really ought not to be killed arbitrarily, certainly not 'exterminated' in vast massacres on the basis of garbage racism. But we cannot be expected to protect them, to put ourselves—or rather, our children—in harm's way to stand between them and their danger. We would need to feel a stronger sense of community before we could find the motivation for such great sacrifice.

Now, to be fair to, and accurate about, Walzer, I hasten to add that Michael Walzer himself advocated military intervention to protect the Rwandans (and the Bosnians), whatever we might think his general theory implies (Walzer 1995: 35–41, also see Walzer 2002: 19–35). His justification took the largely critical form of showing the inapplicability of the ground of his usual objection to intervention, self-determination—people being exterminated are not engaged in a process of self-determination—rather than a constructive account of why the responsibility for protecting the Rwandans fell on us (or who 'us' is), or how we were supposed to be motivated to shoulder it, apart from emphasizing the intrinsic evil of genocide. I prefer his intuition about the case to his general theoretical position, which makes the intuition difficult to incorporate, and, as I was already hinting, it is the theory that needs modifying.

The 'thin' morality that Walzer thinks is universal entails only negative duties; or perhaps he agrees with Miller that the duties to non-compatriots are negative, unless it is impossible for even basic rights to be honoured by a national division of labour. We all think that we all ought not to be exploited, enslaved, manipulated, or murdered; consequently, none of us is allowed to exploit, enslave, manipulate, or murder. I think that what most people believe is that it ought not to be the case that human beings are exploited, enslaved, manipulated, or murdered. They want to live in a world in which these things do not happen to people, themselves included. It is about what happens to people, especially fundamentally decent people, as they take themselves to be, who are vulnerable to dangers like exploitation, murder, and so on, unless society is organized in such a way as to protect them against this kind of thing.[22]

This is why people think that human beings should be acknowledged to have rights, and it is why thinking that people should have rights means thinking that they should receive certain protections. Providing protection involves taking measures to make things secure; consequently, it is not helpfully conceived as entirely 'negative'—simply as agents' choosing to refrain from prohibited interferences.

So there can be no system of rights consisting only of negative duties, and Walzer may not intend the 'thin' universal morality that he sketches to be a system of rights. But those who do believe in universal rights believe in social arrangements that include the provision of a reasonable level of protection against certain dangers, including the danger—highlighted in theory, at least since Hobbes—of sudden death at the hands of hostile others. This means that some people have to do some protecting, which will sometimes be dangerous. Any system of rights providing for physical security requires that some people perform duties that are not only positive, but may get them killed when part of their duty is to resist violence. Nevertheless, people generally do assume that this can be organized one society at a time. This is exactly Miller's picture of actual motivation: duties can be positive, even onerous and dangerous, but only if they are owed only to compatriots.

So, what might it take to convince Western mothers that their sons and daughters should fight militias in Kigali? First, they need to know and to appreciate that often, unless the protection comes from outside the society, there will be no protection. Miller's condition of strict impossibility is in fact fulfilled. Not only is this the case but it is repeatedly, and perhaps increasingly, the case. Statesman-like leaders could explain this persuasively: there is a job to be done and it will not be done unless we contribute a share.

Second, they need to know and to appreciate that their country and their children are in fact being asked to do only a fair share. This is an enormously difficult condition to meet because of what I take to be the normal human tendency to exaggerate one's own contribution to any joint enterprise, from housework to corporate management. That is, even where it is fairly clear what a fair share is and one is, in fact, doing at most one's share, there is some tendency to think one is doing more; this is empirical speculation, obviously. If one asked the average American about the relative contributions of the USA and the Soviet Union to victory in the Second World War, one would probably receive the impression that there was no Eastern Front, nor that twenty million Soviets died, and so on. While a great deal of this may be forgivable national pride or even ethnocentrism essential to more admirable loyalties, it is still a major problem. Nevertheless, it remains true, I would suggest, that necessary conditions here include (a) a clear and sensible understanding of what constitutes a fair share and (b) a perception that one's country and child are being expected to do no more than that.

Manifestly, acknowledging that there could be any fair share would constitute acknowledging some kind of positive, and indeed dangerous, duty to non-compatriots (in the protection of their basic right not to be killed). Now I shall end this discussion here, not under any illusion that I have listed all the necessary conditions—obviously not—or come close to specifying a sufficient set, but in hope of having given added plausibility to two thoughts. First, an acknowledgement of even a limited and carefully specified duty to contribute to the protection of a basic right, like the right not to be killed, for non-compatriots would constitute one important piece of a sense that, besides national societies, there is also an international society with some minimal general duties attached to the most basic rights. It is not the case that people would need first to feel some kind of global oneness, and only then begin to discuss shared principles for governing the already formed society. A shared understanding about the division of moral labour in the protection of basic rights, including the allocation of the default duties without which even the most undeniable rights cannot be protected, would itself constitute at least a slight crystallization of an international society. Whether such a society becomes robust is not independent of which principles would govern it.

Accordingly, I do not believe it is the case that it is pointless to discuss issues like whether Americans and Belgians should have been willing to risk their lives to protect Rwandans because the motivation is not there. The motivation is definitely not there now, and the silences and evasions on the part of Western governments about Bosnia, Somalia, and Rwanda made matters worse. But a clear showing that the performance of a limited role in cooperation with others who were also doing their part is vital in the protection of even the most fundamental human rights, and could be effective in the case at hand, may need to precede any will to act. We might then have the grounds for limiting the sovereignty of powerful states to stand idly by, while genocidal states massacre their own people, a wrong that no one believes a state has a right to commit but no state feels bound to challenge with force. We might conclude that doing nothing in the face of such monstrous evil is also an intolerable wrong because there are fair ways in which to share the resistance.

3

The Humanitarian Responsibilities of Sovereignty: Explaining the Development of a New Norm of Military Intervention for Humanitarian Purposes in International Society

Nicholas J. Wheeler

3.1 Introduction

Is there a 'developing international norm' (Annan 1999*a*: 44) to forcibly protect civilians threatened by genocide, mass killing, and ethnic cleansing as stated by UN Secretary-General Kofi A. Annan in September 1999? The 1990s witnessed a new activism on the part of the Security Council as it extended its chapter VII powers into matters that had previously belonged to the domestic jurisdiction of states. This change in Council practice was pushed by the leading Western states that sought to secure UN legitimacy for interventions to protect civilians in Iraq, Somalia, Haiti, and the Balkans. This was in contrast to the cold war period where humanitarian claims were not employed by states to legitimate the use of force. This prompts the question whether any shift on the legitimacy of humanitarian intervention is confined to the major Western states. Or, did the West successfully promote a new norm of military intervention for humanitarian purposes in international society?

The argument proceeds in three parts. First, I examine the competing theories of the relationship between power and norms advanced by materialist and constructivist writers in the discipline of international relations. Next,

I would like to thank Alex Bellamy, Anne Harris, Ken Berry, and Joel Quirk for their comments on earlier versions of this chapter. I am also grateful to Jennifer Welsh for her helpful suggestions on how to organize the chapter. I benefited from the opportunity to present an early version of the chapter to a seminar held at Oxford University, and I am especially grateful to Andrew Hurrell who acted as discussant and to the rapporteur S. Neil MacFarlane.

I assess the validity of these theories in explaining changing UN practices in relation to armed intervention for civilian protection in the 1990s. Given limits of space, I focus on the two key cases where the Council pushed out the boundaries of legitimate intervention in significant ways, namely, northern Iraq and Somalia. Without the material power of Western states, intervention would not have been possible in either of these cases. But I argue that a materialist based explanation is insufficient because it fails to realize that intervention became possible only because of a changed normative context at the domestic level in Western states. The other case considered here is Rwanda because the Council's abject failure to save Rwandans from genocide illustrates the moral limits of any new norm of civilian protection. The final part of the chapter highlights a further restriction on the operation of the 'developing norm' by focusing on NATO's unilateralism over Kosovo. Even if the Council agrees that the non-intervention principle should be overridden in cases of extreme humanitarian emergency, Kosovo demonstrates the difficulties of reaching a consensus on the application of this principle in specific cases. In the face of divisions within the Council, crucially among the five permanent members (P-5), NATO used force without explicit UN authority. How should we explain the fact that despite breaching specific legal provisions of the UN Charter, the action was not condemned by the Council, or in the wider society of states? Does this suggest that any emerging norm on humanitarian intervention extends even to unilateral action? Or, does it confirm the claim of those who explain world politics in materialist terms, like realism and neo-Marxism? These theories would argue that the strong are always able to dispense with normative restraints when these prove inconvenient.

The conclusion briefly considers the impact of 11 September on the proclivity of states to use force to protect humanitarian values. The 'war against terrorism' risks marginalizing the debate over the legitimacy of humanitarian intervention, but the evidence from Afghanistan and Iraq is that those using force against the threat from terrorism will be looking to bolster their legitimacy by appealing to humanitarian rationales. There are positive and negative interpretations of such a development, and each has bearing on the future status of the norm of civilian protection in international society.

3.2   Norms and power in international society

Constructivist theorizing in international relations defines a norm as the existence of shared understandings as to the permissible limits of state action, and an acceptance that conduct should be justified and appraised in terms set by the norm.[1] The implication being that actors comply with norms because they accept them as legitimate. However, this view of norms is rejected by materialist accounts such as realism and Marxism that emphasize how norms are instruments that states mobilize to serve their purposes.[2] E. H. Carr, a theorist who combined elements of realism and Marxism in his thought, classically developed this materialist or brute power argument. He pointed to the doctrine of the 'harmony of interests' espoused by liberal states in the nineteenth century, and argued that this justification served the particular political and economic interests of Britain. Acknowledging that actors might sincerely believe in the internationalist principles they espouse, Carr's critique is a damning one because he contends that these 'supposedly absolute and universal principles... [are] not principles at all, but the unconscious reflexions of national policy based on a particular interpretation of national interest at a particular time' (Carr 1939: 111). The normative structure of international society depends upon the distribution of power; changes in the latter will lead to normative shifts as new players bring different ideologies to the world stage. Moreover, if weaker states do not comply with the norms supported by dominant states, then they may find these being forcibly imposed upon them.

Alexander Wendt has usefully identified three approaches to explaining norm compliance. He labels these as 'coercion', 'self-interest', and 'legitimacy' (Wendt 1999: 285–90). Wendt suggests that a norm is militarily imposed on states when they do not 'want to comply of their own accord nor see it as in their self-interest'.[3] If the only reason that states complied with a norm were the exercise of preponderant power by a hegemonic state or a group of states, then this would fail to satisfy the constructivist definition of a norm, since it would lack legitimacy among the wider peer group. The second model moves away from violent imposition towards the notion that states rationally calculate the costs and benefits of compliance. The norm is not valued as an end in itself, but rather because it facilitates particular state interests (Wendt 1999: 287–8). This would satisfy the constructivist definition if it could be shown that states were justifying their actions in terms of the norm, and crucially, that this exerted an inhibiting or constraining effect on their behaviour. The 'legitimacy' approach is predicated on the assumption that states adhere to norms because they accept them as valid.[4] At this point, states do not follow norms because they calculate that they will serve their interests. Instead, the norm has served to reconstitute the identity and interests of the actor.

The contention that states comply with norms because they morally approve of them takes constructivism into the realm of what Jürgen Habermas calls communicative action. The latter is characterized by 'action orientated to understanding' (Habermas 1984: 285), in which state actors seek to persuade others to accept new moral positions based on the power of persuasion. There must be openness to the arguments of others and a willingness to change a state's definition of its interests if convinced by what Habermas calls 'the unforced force of the better argument'.[5] Habermasians argue that what counts as a powerful claim should be determined by its moral validity. But they recognize that in practical contexts of argumentation, what can be raised as a reasonable argument is circumscribed by existing norms. How, then, do new norms develop? Martha Finnemore and Kathryn Sikkink consider that this requires particular states to act as 'norm entrepreneurs' who convince other states to embrace the new norm. Drawing on wider currents in social and political theory, they argue that success depends upon framing the new norm as being in conformity with dominant legitimating principles in international society. This approach to language as a tool of political action is strongly associated with the work of Quentin Skinner. He gives the example of how the merchant class in England tried to justify their accumulation of profit in the sixteenth and seventeenth century. Instead of defending a new capitalist ethic as a break with the past, they sought to justify their actions by arguing that they were in conformity with the values of Protestantism that formed the dominant legitimating principle in society. The merchants were manipulating language for strategic purposes, but Skinner's point is that unless they wanted to be exposed as hypocrites, their subsequent actions were constrained by the need to ensure they could plausibly be presented as compatible with the religious values they professed (Skinner 1988: 131–2).

The proposition that state behaviour is inhibited if it cannot be legitimated is a cardinal claim of those constructivists influenced by the linguistic turn in social and political theory. Both realism and Marxism reject this constraining argument, considering that states can always find a convenient rationale to cover their actions. The problem with the realist and Marxist dismissal of norms as constraints is that it ignores how the pursuit of international legitimation can bind future state actions. Although the strongest states are in a position to substitute brute power for legitimacy, what is surprising is how rarely this happens. Even the great powers seek approval from their peers and domestic publics. By entering a public realm of discourse in which their justifications are exposed to criticism and counter-argument, the context can change, as Marc Lynch argues, in ways 'that ... overcome imbalances of material power' (Lynch 1999: 41). If a state is unable to present a persuasive defence of its claims, then it will lose legitimacy in the eyes of its peers. The next section charts how the traditional understanding of state sovereignty as a barrier to international intervention has been robbed of its legitimacy during the 1990s.

3.3   A new norm of Security Council authorized intervention in the 1990s

The fundamental change in normative practice that occurred during the 1990s concerned the Security Council's willingness to define humanitarian emergencies inside a state's borders as a threat to 'international peace and security'. The importance of this shift is that it legitimates military enforcement action under chapter VII of the Charter. This process of change began on 5 April 1991 when the Council decided by ten votes to three (with two abstentions) to name the refugee crisis caused by the Iraqi Government's oppression of the Kurds and Shiites as a threat to the peace. The first operative paragraph of Resolution 688 'condemns the repression of the Iraqi civilian population in many parts of Iraq . . . the consequences of which threaten international peace and security in the region' (SC Res 688, 5 April 1991). The Council demanded that Iraq end its violations of human rights and allow international humanitarian agencies to deliver aid to those in need. Aside from the special cases of Rhodesia and South Africa, this was the first time that the Council had recognized that a state's internal repression could have transboundary consequences that threatened international security.[6] The contrast with the cold war practice of the Council could not be starker. India had argued in March 1971 that the exodus of ten million refugees across its borders—as a consequence of Pakistan's slaughter of tens of thousands of Bengali civilians in East Pakistan—posed a threat to regional security. But the Security Council rejected this claim. The unanimous view taken by Council members was that abuses of human rights within Pakistan's borders were matters that fell within its domestic jurisdiction under Article 2(7) of the UN Charter.[7] Although Cuba, Yemen, and Zimbabwe tried to press this argument in relation to Iraq's treatment of its minorities, the majority of the Council took the view that Article 2(7) was not applicable because of the threat to regional security posed by the refugee crisis.

Resolution 688 was a groundbreaking development, but its significance as a precedent for humanitarian intervention is limited by two factors. The first is that the Council's demands were not backed up by the threat of enforcement action. Resolution 688 determined that the crisis posed a threat to 'international peace and security', but it was not adopted under chapter VII. Russia and China made it clear that they would veto any draft resolution that tried to include enforcement provisions, and even without this threat, it is apparent that many of the non-permanent members would have voted down a tougher resolution. The second reason for being cautious about the precedent set is that the resolution would not have secured the necessary nine votes had it been defended purely on humanitarian grounds. Evidence for this can be seen in the fact that two days earlier, France had tried and failed to secure backing for a resolution to protect the Kurds. This plea fell on deaf ears. Reading the speeches of the six non-permanent members who voted for Resolution 688, it is clear that they were most anxious not to set a precedent that might legitimize Council action on humanitarian grounds alone. Sir David Hannay, Britain's then Permanent Representative on the Council, reflected that it was the security issue of refugees that dominated the deliberations in the Council's 'informal consultations', and which explains why the resolution was adopted.[8]

The Council's demand that Iraq cease its oppression failed to stem the worsening humanitarian crisis. And in the face of mounting media driven pressure from domestic publics in Europe and the United States that action be taken to save the Kurds, the USA, the UK, France and the Netherlands deployed military forces to create 'safe havens' in northern Iraq. The Kurds had sought refuge from Iraqi brutality in the mountains and thousands were dying daily from hypothermia and disease. The idea of the 'safe havens' was to create protected areas so that the Kurds would come down off the mountains. The Western military intervention was explicitly justified on humanitarian grounds, with President George Bush stating that 'I want to underscore that all we are doing is motivated by humanitarian concerns' (quoted in Freedman and Boren 1992: 54). This was the first time since the founding of the UN that a group of states had explicitly defended the use of force in humanitarian terms, and this rationale rested uneasily with the nervousness most states felt towards the doctrine of humanitarian intervention.

Sensitivity to this concern led the Western powers to defend their action as being in conformity with Resolution 688. Thus, Bush stated that the 'safe havens' and northern no-fly zone were 'consistent with United Nations Security Council Resolution 688' (quoted in 'Major's enclave plan for Kurds runs into trouble', *The Times*, 10 April 1991). The crucial passage invoked by intervening states was paragraph six of the resolution that 'appeals to all Member States and to all humanitarian organizations to contribute to these humanitarian relief efforts' (SC Res 688, 5 April 1991). This confirms the validity of Skinner's point that when advancing new norms, actors seek to present their behaviour as compatible with the existing range of legitimating reasons. In this respect, Adam Roberts is correct to point out that 'no right of purely national intervention on humanitarian grounds, without Security Council authority' (Roberts 1993: 437) was asserted. But given that Resolution 688 lacked any enforcement provisions, Western states were through their actions advancing a new claim: the use of force could be justified to enforce compliance with an existing Security Council resolution that demanded respect for human rights. The right of humanitarian intervention asserted was a limited one, and Western governments argued that their intervention was not a breach of Iraq's sovereignty. Nevertheless, military action taken without the consent of the host government clearly challenged traditional interpretations of the sovereignty rule. In so doing, the West was implicitly claiming that the principle of non-intervention was not sacrosanct if it permitted governments to massively abuse human rights within their borders. Despite challenging existing norms of sovereignty in international society, there was no condemnation of Western action in either the Security Council or the General Assembly. Does this mean that Council members were prepared to tacitly legitimate a military response to the humanitarian crisis that they were not prepared to endorse as a point of principle? I will take up this question after considering how far the Somali and Rwandan cases contributed to the developing norm of UN authorized intervention in the 1990s.

In terms of normative evolution, there are two key features of the Somali case. The first is that the debate in the Security Council centred on the humanitarian reasons for acting. Resolution 794 adopted unanimously under chapter VII on 3 December declared that 'the magnitude of the human tragedy caused by the conflict in Somalia, further exacerbated by the obstacles being created to the distribution of humanitarian assistance, constitutes a threat to international peace and security' (SC Res 794, 3 December 1992). The Security Council had to employ the language of chapter VII to justify authorizing intervention, but it was clear from the debate in the Council that the primary justification for acting was humanitarian (Roberts 1993: 440). In the case of the Kurds, the Council had been careful to stress the trans-boundary justification for action. In this case, only the USA and Cape Verde made reference to this aspect of the crisis. Most members focused on the moral responsibility of the Council to end the tragedy.[9] It has to be remembered that the Council was operating on the basis of information supplied by the UN Secretariat that estimated up to two million Somalis could die unless 'security conditions [could be established] that will permit the distribution of relief supplies' (quoted in 'UN offers troops for Somalia', *Guardian*, 27 November 1992). There was consensus that in this situation of extreme emergency, the Council had to will the means to realize its declared ends. Paragraph ten of Resolution 794 authorized Member States 'to use all necessary means to establish ... a secure environment for humanitarian relief operations' (SC Res 794, 3 December 1992). This was the second path-breaking aspect of this case because the willingness to use force contrasted sharply with the position taken over the Kurds. Zimbabwe was the only one of the three dissenting states from April 1991 that remained on the Council. But in a situation where the justification for invoking chapter VII was much more tenuous than in the case of northern Iraq, there was no opposition from it or any other member of the Council to this humanitarian inspired interpretation of chapter VII.

It is tempting to suggest that this case represents the first clear-cut example of UN authorized humanitarian intervention. However, there are good grounds to question such an assessment. Immediately prior to noting that human suffering constitutes a threat to the peace, the resolution recognizes the 'unique' character of the situation requiring an 'exceptional' response (SC Res 794, 3 December 1992). Adam Roberts argues that the case was 'exceptional' because it was 'not a case of intervention against the will of the government, but of intervention when there is a lack of government' (Roberts 1993: 440). This language was inserted by those states that had been sensitive about eroding the principle of sovereignty in relation to Iraq. India and China had abstained on Resolution 688, and both stressed that this case was special because the Somali government had ceased to exist. This was an attempt to place it in a different category to the Iraqi case, where the dispute had centred on the legitimacy of Council intervention against an existing government that was abusing human rights. Nevertheless, whatever the denials to the contrary, this case supported an emerging norm that when states collapse into lawlessness and disorder, a responsibility falls on the Security Council to act.

This emergent norm to protect civilians from the collapse of legitimate state institutions was further reinforced by the international interventions in Bosnia-Herzegovina and Haiti. As Adam Roberts points out in Chapter 5 of this volume, these interventions were characterized by a complex mix of host state consent and varying levels of coercion exercised against non-state actors. For example, in the case of Bosnia, the consent of the internationally recognized government contrasted sharply with the opposition of Bosnian Serb forces to UN operations. The Council was divided in its approach to Bosnia but this stemmed from different attitudes to the use of force rather than concerns about whether the Council had a firm legal basis for authorizing such actions.

The case that best illustrates both the development of a new norm and its moral limits is Rwanda. The UN's catastrophic failure to protect Rwandans has been well documented. But what is relevant for this discussion is how the principle of sovereignty was never raised in the Council as a barrier to military intervention to end the genocide. In 1971, the Council had hidden behind Article 2(7) as Pakistan slaughtered the Bengalis. In 1994, the Council once again failed to stop mass killing, but no state tried to defend the UN's stance of non-intervention on the grounds that genocide fell within Rwanda's domestic jurisdiction. This was recognized by Annan who pointed out in his 1999 Annual Report to the General Assembly that the reason why there was no intervention to end the Rwandan genocide was because UN Member States were reluctant 'to pay the human and other costs of intervention, and by doubts that the use of force would be successful, than *by concerns about sovereignty*' (Annan 1999*b*: 21 [emphasis added]). It is simply inconceivable that the Security Council would have blocked any state or group of states from intervening to stop the genocide in those crucial weeks in April and May when outside military intervention could have saved hundreds of thousands of lives.

The idea that there is a relationship between internal and external legitimacy has existed since the origins of the global human rights regime in the late 1940s. What is new is the claim that in the most appalling cases of brutality and slaughter, a state should temporarily forfeit the right to protection from the norm of non-intervention. Although many Council members will seek the UN Charter's reassurance of justifying this in terms of the threat posed to wider peace and security, supporters of this norm argue that it is defensible on humanitarian grounds alone. This proposition is often presented by its critics as one of privileging human rights concerns over state sovereignty.[10] But this is an erroneous reading. Sovereignty—and its logical corollary the rule of non-intervention—remains the dominant legitimating principle. However, it is no longer conceived as an inherent right. Instead, states that claim this entitlement must recognize concomitant responsibilities for the protection of citizens. The Special Representative of the UN Secretary-General for Internally Displaced Persons, Francis M. Deng, has called this approach 'sovereignty as responsibility' (Deng 1993, 1995; Deng et al. (eds.) 1996). The International Commission on Intervention and State Sovereignty (ICISS) that reported in late 2001 took up this idea as its underlying theoretical assumption. It argued that the debate over sovereignty versus intervention should be reframed in terms of the 'responsibility to protect'. States are entrusted with the primary responsibility to protect the security of their citizens. However, should states fail to exercise this responsibility, then 'the principle of non-intervention yields to the international responsibility to protect' (ICISS 2001a: p. xi). Although this norm was not explicitly invoked by Western states to justify their intervention in northern Iraq and Somalia, and nor was it evident in the Council deliberations over Resolutions 688 and 794, it is hard to resist the conclusion that the Council was—albeit tentatively—applying the principle of 'sovereignty as responsibility' in its actions over Iraq and especially Somalia.

How, then, should we explain the Security Council's new practice relating to intervention in the 1990s? Since realists have not preoccupied themselves with this question, we have to look to neo-Marxist writers for a materialist explanation. The left-wing public intellectual Noam Chomsky argues that the United States was able to manipulate the rhetoric of anti-communism to justify its political and economic hegemony during the cold war. But the end of the cold war robbed the United States of this normative justification. Consequently, the Western bloc required a new discourse to legitimate its dominant position. Chomsky asserts that humanitarian ideals have been deliberately pressed into service to achieve this. He considers that, 'With the Soviet deterrent in decline, the cold war victors are more free to exercise their will under the cloak of good intentions but in pursuit of interests that have a very familiar ring outside the realm of enlightenment'.[11] With the demise of the Soviet Union, there was no power capable of blocking US manipulation of the UN to provide legitimating cover for its interventions in Iraq, Somalia, and the Balkans.

Military force is the ultimate means of securing compliance, and when the USA has confronted direct threats to its hegemony (as with Iraq), violence has been exercised against the offending government. However, materialists would argue that US power does not have to be overtly threatened to be

effective in producing obedient behaviour. The very fact that American political, economic, and military power casts such a large shadow over world politics ensures that the USA can bend the UN to its will. This illustrates a key
limitation in the framework of norm compliance developed by Wendt: if
power operates in this way, it is very difficult to draw a clear distinction
between explanations of coercion and self-interest. To take the example of
decision-making in the Security Council, a materialist analysis would hypoth-
esize that the non-permanent members supported Western positions on
humanitarian intervention out of fear that a failure to comply could lead to
American economic and political power being exercised against them. The
implication being that there has been no underlying change of norm in relation to military intervention for civilian protection since the Council's stamp
of legitimacy was a convenient fiction produced solely by the exercise of
Western power.

There are three objections to the materialist explanation. First, the claim
that Western states intentionally employed humanitarian claims to mask
power political interests ignores the extent to which they were impelled to act
as 'norm entrepreneurs' by their domestic publics. In the case of Somalia,
Chomsky's neo-Marxist account fails to explain how it was that the United
States came to intervene in a country that held no strategic or economic value
to America. To understand how intervention became possible in Somalia, it is
necessary to focus on how changing moral sensibilities at the domestic level
pressured the administration of George Bush senior into taking an action that
pushed out the boundaries of legitimate intervention at the global level.
By transmitting television images of cruelty and slaughter into the homes of
citizens in liberal states, the media was able to mobilize a powerful constituency behind intervention in the cases of both Somalia and northern Iraq.
Martin Shaw argues that media coverage of the suffering of the Kurds 'compelled intervention by the Western powers' (Shaw 1996: 156). Whilst this
goes too far since state leaders could have acted differently, what is clear is
that without the media coverage, it is highly unlikely that Bush would have
repositioned himself behind an action that he had previously ruled out.[12] The
same story can be told in relation to Somalia: The administration focused
attention on the humanitarian crisis during the 1992 Presidential election
campaign, but no one on the Bush team seriously expected American forces
to be sent to Somalia. What changed this expectation was media coverage of
starving Somalis that pricked at the conscience of Americans. Lawrence
Eagleburger, acting Secretary of State during the Somali crisis, opined in 1994
that 'television had a great deal to do with President Bush's decision to go in'
(quoted in Minear, Scott, and Weiss 1996: 54–5). Andrew Natsios, the then
Director of the Office of Foreign Disaster Assistance (OFDA), also subsequently claimed that 'sustained media coverage of the anarchy and starvation
in Somalia certainly contributed mightily to the Bush Administration's decision

to deploy Operation Restore Hope' (Natsios 1996: 159). Although Bush Sr. had lost the election by the time he came to intervene in Somalia, he was conscious that a failure to act in the face of public demands for action would lead to charges that his vision of a 'new world order' was empty rhetoric. After all the criticisms of the administration for its inaction over Bosnia, Somalia appeared to provide an opportunity to end his Presidency on a moral high note.

The role of new ideas—a growing moral awareness among citizens in the West as to the plight of distant strangers—is crucial in explaining how US intervention became possible in both northern Iraq and Somalia. But ideas are not enough by themselves, since they have to acquire what Daniel Philpott calls 'social power'. He defines this as *'the ability of believers in ideas to alter the costs and benefits facing those who are in a position to promote or hinder the policies that the ideas demand'* (Philpott 2001: 58 [original emphasis]). By raising the moral consciousness of Americans, the media networks exercised a form of 'social power' over the Bush Administration that was pivotal in persuading it to change its calculations on the costs and benefits of intervention in both northern Iraq and Somalia.

The second problem with a materialist explanation is that it does not sufficiently distinguish between power based on relations of domination and power that rests on shared norms. A good example of this is the fact that no Council member challenged the West's interpretation of Resolution 688 as justifying the safe havens in Iraq. Realism would explain this in terms of powerful states always being able to find convenient pretexts to justify their breach of the rules, and cite the acquiescence of other states as evidence of the West's implicit or explicit exercise of material power. However, an alternative account would emphasize how Western action benefited from what I have called the 'shaming power of humanitarian norms'. This is a form of power not derived from the political, economic, and military strength of the West. Instead, it stems from the fact that even repressive governments recognize the need to legitimate their actions as being in conformity with global humanitarian values. Non-Western governments that were uncomfortable with what they viewed as the West's erosion of the non-intervention principle calculated that they would suffer political costs if they challenged Western intervention, and so they acquiesced in it. But what is important is that these calculations only make sense in a global social context in which protection of basic humanitarian values is becoming a *sine qua non* of legitimate statehood. Thus, in the case of northern Iraq, no member of the Council wanted to be seen as opposing a military action that was clearly saving lives. As a result, even those governments who were most uncomfortable with the West's use of force against Iraq were shamed into silence.

The third criticism of the materialist position is that it overlooks the possibility that state leaders might approve a new norm because they sincerely believe in it. Identifying when a government has genuinely accepted a norm is methodologically very difficult, but two tests can be applied: first, does it publicly endorse the norm in its domestic and international statements, and second, is there any evidence to support the materialist explanation that the state is only adhering to it because of the exercise of power against it?[13] On the first point, the best evidence for a change of norm in relation to the legitimacy of using force to protect civilians in danger are the statements of many governments at the 54th General Assembly in September 1999. Although some states, notably Russia, China, and India, defended the principle of sovereignty against what they viewed as human rights imperialism by the West, a large majority considered that Council authorized intervention even without the consent of the target state was permissible in cases of extreme humanitarian crisis. However, what remained completely beyond the pale was the idea that there existed a right of unilateral humanitarian intervention: No government advocated this position, and many governments that accepted the legitimacy of UN authorized actions spoke out strongly against such a claim.

Turning to the second test of whether a norm is accepted on moral grounds, there is no evidence to support the charge that the non-permanent members of the Council refrained from criticizing Western interventions in the 1990s because of concerns that this would lead to coercive pressures being mobilized against them by the USA and other Western states. Materialists could reply that power does not have to be used to be effective, but in the absence of any empirical evidence to support this claim, it remains a hypothesis that needs more rigorous testing. One important piece of evidence that refutes the materialist position is that had Western power been as omnipotent as they suggest, would Yemen and Zimbabwe have voted against Resolution 688?[14] These governments morally opposed the new norm of Council action pressed by Western states, indicating that they were not influenced by the worry that Western power might be employed against them. What was at stake in April 1991 was a battle of ideas concerning the legitimate boundaries of Security Council action in humanitarian crises. The success of Western governments lay in persuading other members of the Council that the UN had a moral responsibility to protect the Kurds, and then in deploying force in a manner that was clearly saving lives. Material power played little— if any role—in deciding the outcome of this clash between supporters and opponents of Resolution 688.

It is apparent that there are good reasons for rejecting an exclusively materialist based explanation for the changing practice of Security Council intervention in the 1990s. It is also evident that the pressure for changing the boundaries of legitimate intervention has come from Western governments, who in turn, have been responding to pressures from domestic publics. In the case of the safe havens in northern Iraq, there had been no major opposition from Council members to the West's stretching of Resolution 688 to justify intervention. But when the USA, UK, and France tried to employ the same device over Kosovo, significant divisions opened up between the P-5. These divisions pointed up the significant limits to any developing norm of intervention in post-cold war international society.

3.4   Kosovo and the limits of the doctrine of 'sovereignty as responsibility'

The significance of NATO's use of force against the Federal Republic of Yugoslavia in March 1999 is that this was the first time since the founding of the UN that a group of states had explicitly justified bombing another state in the name of protecting a minority within that state. Moreover, the action lacked explicit authorization from the Council, and was condemned by Russia and China as a flagrant breach of international law. The divisions in the Council alert us to a crucial point. Even if there is agreement that states, which commit gross and systematic violations of human rights, should forfeit the right to protection of the norm of non-intervention, how should the UN proceed if Council members—especially the permanent members—are divided over whether a particular case warrants armed intervention? And if the Council is paralysed from acting because of the power of the veto, how should the international community judge a state, or group of states, that justify the use of force as preventing an impending humanitarian catastrophe? This is the moral and legal conundrum that is posed by NATO's action in Kosovo.

Realism and Marxism would argue that NATO's decision to act without explicit Security Council authority demonstrates the weakness of the constructivist claim that norms and law constrain state actions. NATO felt impelled to act over Kosovo and cast around for 'scripts'[15] that it could use to defend its actions before domestic and international public opinion. At first glance, NATO's action appears to pose some serious problems for the proposition that norms inhibit state actions. After all, if NATO had defended non-intervention in Kosovo on the grounds that it lacked a legal mandate, then constructivists would cite this as evidence that legal rules constrain even the most powerful states. The then British Foreign Secretary, Robin Cook, had stated publicly in early June 1998 that NATO needed Council authority to act, and so what has to be explained is how it was that the Alliance was able to act without an explicit mandate from the UN.

The first reply to the above criticism is that interventions, which would appear prima facie to break existing law, do not necessarily disprove the claim that legitimacy concerns limit state actions. The constructivist thesis is that actions will be inhibited if they cannot be legitimated. This opens up the intriguing possibility that actions might be legitimate but illegal, a position that has been directly invoked to describe NATO's action over Kosovo.[16] The second point that the materialist criticism misses is that some 'scripts' are more persuasive than others. And in the case of Kosovo, as I argue below, NATO could draw on some powerful legitimating arguments. This reflects the fact that the Charter embodies conflicting norms when it comes to the protection of human rights. On the one hand, the Charter requires states to protect human rights within their jurisdictions. But on the other hand, it prohibits the use of force as an instrument for individual states to defend these human rights norms (see Roberts, this volume). This conflict of norms was revealed in a particularly acute manner over Kosovo. There was no disagreement in the Council that the Milošević regime was massively violating basic humanitarian standards through its forced expulsion of Kosovar Albanians, but nor was there a consensus that the only solution to the humanitarian crisis was the use of force.[17]

If law was purely a handmaiden of power as realism and Marxism argue, then the USA might have tried to defend its use of force against Yugoslavia as one of self-defence. However, State Department lawyers acknowledged that such a justification would lack credibility, and so a debate took place inside the Clinton Administration concerning whether the United States should invoke the legal doctrine of unilateral humanitarian intervention. These deliberations brought together lawyers and other high-ranking officials from the Departments of State and Defence. As a result of these, the administration rejected employing humanitarian intervention as a legal basis for the action. There were two factors underpinning this decision: First, the legal advisers emphasized the risk that this precedent might be used by others to justify interventions that would undermine the fabric of international order to the detriment of US interests.[18] The second reason was that the United States wanted to maintain its freedom of action over whether it engaged in such actions, and it worried that relying on the doctrine of humanitarian intervention would generate expectations of similar US action in other crises.

Having ruled out the rationales of self-defence and humanitarian intervention, the USA justified its action by citing a series of contextual considerations. These underpinned a claim to legitimacy, but no explicit claim to legality was made.[19] The US and other NATO governments cited the following three factors: the Milošević government's ethnic cleansing of Kosovar Albanians; the consequences of which was creating a humanitarian emergency that threatened peace and security in the region; and the fact that the Security Council had previously adopted three chapter VII resolutions demanding a halt to Yugoslavia's gross and systematic violations of human rights.

Skinner's claim that actors seek to justify actions that break existing norms by defending them in terms of the dominant legitimating language of a society is well illustrated by US appeals to the human rights principles in the Charter. Thus, the US Permanent Representative stated on 26 March in the

Council that 'The United Nations Charter does not sanction armed assaults upon ethnic groups, or imply that the international community should turn a blind eye to a growing humanitarian disaster' (S/PV.3989, 26 March 1999, p. 5). These arguments failed to persuade Russia, China, and India (the latter was not a member of the Council but had asked to participate in the debate). The Russian Permanent Representative stated that while his government did not defend Yugoslavia's violations of international humanitarian law, 'Attempts to apply a different standard to international law and to disregard its basic norms and principles create a dangerous precedent that could cause acute destabilization and chaos on the regional and global level' (S/PV.3988, 24 March 1999, p. 3). Similarly, the Chinese Ambassador declared NATO's action a 'violation of the principles of the Charter... and of international law, as well as a challenge to the authority of the Security Council' (S/PV.3989, 26 March 1999, p. 9). India supported this position arguing that, 'It is clear that NATO will not listen to the Security Council. It would appear that it believes itself to be above the law... Those who take the law into their hands have never improved civic peace within nations; neither will they help in international relations' (S/PV.3989, 26 March 1999, p. 16). What is significant about the different positions taken in the Council by NATO on the one hand, and Russia, China, and India on the other, is that they all relied on claims as to what was the proper interpretation of the UN Charter as it pertained to the facts of the Kosovo case.

One theme that underlay some of the statements in the Council during the Kosovo crisis was that Russia and China had behaved irresponsibly by threatening to veto a draft resolution authorizing NATO's use of force. For example, the Slovenian Permanent Representative expressed his regret that NATO's action had been necessitated because 'not all permanent members were willing to act in accordance with their special responsibility for the maintenance of international peace and security under the United Nations Charter' (S/PV.3988, 24 March 1999, pp. 6–7). The problem with this argument, as Simon Chesterman points out, is that it refuses to accept that Russia might have had genuine misgivings about the use of force (Chesterman 2001: 221). The disagreements in the Council over Kosovo illustrate the playing out of the conflicting norms regarding human rights and sovereignty that are built into the UN Charter. What is important about the debate in the Council is that all the participants relied on legal and moral arguments that were anchored in the normative framework supplied by the UN Charter (Johnstone, forthcoming). Nevertheless, by intervening in a context where there was no explicit Council authorization, NATO accepted, in former US legal advisor Abraham Sofaer's words, the burden of persuading governments, courts, and the public of the propriety of its actions'.[20] How successful was NATO in carrying this 'burden of persuading' in the case of Kosovo?

In any analysis of the international reaction, what has to be explained is how it was that on 26 March 1999 a Russian draft resolution demanding a halt to the bombing was comprehensively defeated by twelve votes to three (Russia, China, and Namibia). Five states on the Council were members of NATO, but the other seven votes were cast by Slovenia (a friend of the West and strongly opposed to Milošević), Argentina, Brazil, Bahrain, Malaysia, Gabon, and Gambia. Did the vote signify an acceptance on the part of these states as to the legitimacy of humanitarian intervention in cases where the Council was blocked from acting by the threat of the veto? Or, was it, as the Cuban Ambassador argued, a reflection of US hegemony in the global system? He declared the vote as 'shameful' and considered that 'never before has the unipolar order imposed by the USA been so obvious and so disturbing' (S/PV.3989, 26 March 1999, p. 13). On this view, the votes cast against Russia are to be explained in terms of the calculations Council members made about the costs of challenging US power.

Set against this, the Permanent Representative for the Netherlands was in no doubt that the defeat of the Russian resolution reflected growing acceptance of the norm of 'sovereignty as responsibility':

Today, we regard it as a generally accepted rule of international law that no sovereign State has the right to terrorize its own citizens. Only if that shift is a reality can we explain how on 26 March the Russian-Chinese draft resolution branding NATO air strikes a violation of the Charter could be so decisively rejected by 12 votes to 3 ... Times have changed, and they will not change back   (S/PV.4011, 10 June 1999, pp. 12–13).

The problem with this interpretation of the vote is that it overlooks the fact that outside of the five NATO states and Slovenia, only Argentina publicly approved the action on grounds of sovereignty as responsibility. The Argentinian Ambassador stated that 'Argentina ... wishes to stress that the fulfilment of the legal norms of international humanitarian law and human rights ... falls to everyone' (S/PV.3989, 26 March 1999, p. 7). Its growing commitment to democratic values at home was reflected in a commitment to defend human rights internationally. The argument that Argentina accepted the legitimacy of NATO's action is not incompatible with the view that it also acted out of self-interest. Wendt implies that a choice has to be made between legitimacy and self-interest in explaining why states comply with a norm. But this is curious given his general thesis in *Social Theory of International Politics* that identities are constitutive of interests. By voting with the USA over Kosovo, Argentina strengthened its claim to be part of the Western orbit, an identity that promised to bring tangible political and economic benefits.

Gabon and Gambia were silent in the debate over the Russian draft resolution, but Bahrain and Malaysia contributed to it. In a short statement, the Permanent Representative for Bahrain claimed that his government was unable to support the resolution because this would have done nothing to rectify the 'humanitarian crisis of tremendous proportions' (S/PV.3989, 26 March 1999, p. 9) facing the Kosovars. It was anticipated that Malaysia might abstain on the vote, but in the end, it voted against the resolution. Its Deputy Permanent Representative tried in his statement to balance the conflicting principles at stake: on the one hand, he affirmed his government's view that force 'should be sanctioned by the Security Council', but on the other, he considered that the 'immense humanitarian catastrophe' and the 'irreconcilable differences in the Council' necessitated 'measures to be taken outside of the Council' (S/PV.3989, 26 March 1999, p. 9). These statements clearly provide no support for the idea that there is a legal right of humanitarian intervention in the absence of express Council authorization. However, it is equally problematic to explain the votes cast by Malaysia and Bahrain in terms of the operation of American hegemony as the Cuban Ambassador argued. If this was the case, then why did Malaysia and Bahrain feel the need to make a public statement rather than remain silent, as was the case with other members like Brazil who also cast a vote against the Russian resolution? What is lacking from both the 'sovereignty as responsibility' and a materialist explanation is recognition of the specific contextual factors that led to the voting.

The majority of Council members (excluding the five NATO states and Slovenia) rejected the Russian resolution because they accepted that NATO's action was justifiable on humanitarian grounds. Having witnessed the horrific consequences of Serb ethnic cleansing in Bosnia, and fearful that this was about to be repeated in Kosovo, they were persuaded that such atrocities could not be tolerated again. The conundrum that faced Council members was that whilst NATO's intervention was a clear breach of specific provisions of the Charter, the illegality of its action had to be weighed against the moral imperative to rescue the Kosovars. The result was that the majority of non-Western states on the Council operated an international equivalent of mitigation in domestic law systems.[21] Thomas Franck argues that 'the essence of mitigation is that the law recognises the continuing force of the rule in general, while also accepting that in extraordinary circumstances, condoning a carefully calibrated and justifiable violation may do more to rescue the law's legitimacy than would its rigorous implementation' (Franck 2002: 185). The analogy with domestic law should not be pressed too far: At no point did any of the five NATO members on the Council argue that the Alliance's recourse to force was a breach of the law that was justified on moral grounds.[22] Equally significant is the fact that none of the seven non-permanent members who voted down the Russian resolution defended their vote explicitly in these terms. On the other hand, NATO did not rely on an explicit legal rationale, and its claim to be acting to prevent a humanitarian emergency could be interpreted as a plea in mitigation. Franck argues that when faced with such pleas, the role of the UN's political organs—crucially the Council—is to act as 'a global jury' (Franck 2002: 186) in which the text of the Charter is balanced against the moral necessities of the case. There is nothing objective about such a balancing of legality and morality. Indeed, a different grouping of non-permanent members with a different set of interests and values might have interpreted the facts of the Kosovo case very differently, leading to a more positive assessment of the resolution proposed by Russia.

The other crucial point about the practice of mitigation exercised by Council members over Kosovo is that it does not represent approval of a new legal principle of unilateral humanitarian intervention. This judgment is supported by the statement made by the foreign ministers of the non-aligned countries at their meeting in Cartagena in April 2000. They repeated their long-standing opposition to the doctrine of humanitarian intervention:

> We also want to reiterate our firm condemnation of all unilateral military actions without proper authorisation from the United Nations Security Council...We reject the so-called 'right' of humanitarian intervention, which has no legal basis in the UN Charter or in the general principles of international law   (Foreign Ministers Statement at a meeting of the Non-Aligned Movement, Cartegena, April 2000).

Yet it is clear from the Council's response to NATO's use of force against Yugoslavia that such ringing statements of principle are not necessarily a reliable guide to how states will react in specific cases where they have to balance conflicting legal and moral concerns. The lesson of Kosovo is that the Council is not ready to formally endorse intervention for humanitarian purposes by individual states or 'coalitions of the willing' when the Council itself has not expressly authorized it. But neither is it always going to condemn it. The moral and legal responsibility that falls on those who intervene without Council authority is to persuade the Council—and wider global opinion— that its action should be excused or tolerated on humanitarian grounds. And if states are not condemned for breaking the law in such cases, or only pay a minor penalty for such infractions, it seems reasonable to conclude that the Council would be operating a principle of mitigation as it did over Kosovo.

The lesson that many draw from Kosovo is the importance of making the Security Council work better so that it can avoid a future situation where the permanent members are divided on the merits of using force to end a humanitarian crisis. The ICISS in its report proposed that the Council agree on the principles that should determine when military intervention is justifiable on humanitarian grounds. This idea had been championed by the UK in late 1999. The British Foreign Secretary, Robin Cook, had instructed officials to draw up a paper on guidelines for intervention that was circulated to the other permanent members of the Council. The paper has not been made public but it is possible to glean its key aspects from a speech Cook made in July 2000.[23] The Foreign Secretary identified the following parameters

for defining a legitimate intervention: the existence of an extreme humanitarian emergency; the exhaustion of all peaceful remedies; an 'objective determination' that force is the only means to avoid a humanitarian catastrophe;
and the conduct of an operation so as to satisfy the principles of international
humanitarian law. The British hoped that agreement on such principles
would help the Council respond in a united and effective way the next time
it was faced with an urgent humanitarian crisis. The problem with this
approach is that even if the Council could reach agreement on the criteria to
be applied, this does not guarantee agreement over whether these have been
met in specific cases. The fact is that had an agreed document based on the
UK criteria existed at the time of Kosovo, this would not have resolved
the disagreements among the P-5. The same response can be made to the rec-
ommendation in the ICISS report that the P-5 agree not to exercise the veto
to obstruct a resolution with majority support aimed at stopping or
preventing 'a significant humanitarian crisis...where [their] vital national
interests were not claimed to be involved' (ICISS 2001a: 51). Given that the
key disagreement in the Council was over whether the humanitarian crisis in
Kosovo met the threshold that should trigger UN military intervention,
the ICISS's proposal to restrict the veto fails to address the root cause of the
divisions over Kosovo.

   This does not mean that there is no value in seeking a consensus on
criteria within the Council. Were the latter to agree on a set of norms governing
permissible interventions, this would provide it with a common framework
when deciding the merits of humanitarian interventions that are taken outside of explicit Council authority. As such, it might help the Council exercise
its function as a 'global jury'. This view finds support in Ian Johnstone's
assessment that 'deliberation on these questions could enhance the power of
persuasion based on law, and give "the better argument" a fighting chance in
Security Council decision-making' (Johnstone, forthcoming). Criteria would
not guarantee consistency in approach, since Council actions will always be
subject to the play of power and interests. Nor would it resolve thorny
disputes over the application of the principles as arose over Kosovo. What it
would do is send a signal to states that interventions, which could not
reasonably be defended in terms of this framework, would lack credibility.
Moreover, governments that tried to press such claims would risk being
condemned—and perhaps sanctioned—by the Council.

   The ICISS report suggested that the prospect of future unilateral actions
could be helpful in sending a clear message to the Council that it would
undermine its authority if it failed 'to discharge its responsibility in
conscience-shocking situations crying out for action' (ICISS 2001a: 55). If this
was a veiled reference to Kosovo, then it overlooked the fact that the Council
was divided on what constituted the proper exercise of its 'responsibility' in
this case. The statement in the report would have been more pertinent had it

been specifically related to Rwanda, since this is where the Council was most derelict in its responsibilities. But it is also a case where there was no unilateral action by concerned states determined to prevent or end genocide.[24]

3.5 Conclusion

By mapping the changing boundaries of Security Council intervention in the 1990s, this chapter has provided support for Annan's claim that there is a new norm of intervention to protect civilians in peril. It is virtually inconceivable that Russia and China (unless they had vital interests at stake) would veto Council action in a clear-cut case of genocide or wholesale slaughter. The fact that even China felt unable to veto two chapter VII resolutions that demanded Yugoslavia respect its international humanitarian obligations in relation to the Kosovars is indicative of how traditional meanings of sovereignty are changing as a consequence of the growth of human rights values in world politics. Council members remain fiercely protective of the non-intervention principle, and those most sensitive about the doctrine of humanitarian intervention, will look to justify action in terms of the chapter VII requirement that it contributes to 'international peace and security'. But the importance of the humanitarian norm in constraining state actions is revealed by the fact that even the most powerful non-Western states have been reluctant to directly oppose intervention in cases of extreme humanitarian need. Nevertheless, the extent of this normative change should not be pushed too far. There is still no case where the Council has explicitly sanctioned military humanitarian intervention in the absence of some form of consent from the target state.

The development of a new norm of UN intervention has been led by Western states that have played the role of 'norm entrepreneurs'. Realists like Stephen Krasner are right to argue that norms depend for their enforcement upon powerful states, and without the West's ascendancy at the end of the cold war, there would have been no interventions in northern Iraq, Somalia, and especially Kosovo. NATO's unilateral use of force against Yugoslavia antagonized Russia and the fact that this did not lead to a crisis in US–Russian relations reflects the massive imbalance of power between the two states in the post-cold war world. But what is missing from this materialist account is that the mobilization of capabilities for humanitarian purposes only became possible when domestic political pressures compelled Western governments to act. This effect on policy was least influential in the case of Kosovo where Clinton and Blair took the lead in forging domestic support for intervention. A mix of humanitarian and security imperatives led the major NATO states to use force against Yugoslavia, but it is too easy to present the Alliance's humanitarian rationales as window dressing to disguise the projection of American power in the Balkans. The Clinton Administration had been stung by criticisms of its inaction over Rwanda and especially Bosnia, and it was determined to prevent another humanitarian catastrophe in Kosovo. This conviction on the part of Clinton and Blair that they had a moral responsibility to defend liberal values led them to define Western interests very differently than had been the case with US and UK policy in relation to Bosnia.

In seeking to legitimate new actions that challenged existing norms of intervention, Western governments were careful to frame these in terms that were compatible with the normative framework of the UN Charter. The most controversial example of this was Kosovo. The five NATO members on the Council—reluctant to advance a legal doctrine of unilateral humanitarian intervention—invoked the claim that they were acting in support of the humanitarian purposes embodied in existing resolutions—none of which explicitly authorized the use of force. Russia and China were prepared to acquiesce in the West's stretching of resolutions when this could be defended on humanitarian grounds as in northern Iraq. But they drew the line when NATO attempted to justify the bombing of Yugoslavia on this basis, considering that the Alliance's recourse to force was both flagrantly illegal and the antithesis of humanitarianism.

The fundamental issue at stake over Kosovo was who should decide when a humanitarian crisis has reached the point that recourse to force is justifiable: Russia, China, and India were emphatic that this decision must always rest with the Council. Set against this, NATO took the view that in situations where it believed there was an extreme humanitarian crisis, and where the Council was paralysed by the threat of the veto, it had the moral authority to act. The best defence of NATO's intervention in Kosovo is that it was an anticipatory one aimed at preventing a humanitarian catastrophe. Had NATO waited until its intelligence predicting an escalation of the ethnic cleansing had been proven correct, Russia and China might have supported the use of force. But armed intervention would have come too late to save many Kosovars. Given that the risk of states abusing humanitarian claims for ulterior purposes is greatest in relation to preventive action, the challenge facing the UN is to devise a framework for judging the legitimacy of anticipatory humanitarian interventions. The fact that seven of the ten non-NATO states on the Council voted against the Russian resolution condemning NATO's action indicates that they were persuaded that NATO had carried the burden of justifying the use of force on these grounds.

The votes cast in the Security Council on 26 March 1999 in no way marked acceptance of the legitimacy of non-Security Council authorized intervention. Rather, they are best viewed in terms of the majority of non-permanent members deciding on moral grounds to excuse NATO's breach of UN Charter rules governing the use of force. It is conceivable that future cases will arise where the Council has to pronounce again on the legality of unilateral intervention justified on humanitarian grounds, and this could lead it to exercise a form of mitigation as it did over Kosovo. If a number of precedents build up of this kind, then this might, as Jane Stromseth suggests, lead to the gradual emergence of a 'new normative consensus regarding [non-Security Council authorized] interventions for humanitarian purposes... In this gradual process of normative evolution, any conflicts between the non-intervention and the human rights principles at the heart of the UN Charter are best addressed in concrete situations...' (Stromseth 2003: 271). The problem with this customary law solution is that no new 'normative consensus' is going to resolve the kind of moral and political differences that existed in the Council over Kosovo.

The extent to which the Council will be called upon to exercise its 'jury-ing' function in the future depends upon whether we should expect to see new anticipatory interventions that are defended in terms of human rights principles. As noted above, NATO's intervention in Kosovo occurred because the humanitarian impulse was joined by a hard-headed security interest in confronting Milošević. The viability of any 'developing international norm' depends upon the most powerful states being prepared to use force to protect humanitarian values when they are most endangered. But it also crucially depends upon being able to show that force can save lives if it is employed in a proportionate and discriminate manner. An opportunity to demonstrate that violence is sometimes the only means to protect humans from terrible slaughter was provided by the genocide in Rwanda. And it is the failure of the Council—crucially its most powerful Western members—to do more to end the killings in Rwanda that best illustrates the moral limits of the new norm of military intervention for humanitarian purposes in international society. For some, this suggests the irrelevance of norms as in David Rieff's grim obser-vation on the twentieth century—'no century has had better norms and worse realities' (Rieff 2002: 70). On the other hand, the ICISS report argues that if the norm of 'sovereignty as responsibility' can secure a firm hold over the thinking of governments and their citizens, this will generate the neces-sary political will to ensure that action is taken by the UN the next time it confronts genocide and mass slaughter (see ICISS 2001a).

The problem with this prognosis is that the US reaction to 11 September suggests that the major debate over humanitarian intervention triggered by Kosovo is being fundamentally recast in the light of the 'war against terrorism'. For those committed to entrenching the norm of 'sovereignty as respons-ibility', a pessimistic reading of 11 September is that it spells the end of Western intervention for the purposes of protecting individuals and minor-ities in danger. The concern is that the Bush Administration would be so preoccupied with fighting the spectre posed by global terrorism that it would have little or no enthusiasm to launch interventions, or support others in such endeavours. After the collapse of the twin towers, the luxury of choosing whether to save strangers has been replaced by the urgency of using force to counter the perils posed by global terrorism and weapons of mass destruction. Liberal internationalists like British Prime Minister Tony Blair might assert that 11 September should not distract the international community from its compelling 'moral duty'[25] to stop future genocide. But given the priorities driving the White House of George W. Bush, there is little reason to think that the West's response to a future Rwanda would be any different than it was in April 1994.

Yet, it would be misleading to conclude from this that humanitarian claims are irrelevant in thinking about the 'war against terrorism'. As Simon Chesterman shows in Chapter 9 of this book, humanitarian justifications have played a role in the first two prominent phases of the new war against terror—Afghanistan[26] and Iraq. On the most positive reading, reliance on humanitarian rationales by the USA and its allies could help in holding these states accountable for their protection of civilians in states targeted for intervention. But this compromise between the two agendas of intervention is deeply problematic from a moral point of view if it leads to a situation where intervention to save civilians is only possible if this is a by-product of a counter-terrorist inspired intervention. Moreover, the worry about the US invocation of humanitarian claims is that far from constraining American power, this becomes a legitimating device to cover the fact that violence is being used for American strategic purposes in ways that are detrimental to humanitarian values.

It is evident that the Bush Administration's 'war against terrorism' represents a major challenge to the doctrine of 'sovereignty as responsibility' that Annan has been pressing on the UN membership—and which finds its most eloquent expression in the ICISS report. The challenge for those governments wishing to promote this idea is to persuade other governments, the non-governmental humanitarian community, and wider global opinion that humanitarian intervention remains a moral imperative irrespective of whether this is defensible in terms of defeating the threat from global terrorism.

4

Taking Consequences Seriously: Objections to Humanitarian Intervention

Jennifer M. Welsh

4.1   Introduction

In Chapter 3, Nicholas Wheeler argued that a new norm supporting humanitarian intervention has developed in international society over the course of
the last decade.[1] In essence, this norm asserts that—when all other diplomatic actions have failed—states have the right and responsibility to employ
military force against another state in order to protect civilians in danger.
Wheeler's contention reflects, in the language of international relations
theory, a 'solidarist'[2] understanding of the nature of international society:
its conditions for membership, its normative depth, and its capacity to engage
in collective action.

More specifically, the emerging norm of humanitarian intervention is
alleged to derive from a fundamental shift in the understanding of
sovereignty in international relations—a move from 'sovereignty as authority'
to 'sovereignty as responsibility'.[3] The former defines sovereignty as unrivalled
control over a delimited territory and the population residing within it, while
the latter suggests that sovereignty is conditional upon a state demonstrating
respect for a minimum standard of human rights. What happens when these
responsibilities are not fulfilled? If we draw upon Henry Shue's formulation
from Chapter 2, every effective system of rights (including the rights of sovereignty) requires some default duties—that is, 'duties that constitute a second-
line of defense requiring someone to step into the breach when those with
the primary duty...fail to perform it.'[4] In our anarchical international system, there is no centralized police force to perform such duties. As the report
of the International Commission on Intervention and State Sovereignty
(ICISS) concludes: 'Sovereign states have a responsibility to protect their own
citizens from avoidable catastrophe...but when they are unwilling or unable

to do so, that responsibility must be borne by the broader community of states' (ICISS 2001*a*).

This chapter will argue that the most compelling objections to humanitarian intervention operate at this deeper, philosophical level. They question not only whether the doctrine of 'sovereignty as responsibility' *has* taken hold as a prevailing concept in international society, but also whether it *should* take hold—particularly in the form suggested by Western states. The consequences of this new understanding of sovereignty, they argue, would destroy the very pillars of international order without offering a robust alternative.

The philosophy underlining objections to humanitarian intervention is essentially a philosophy of limits: limits on the consensus that exists internationally about the link between a state's legitimacy and its protection and advancement of human rights; limits on the willingness of intervening states to engage in long-term efforts to address root causes; and finally, limits on the degree to which we can say that humanitarian interventions have been undertaken in the name of the 'international community'. Indeed, those that have opposed instances of humanitarian intervention have frequently raised concerns about who is doing the intervening—and on what grounds. This philosophy of limits is well captured by ethical philosopher Tzvetan Todorov in his 2001 Amnesty Lecture: 'individual human beings still get much more as citizens of a state than they do as citizens of the world'.[5] As I will show, the debate over humanitarian intervention is not a black and white one, between those who are concerned about human rights and those who turn a blind eye to human suffering. Rather, it is a debate about the boundaries of moral community, the consequences of intervention, and the density of values that underpin international society.

My argument proceeds as follows. First, I analyse two sets of objections to humanitarian intervention that dominate the international relations debate: legal and ethical. In so doing, I evaluate the strength of each challenge and establish that the ethical position of pluralism—particularly as articulated by non-Western states—mounts the most compelling objection. In the conclusion, I offer a response to pluralism that defends humanitarian intervention in extreme cases and suggest ways in which such action could gain greater legitimacy in international society.

4.2   Objections to humanitarian intervention

As demonstrated in the Introduction to this book, a number of 'push' and 'pull' factors have operated since the end of the cold war to facilitate intervention in the affairs of conflict-ridden societies. Most salient among these are: the end of superpower rivalry, which makes it possible for a collective 'international will' to be expressed; changing notions of security; revolutions in information and technology, which make the suffering of 'others' more visible and accessible; and the evolution of human rights norms and international humanitarian law. While there is clearly a climate of increased expectation for action, there are a series of reasons why one might oppose a new norm of humanitarian intervention. These reasons are found not only in the scholarly literature, but also in the rationale which states offer in their statements—whether in the UN or in the domestic political arena.

4.2.1 Legal objections

The 1999 NATO bombing of Kosovo has become famous for the volume of legal debate that it generated. Lawyers analysing the case have reached surprisingly different conclusions, even after reviewing the same kinds of evidence.[6] The level of controversy is significant, since as international lawyers Byers and Chesterman note: 'On the basis of traditional approaches to the interpretation of treaties and the analysis of customary rules... the Kosovo intervention was clearly illegal, and regarded as such by enough states that it could not possibly have contributed to a change in the law' (Byers and Chesterman 2003: 178). This suggests two possibilities: either those arguing for legality are speaking for a larger political agenda, or the nature of legal arguments is changing. Whichever view one holds, it is clear there is a legal divide on the question of humanitarian intervention.[7]

Let us look first at the relevant treaty law. The basic presumption of international law post-1945, according to the key articles of the UN Charter,[8] is that the use of force is illegal. The qualifications to this rule are claims made in the name of self-defence or collective security; in the latter case the Security Council may authorize the use of force if it does so explicitly through a resolution adopted under chapter VII. Up until the 1990s, most international lawyers agreed that intervention for the purposes of humanitarianism or democracy building did not pass these two hurdles. This interpretation is strengthened by the UN Charter's context and purpose—an effort to delegitimize individual acts of war and transfer authority for the use of force to the Security Council.[9]

The evolution of international humanitarian law suggests that responses to genocide could be seen as another legitimate exception to Article 2(4). Most states in the international community have accepted, through their ratification of the 1948 Genocide Convention, an obligation 'to prevent and to punish' such acts. This suggests that genocide has been placed beyond the protection of the domestic jurisdiction clause of the UN Charter—Article 2(7)—and must be viewed as an *international* crime. However, three caveats are in order. First, while the authors of the Convention sought to create an obligation to repress genocide, they explicitly chose *not* to establish universal jurisdiction.[10]

Although contemporary state practice is evolving on this question, particularly in the wake of the establishment of War Crimes Tribunals, it still suggests that prosecution by national courts is the preferred course in international law. Second, while legal analysis affirms that intervention in respect of genocide may include military action, 'this is viewed as a right rather than as an obligation'.[11] Finally, the law offers little support for states acting *individually* in response to acts of genocide. Article VIII of the Genocide Convention suggests that only multilateral responses are legitimate, stating that the signatories can 'call upon the competent organs of the United Nations to take such action under the Charter of the United Nations as they consider appropriate for the prevention and suppression of acts of genocide'.[12]

Those subscribing to 'legal realism'[13] suggest that the general prohibition on the use of force, enshrined in Article 2(4), could and should be stretched to accommodate other important principles of the UN such as human rights.[14] In other words, the original objective of outlawing force must be amended to permit interventions that promote a humanitarian purpose. Legal scholars who oppose this expansion of 2(4) argue that neither treaty nor customary law supports a change in priorities between the different goals of the UN; while there have been great strides in the development of measures to protect human rights over the last fifty years, such measures have not influenced the interpretation of Article 2(4) (see Hilpold 2001: 451–2). Furthermore, although human rights are listed as a principle in the early articles of the Charter, so too are other principles. If we are not arguing for the use of force to further those aims, why should humanitarian goals be any exception? These classical or 'restrictionist' lawyers[15] reason that the lawful exceptions to the prohibition on the use of force should remain limited to self-defence, and that the use of force for humanitarian purposes should be rendered impermissible.

An alternative legal argument favouring a more flexible interpretation of Article 2(4) focuses on the accumulated state practice of intervention since the end of the cold war. These 'counter-restrictionist' lawyers[16] point to a series of cases from the 1990s (particularly Liberia, Northern Iraq, Somalia, and Kosovo) as state practice supportive of a new customary rule, with statements by Western governments articulating humanitarian motives presented as evidence of an accompanying *opinio juris*. The problem with such an approach is that it privileges custom over treaty—a move which is controversial from the perspective of the Vienna Convention.[17] In addition, non-Western legal opinion opposes this interpretation of the customary law on intervention, since it seems to suggest that certain types of practice count more than others—that is, the actions of Western states versus the stated opposition from those such as China, Russia, and India. Indeed, the case for *opinio juris* in support of a new right of humanitarian intervention is difficult to make in the face of a series of General Assembly Resolutions that explicitly reject such a right.[18]

The legal objections to humanitarian intervention, while well reasoned, ultimately fail to satisfy. This is partly due to the standoff that exists within the legal community itself. More importantly, however, opposing humanitarian intervention because it is illegal does not take us to the heart of the debate. Frequently, there are deeper and more significant objections lying underneath legal arguments—whether they be about the strength of developing norms or larger objections to *any* use of force in international relations. Indeed, in his study of the legality of humanitarian intervention, Chesterman acknowledges that lawyers arguing in favour of a new right usually rest their case on moral grounds—the need to 'do something' in the face of evil (Chesterman 2001: 236).

Furthermore, the legal case against humanitarian intervention offers little help in evaluating the changing behaviours and expectations of states. Although the lawyers supporting a new customary right of humanitarian intervention overstate their case, there is a body of post-1990 practice that demonstrates support—or at least toleration—for UN-authorized actions with an expressly humanitarian purpose. This can be seen not only through the use of Security Council Resolutions which authorize the 'use of all means necessary' to secure humanitarian objectives, but also in the *ex post facto* UN endorsements given to interventions carried out by regional coalitions of states, such as that led by ECOWAS in Liberia in 1990.[19]

The cases, many of which are examined in this volume, reveal four important trends. First, contrary to what is commonly believed, state practice reveals a less clear-cut conflict between sovereignty and humanitarian intervention. In most legal definitions of humanitarian intervention, for intervention to truly be intervention, the state on the receiving end must *not* consent to the action. Yet, the state practice of the post-cold war period involves some degree of state consent—albeit in some senses coerced—for humanitarian actions. As Nicholas Morris notes in Chapter 6, the Bosnian regime did consent to the original placement of UN forces, although they were designed for impartial peacekeeping. Similarly, as Ian Martin's discussion of East Timor demonstrates, the Habibie government's consent was taken as a necessary condition before an international mission could proceed. In these and other cases, it is not clear that a right of humanitarian intervention, in the legal sense, is being asserted.

Second, most of the instances of intervention in the post-cold war period (Kosovo being the biggest exception) have involved Security Council resolutions that invoke chapter VII—that is, a threat to international peace and security. One reading of this trend is to suggest that states are still uncomfortable asserting that a human rights violation by a government against its own people is, in itself, a sufficient justification for the use of force. Instead, the rationale for using force is beefed up by the claim that international stability is being threatened by those violations—either through the flow of refugees or the spillover effects of civil war. Such an expansion could be made compatible with a doctrine of state sovereignty, and thereby enable trad-itionally non-interventionist states to support UN action.[20]

This leads to a third point: the legality of interventions for humanitarian purposes currently rests upon the condition of Security Council authoriza-tion. The foundational principle for international order, non-intervention, is set out clearly in Articles 2(4) and 2(7) of the Charter; it can only be qualified by Article 24, which gives the Security Council 'primary responsibility for the maintenance of international peace and security'. The presumption in law, therefore, is that action must be multilateral; you 'can't go it alone' and engage in unilateral humanitarian intervention.[21] ICISS has endorsed this reading of 'proper authority':

There is no better or more appropriate body than the United Nations Security Council to authorise military intervention for human protection purposes. The task is not to define alternatives to the Security Council as a source of authority, but to make the Council work better than it has   (ICISS 2001a: p. xii).

The ICISS conclusion is driven by a desire to maintain the Security Council's pre-eminent status within international society, and to avoid any further erosion of the 'social capital' it draws upon to encourage the cooperation of UN member states (Hurd 2002: 35). However, as Adam Roberts notes, it fails to address the deeper problems of politicization and lack of transparency that undermine the legitimacy of Council decisions.[22]

Finally, the cases of intervention over the past decade reveal that the thorniest issues around sovereignty come to the fore not so much at the moment of intervention, but rather *after* military force has been used, and the participating states are deciding how long their commitment should last. Since the mid-1990s, states engaged in missions for humanitarian pur-poses have found themselves rebuilding conflict-ridden societies. In the process, their actions have raised serious questions about the legitimacy and viability of international civil authorities, as well as charges that we are returning to a world of imperialist protectorates.[23] The legal literature on humanitarian intervention, in its quest to establish whether there is a 'right to intervene', has tended to overlook these dilemmas. As Robert Keohane puts it: 'classical notions of sovereignty provide a poor basis for policy with respect to the post-intervention political decisions in troubled societies' (Keohane 2003: 276).

4.2.2 Ethical objections

The ethical objections to humanitarian intervention fall into three broad categories: those arguing that the moral duty of the statesman is to his own citizens; those arguing that self-determination is compromised by intervention;

and those arguing that humanitarian intervention has negative consequences which overrule its noble intentions.

4.2.3 *Raison d'état*

As its name suggests, the realist school of international relations stakes its reputation on having a 'realistic' view of world politics. And that interpretation of what's *really* going on in the world doubts whether states act in moral or selfless ways. Even if states claim they are intervening on humanitarian grounds, they are actually attempting to further their own self-interest. In the case of Kosovo, realists argue that intervention was ultimately about upholding the credibility of NATO, and therefore, not really about upholding human rights.

This popular rendition of realism is problematic for two reasons. First, it sets up the 'straw man' of a humanitarian intervention driven by pure motives. It is an empirical fact that states have used humanitarian rationale for their actions. Undoubtedly, there have been mixed motives at work; we would look forever for a pure case of humanitarian intervention. The question is not whether states actually engage in humanitarian intervention, but whether they should. Realism, whether it admits it or not, does take a stand on this normative question.[24] Second, and more useful for our purposes, the realist position described above masks the ethical position that underpins this school of thought.

The classical realist notion of *raison d'état* maintains that the proper function of the state—and therefore, the primary responsibility of the statesman—is to protect and further the national interest. To put it in Hobbesian terms, this is what state leaders have been authorized to do. But scratching a bit deeper, one finds that this pursuit of the national interest is also a moral enterprise—albeit a different kind of morality. *Raison d'état* asserts that state leaders occupy a particular role, which raises new and different moral dilemmas from those that face ordinary individuals. It is this sense of 'political morality' (Wight 1966: 128)—and not any notion of natural law or international morality—that should drive the action of state leaders. Statesmen are entrusted with the fate of those who form part of their political community, and must base their foreign policy decisions on whatever serves the well being of their own citizens.

The privileging of the national interest over any universal moral claims can be traced to two important traditions in Western thought. The first and most extreme statement is found in the writings of Hegel, who conceives of the state as the ultimate source of morality.[25] In this formulation, sovereignty is intrinsically valuable and all forms of external intervention are viewed as illegitimate infringements on the moral freedom of states.

The other—and I would argue more compelling—tradition is social contract theory. According to contractarianism, the state exists as a discretionary association for the mutual advantage of its members, and the government as an agent whose duty is to serve the basic interests of those members. As political philosopher Allen Buchanan puts it: 'The justifying function of the state—what justifies the interference with liberty that it entails—is the well-being and freedom of its members. There is no suggestion that the state must do anything to serve the cause of justice in the world at large...' (Buchanan 1999: 75). Thus, state leaders have an 'overriding fiduciary obligation' to serve the interests of their own citizens and cannot use the resources of state to improve the lot of outsiders. This view has become prominent in many Western democracies, when state leaders are criticized for 'globe-trotting' rather than focusing on domestic policy priorities.

There are two main responses to *raison d'état*'s conception of obligations and interests. First, I would argue that a contractarian basis for the state does not necessarily restrict its ethical concerns to its own citizens. There are also important duties to outsiders. As Buchanan skilfully demonstrates, the depiction of the state as a discretionary association is plagued by incoherence. On the one hand, it justifies the state and its coercive apparatus by the need to protect universal interests—that is, the basic human rights of life, liberty, and property. On the other, it limits the right of the state to exercise that coercive power to the protection of particular individuals, 'identified by the purely contingent characteristic of happening to be members of the same political society' (Buchanan 1999: 79). Additionally, most versions of the discretionary association position recognize that states have certain negative duties to outsiders—namely, an obligation not to harm the innocent civilians of other states. Yet, this concession hints at a deeper belief in the moral worth of human beings, whose safeguarding may require *positive* actions as well. As Buchanan states: 'it is arbitrary to soften the harsh implications of the discretionary association view by admitting negative duties to noncitizens while denying any positive duties to noncitizens'.[26] In sum, while a state must fulfil its primary duties to its citizens, it also has, in the words of John Rawls, a natural duty 'to assist in the establishment of just arrangements when they do not exist, at least when this can be done with little cost to ourselves'.[27] Such an obligation is heightened when domestic opinion calls for foreign policy action to address suffering elsewhere, as it did in the United States during the crisis in Somalia. It is also supported by the current state of international humanitarian law and by the evolution of international human rights norms.

Second, as members of the constructivist school[28] have powerfully shown, the national interest is not magically and exogenously given, but rather constructed by a host of forces inside and outside a state. It is, therefore, conceivable, as in the case of New Labour in Britain, to expand the meaning. During the Kosovo crisis of 1999, representatives of the British government argued that a response to ethnic cleansing in the Balkans could be made compatible with the national interest if the notion of nation was widened to include the principles that Britain stood for. Britain, as a 'civilized nation', had an obligation to demonstrate horror in the face of 'uncivilized' acts. In a similar way, New Labour has argued that changes in the international system, driven by the forces of globalization, make it legitimate and necessary to widen the scope of the national interest. Tony Blair gave voice to this view in his 2001 speech to Labour Party Conference: '[w]hat is the lesson of financial markets, climate change, international terrorism, nuclear proliferation or world trade? It is that our self-interest and our mutual interests are today inextricably woven together' (Prime Minister Tony Blair, Speech to the Labour Party Conference, *Guardian*, 3 October 2001, p. 4). As a result, pursuit of national interest involves actions designed to minimize political, economic, and social instability elsewhere in the world. Humanitarian interventions are just one manifestation of this strategy.

4.2.4 Self-determination

The second ethical objection to humanitarian intervention, enunciated in the nineteenth century by J. S. Mill, is based on the belief that our highest moral duty is to respect the right of self-determination (Mill 1875: 153–78). It is through the act of self-government that political communities—and by extension, individuals—realize freedom and virtue. Outsiders cannot and should not interfere with this process, for as Mill writes: 'It is during an arduous struggle to become free by their own efforts that these virtues have the best chance of springing up.'[29]

The strongest modern proponent of this view, Michael Walzer, bases his objections to intervention on a strong understanding of communal integrity. He argues that sovereign states are moral entities and should therefore enjoy the presumptive right of non-intervention.[30] States are, in his words, 'the arena within which self-determination is worked out and from which, therefore, foreign armies have to be excluded'. But it is crucial to underscore that for Walzer it is the political communities that underpin states—and not the more surface-level state borders—which deserve of our moral concern. He clearly states that the standing of states and governments derive from the standing with their own citizens.

Walzer's critics suggest that his notion of communal integrity has conservative implications by shoring up the authority of illegitimate regimes.[31] But if Walzer's views are conservative, I would place them in a more Burkean camp. He adopts Burke's sense of political community as a historical contract that exists among 'the living, the dead, and those who are yet to be born' (Burke 1981: 146–7). A community's process of self-determination is a long one, marked by bumps in the road, and those who live outside that community cannot shorten or smooth it. Instead, we must make a moral presumption: 'that there exists a certain "fit" between the community and its government and that the state is "legitimate"'.

Walzer acknowledges that we are left with a strange situation: states are presumed to be legitimate in international society, even when they might actually be illegitimate at home. He argues that we should accept this—not for utilitarian reasons, but for moral ones. In his view, the claim that only liberal or democratic states should have a right against external intervention is akin to saying that protection should be offered only to individuals who have arrived at certain opinions or lifestyles. The rule of non-intervention is the respect that foreigners owe to a historic community and to its internal life.

Despite the power of this ethical objection, the argument breaks down once the notion of communal autonomy is questioned—that is, if there is a clear absence of 'fit' between the government and community. Walzer himself sets out two exceptions to the general presumption,[32] which he has further elaborated in writings after Bosnia and Somalia (Walzer 1995). First, when a community fragments, and there are competing factions in active revolt, the rule of non-intervention no longer holds—particularly, if another outside power has already intervened. Thus, for example, Walzer allows for intervention in cases where empires or multinational states are crumbling. Second, when the rights of individuals within a community are seriously threatened, such that they are no longer truly self-determining, outside intervention to protect basic individual rights is morally defensible. Walzer speaks of the legitimacy of intervention in cases of 'massacre' and 'enslavement'—to which he adds the expulsion of large numbers of people.

In these instances, the question is not *whether* humanitarian intervention is justifiable but rather *when?* It is important to underscore that the moral legitimacy of intervention is limited to extreme cases. If the right of self-determination is to be respected, then Western policymakers must clearly separate a minimalist conception of human rights protection from a maximalist intention to reshape societies in a Western, liberal-democratic image. In this regard, it is interesting to note that while liberals such as Michael Ignatieff supported the USA-led war against Saddam Hussein in 2003, Walzer insisted that the moral threshold had not been crossed. The ICISS report demonstrates how difficult it is to establish scientific measures of what constitutes 'extreme'; generally expressed, the threshold is those instances of violence which 'shock the conscience of mankind' or present an overwhelming threat to international security. More specifically, a moral defence of intervention can be mounted in two cases: where there is a large-scale loss of life—with or without genocidal intent—that results from deliberate state action or the massive failure of state structures; and where there is large scale 'ethnic cleansing' carried out by killing, rape, torture, or mass expulsion (ICISS 2001*a*).

There is another aspect of Walzer's argument that stresses not so much the sanctity of the community, but the value of pluralism. For Walzer, that value is inherent: he seems to enjoy looking around the world and seeing diverse communities. But in the hands of other philosophers, such as Todorov, the moral argument for diversity looks slightly different. Here, the search for a single truth is the enemy, for it inevitably leads to conquest and bloodshed. Far better, it is argued, to have a variety of entities claiming to know the truth—coexisting in a peaceful condition of mutual toleration. To put it another way, the moral argument for diversity inverts the Democratic Peace Thesis: attempts to remake the world's political communities into liberal democracies are likely to lead to war, not peace. This variation on Walzer, which points to consequences, is a more serious objection to humanitarian intervention and is closely linked to the pluralist position that I consider below.

4.2.5 Consequentialism

The third set of ethical objections to humanitarian intervention is consequentialist. Even if one could establish minimal obligations to outsiders and overcome concerns about self-determination, intervention is opposed because of the negative consequences it can bring. There are two different kinds of consequentialist arguments that have been levelled against humanitarian intervention: realist and pluralist.

4.2.6 Realism

In arguing for the national interest, some realists move beyond the script provided by *raison d'état* toward utilitarian calculations: states should further their own national interest because (if all states do this) it is likely to produce the best overall outcome.[33] In formulating foreign policy statesmen should not aim to maximize global well-being directly, but rather focus on the immediate interests of their own citizens.

For realist consequentialists, humanitarian interventions make irrational policy. There are simply too many unknown variables that the intervening state will not be able to control. More importantly, by intervening militarily in the name of abstract principles, we may create more problems than we solve. Hans Morgenthau's critique of US foreign policy in the 1960s nicely illustrates this argument. In his classic article, 'To Intervene Or Not To Intervene', Morgenthau alleges that failure to understand the distinction between abstract principles and national interests led to the Bay of Pigs Fiasco for the USA in 1961. 'Had the United States approached the problem of intervening in Cuba in a rational fashion, it would have asked itself which was more important: to succeed in the intervention or to prevent a temporary loss of prestige among the new and emerging nations.' The problem, according to Morgenthau, was that the USA failed to assign priority to these two considerations. 'Instead, it sought the best of both worlds and got the worst' (Morgenthau 1967: 431).

A variety of 'new problems' are envisaged by realist consequentialists. Opposition may be created on the ground in the course of engaging in military action. Expectations may be inflated among those suffering from oppression elsewhere in the world, who will quickly level the charge of selectivity if there is no intervention to support their cause. Anxiety and hostility may be provoked among other governments that fear they might suffer the same treatment. Or, as many consequentialist critics of recent interventions argue, military action will lead to a prolonged foreign presence, in the form of a quasi-protectorate, for which Western governments have little appetite (see, for example, Kissinger 2001: 270). Under any of these circumstances, the consequences will be disillusionment and resentment—the breeding ground for new enemies.

Consequentialist arguments of this kind are finding favour in many Western capitals, as governments debate the pros and cons of engagement in war-torn societies and search feverishly for exit strategies. Nonetheless, this objection to humanitarian intervention fails to convince. As suggested above, it is possible to conceive of a limited practice of humanitarian intervention, designed to address extreme cases. One could never completely erase the possibility of abuse or the selective application of the practice. But these objections in and of themselves are not strong enough, and should not prevent action where 'right' motive joins together with the capacity to make a difference. The same charges of abuse and selectivity accompany other uses of force in international relations. Arguments about the 'indivisibility of humanity' in many ways echo the claims about 'indivisibility of peace' that accompanied the development of collective security. Furthermore, the empirical evidence from the 1990s does not prove that abuse and selectivity have actually had negative consequences for the international system *as a whole*— which is the frame of reference for realist consequentialism.

In addition, while it is true that one cannot know in advance whether an intervention will succeed and not incur unacceptable damage and death, this does not completely rule out the use of force for humanitarian objectives. However controversial, there is a tradition of norms governing the use of force to which states have appealed when weighing risks against potential gains. ICISS, drawing on older traditions of just war theory, developed a set of six criteria to facilitate morally justifiable intervention: right authority, right cause, right intention, last resort, proportionate means, and reasonable prospects (ICISS 2001a). It is possible to conceive of cases—Rwanda being one of them—in which the timely use of force applied against humanitarian objectives could succeed in preventing or alleviating mass human suffering.

4.2.7 Pluralism

It is one thing to say that a limited and regulated practice of humanitarian intervention is conceivable, and quite another to say that it is legitimate in today's international system. This brings me to my final and most compelling critique—that of the pluralists.

Pluralist consequentialism rests on a deeper set of beliefs about the nature of international society. More specifically, it contends that the consensus that underpins international society is a *procedural* rather than *substantive* one[34]— limited to agreements about what constitutes acceptable external behaviour and reciprocal rules like non-intervention. In short, the bases for international order begin and end at state frontiers, and do not extend to a deeper homogeneity in political, social, or cultural values.

For pluralists, sovereign states are unlikely to concur on what counts as injustice or oppression inside a state, and hence unlikely to agree when humanitarian intervention would be justified.[35] Hedley Bull, writing in 1984, asserted that the consensus uniting states in the matter of human rights was a very slender one—even if they appeared to be speaking the same language. For him, the reluctance of the international community to endorse humanitarian intervention during the cold war period reflected 'not only an unwillingness to jeopardise the rules of sovereignty and non-intervention... but also the lack of any agreed doctrine as to what human rights are' (Bull 1984*b*: 193).

But pluralists go even one step further. Drawing on the moral argument for diversity I outlined earlier, they suggest that attempts to assert a consensus on human rights may undermine the fragile order that *does* exist in international society. This order, based on mutual toleration of difference, is viewed as a precondition for the protection and promotion of individual well being. Hence, in a twist on realist consequentialism, pluralists argue that the best international outcome derives from each state adhering to the norm of non-intervention (Mason and Wheeler 1996: 102; see also Holzgrefe 2003: 23–4). Considerations of stability must trump concern for justice.

Pluralists such as Robert Jackson are particularly concerned that humanitarian intervention might slide into a wider conflict. While states have a responsibility to pursue international justice where they can, they cannot jeopardize other fundamental values in the process. And here, international peace should have particular weight, since it is in situations of war—particularly war between great powers—where humanitarian values are most likely to be threatened (Jackson 2000: 291–2). In other words, there is a moral obligation to prevent war, which overrules the moral obligation to promote human rights elsewhere. Proponents of this view emphasize that the overriding aim of statesmen after 1945 was to prevent another disastrous war; accordingly, the UN was charged with the maintenance of international peace and security as a first priority. Echoing the restrictionist international lawyers, they argue that the only legitimate exceptions to the ban on the use of force are self-defence and collective security.

Pluralist arguments about consequences are the most difficult to counter, both conceptually and practically. Imagine a situation where the moral case for action is strong and the exit strategy is clearly laid out. States still might hesitate to act, for fear of fundamentally undermining international order—the rules and norms that allow members of international society to coexist and prosper. Indeed, Western hesitation to intervene in Chechnya is a possible example.

While Bull's and Jackson's pluralist objections to humanitarian intervention are formidable, I argue that they do not necessarily preclude action in cases of humanitarian catastrophe or mass violations of human rights. There are two ways of making this case.

First, Bull's cold war assessment requires updating. His commentary on humanitarian intervention grew out of a context in which the right had been asserted primarily by states that had intervened to rescue their own nationals.[36] Furthermore, his writing emphasized the difference between Western notions about the rights of individual persons against the state, versus the Soviet conception of rights as conditions brought about *by* the state and the Third World emphasis on collective rights. The post-cold war period has seen less tension between individual and collective rights[37]—although the question of whether the state must ultimately be the provider of human rights is still very much alive. Thus, while diversity continues to characterize international society in the twenty-first century, there is a greater degree of consensus today on the meaning of sovereignty and human rights than pluralists suggest. This view has been endorsed by the findings of the ICISS: 'The defence of state sovereignty, by even its strongest supporters, does not include any claim of the unlimited power of a state to do what it wants to its own people' (ICISS 2001*a*: 8).

Second, while the potential for inter-state war should be considered and guarded against, it is arguably not the most significant threat to humanitarian values in contemporary international society. If we look at the landscape of the twentieth century, we see that while roughly thirty-five million people were killed in armed conflict, somewhere in the neighbourhood of 150–170 million people have been killed by their *own* governments, through political murder or mass misery (Rummel 1996). If humanitarian values are our concern, then developing strategies to address their greatest enemy—even if it exists within the domestic jurisdiction of another state—is surely the biggest ethical dilemma of our time.

But pluralism is not so easily dispensed with. A strong, non-Western version has recently been articulated by Mohammed Ayoob, who sees the practice of humanitarian intervention as the greatest challenge to international society (Ayoob 2002: 81–2). Ayoob contends that the norm of non-intervention is more important today than ever, since international society has seen a rapid increase in its membership and erosion of the European culture than once underpinned it. Further, he strongly rejects any movement toward 'sovereignty as responsibility', arguing that it carries shades of the old 'standard of civilization' mindset.[38] For Ayoob, this contemporary revival of imperialism is particularly tragic, since it threatens to 'erode the legitimacy of an international society that for the first time has become truly global in character' (Ayoob 2002).

Ayoob's pluralist perspective on humanitarian intervention is reflected in the lukewarm reception given to the issue by developing countries. Indeed, while the concept of sovereignty has its roots in Europe, some of its most vocal defenders are found in the developing world.[39] Examples of the strong attachment to sovereignty and non-intervention can be found in the final communiqué of the meeting of the foreign ministers of the Non-Aligned Movement (1999 September) and of the Havana Group of 77 Summit (April 2000), both of which categorically rejected the so-called right of humanitarian intervention. China, the most powerful developing country in contemporary international society, has expressed this opposition to humanitarian intervention at the Security Council table, particularly during the Kosovo crisis.[40] As one Chinese commentator put it: 'As a matter of fact, interventionism is not at all "new". The Chinese are very familiar with such "humanitarian intervention" in their past and see it as a tool that was often used by advanced countries to conquer so-called "barbarous ones" and to impose "civilised standards".'[41]

What is noteworthy about non-Western pluralism is that it emphasizes the justice function that non-intervention can play in an empirically unequal world. Ayoob observes that sovereignty is constituted not only by attributes, but also by peer recognition. Sovereign recognition provides a shield for weak states against the interventionist and 'predatory instincts' of the great powers. In other words, his conception of justice is one of equality of status, rather than economic redistribution.[42] This leads Ayoob to an apocalyptic conclusion about the consequences of tinkering with sovereign equality and legitimating intervention—even for humanitarian purposes: 'International society is based on a set of normative structures, with sovereignty being the foremost among them. If these structures are undermined, it may lead to either unadulterated anarchy or unmitigated hegemony or a combination of the two— anarchy within and hegemony without' (Ayoob 2002: 82–3). In this sense, Ayoob comes very close to Todorov's observation that states still have the greatest capacity to provide protection and welfare for individuals. Other organizations, whether international or non-governmental, have not yet demonstrated they can establish or maintain political order. And until they can, he warns, we should not impair the ability of sovereign states to do so.

In sum, Ayoob's pluralism raises two fundamental questions for the humanitarian intervention debate: whether the values underpinning recent interventions are truly universal, reflecting a consensus on how to define 'sovereignty as responsibility'; and, whether such interventions can be said to represent the will of the international community. Who is it that decides when a state has not fulfilled its responsibilities, and determines that only force can bring about its compliance?

4.3 Conclusion: the response to pluralism

This chapter has argued that of the legal and ethical objections to humanitarian intervention, the pluralist position is the most compelling. Questions about 'sovereignty as responsibility' lead directly to questions about the legitimacy of intervening with force in a sovereign state on humanitarian grounds. They also raise important questions about who should play the role of judge and enforcer in contemporary international relations.

This leads me to three sets of conclusions about humanitarian intervention and international society. First, if we retain a very limited notion of 'sovereignty as responsibility', and resist the temptation to conflate a minimal protection of human rights with the right to liberal-democracy, the consensus on those exceptional cases that justify humanitarian intervention will be easier to achieve. Under such a scenario, we are likely to see much greater support for humanitarian intervention in situations of complex emergency when states are collapsing (Somalia and Sierra Leone) than in cases aimed at regime change or punishment for actions against minorities (Haiti and Kosovo). As we move into the twenty-first century, the issue of humanitarian intervention is more likely to occur, to use Ignatieff's words, 'in the context of chaos rather than tyranny' (Ignatieff 2003: 305). Humanitarian intervention will remain a rare occurrence in international society, and will be treated as a nuanced exception (Franck 2003: 227) to the general prohibition against the use of force in international law.

This first conclusion acknowledges that there remains a very strong conviction—not only in non-Western circles—that the state is still the best agent to promote and protect human rights. Where pluralists such as Ayoob go too far, however, is in arguing that developing states should enjoy a kind of 'grace period', during which they can employ all means necessary to complete their state building process and ensure domestic order.[43] We can no longer accept mass murder or the killing of innocent civilians as a necessary part of what he calls the 'historical trajectory of state-making'—not only because it may threaten international peace and security, but also because the citizens inside such states should enjoy the same basic rights as those in the developed world (Makinda 2002). In fact, if the international community endows states with supreme moral force, and gives no attention to individual rights, it may unwittingly provide incentives for secession and further conflict. Individuals who feel threatened by another group within their state will conclude that the only path to survival is to band together and create a state of their own.[44] Finally, not all non-Western states are as weak as Ayoob suggests, or equally dependent on the protective shell of non-intervention. Indeed, greater clarity is needed as to what 'weak' and 'strong' mean in contemporary international society. It might be argued, for example, that China is in fact a strong state; unlike many developing countries in Africa, it possesses the capacity to provide for basic human rights—but in some cases its government chooses not to.

My second conclusion is that statesmen and policymakers must become more serious about improving the representativeness and effectiveness of the UN Security Council if they are to alleviate growing concerns about who speaks for the international community. As Adam Roberts suggests in the next chapter, it is questionable whether the Council can apply uniform criteria to instances of humanitarian crisis. It is also unclear whether the political bargaining that currently takes place in New York can continue to produce legitimate outcomes in the eyes of international society. The veto-bearing Permanent Five can rest easy; they will not be on the receiving end of an intervention. At the same time, however, they can prevent interventions or other kinds of UN action for narrow political reasons.[45]

Finally, if one believes in the notion of 'sovereignty as responsibility'—as I do—then more attention needs to be paid to the non-military means of operationalizing it. One of the major difficulties in legitimating humanitarian intervention has been the effectiveness of the cases in the 1990s. Situations like Kosovo demonstrate that humanitarian interventions can have tricky outcomes; because of the military component, they require the interveners to ally with forces on the ground (who are sometimes dubious) and can substantially weaken states in the short term. Moreover, interventions to safeguard the rights of one ethnic group may in the long run facilitate new acts of oppression—as witnessed by growing concern about the fate of the Serbian minority in Kosovo.

Given these high stakes and unintended consequences, alternative measures—whether diplomatic or economic—must continue to be pursued vigorously. Rather than punishing those states that are not responsible to their citizens, should we think more about how we can build the capacity of states to be responsible? If 'sovereignty as responsibility' is only meaningful in a negative sense, it is unlikely to take hold as a powerful norm in international society.

PART TWO

The Politics and Practice of Humanitarian Intervention

5

The United Nations and Humanitarian Intervention

Sir Adam Roberts

Since the end of the cold war, in territories ranging from northern Iraq to East Timor, a succession of urgent situations involving mass suffering has resulted in external military interventions that were justified on largely humanitarian grounds. There have also been situations, of which Rwanda and Bosnia are examples, in which there was a strong case for such intervention, but either no action followed or any action taken was too little and too late. All these situations involved the United Nations in numerous and complex ways: the UN has been at the centre of an unprecedented number of field operations and policy debates relating to humanitarian intervention. Member states of the UN disagree strongly on this issue, and different UN bodies have had different, and sometimes opposing, views and roles in respect of it. The subject refuses to go away, and has ominous implications for the UN.

At the heart of the UN's difficulty with humanitarian intervention lies a paradox. For its first 45 years the UN was firmly associated with the principle of non-intervention in the internal affairs of sovereign states—a fact that helped to explain the support that the UN received from governments of post-colonial states. Then, in the post-cold war era, the UN became associated with a pattern of interventionism, often on at least partly humanitarian grounds. From being an institution for the non-use of force, it became an instrument for the use of force. This chapter explores the history, causes, and consequences of this extraordinary and fateful change. I begin by examining the provisions for the use of force in the UN Charter, along with the development of human rights law and the laws of war since 1945. The chapter then reviews UN doctrine and practice on humanitarian intervention both during and after the cold war. The chapter concludes by identifying issues and controversies associated with humanitarian intervention that have arisen at the United Nations, including Kofi Annan's bold call to take the issue seriously, the UN General Assembly's not-so-bold response to a developing practice and doctrine of intervention, and the challenge posed by the Bush

Doctrine of September 2002. The question is raised: Could the problems associated with humanitarian intervention weaken or even destroy the UN?

The starting point of this chapter is that there is not now, and probably cannot be, a definite general answer in international law to the perennial question of whether states have a right of humanitarian intervention in the classical sense.[1] States and individuals continue to have radically different views of the matter. However, within the UN context the question has acquired certain new dimensions, some of which may be capable of being answered. Humanitarian intervention has affected the UN deeply, not just because it is a contentious issue, but also because it has proved to be an occasionally necessary, and almost always problematical, practice.

5.1   The United Nations Charter

In 1942–5, when they were making plans for what became the UN, the major members of the wartime alliance (itself called 'the United Nations') were engaged in a world war against the Axis powers.[2] It might seem logical that in such circumstances discussions for an international organization ought to have encompassed the right of intervention against any tyrannical regime that kills huge numbers of people. As some of their wartime declarations show, the allies were aware that the Nazi regime was committing large-scale killings. Yet, humanitarian intervention was not explicitly an issue in the debates and diplomacy leading to the conclusion of the UN Charter. Among the many reasons for this was the fact that the war was perceived more as a war against external aggression than against tyranny as such. Moreover, there was a natural concern not to frighten off the very entities, namely states, of which the UN was to be formed. As President Roosevelt said in 1944: 'We are not thinking of a superstate with its own police forces and other paraphernalia of coercive power.'[3]

The Charter is widely seen as fundamentally non-interventionist in its approach. Taken as a whole the Charter essentially limits the right of states to use force internationally to cases of, first, individual or collective self-defence, and second, assistance in UN-authorized or controlled military operations. Nowhere does the Charter address directly the question of humanitarian intervention, whether under UN auspices or by states acting independently. However, the Charter does set forth a number of purposes and rules, which are germane to humanitarian intervention. Some of these can be in conflict with others.

The strongest and most frequently cited prohibitions on intervention are those in Article 2. Article 2(4) states: 'All Members shall refrain in their international relations from the threat or use of force against the territorial integrity or political independence of any state, or in any other manner inconsistent with the Purposes of the United Nations.' Article 2(7) states: 'Nothing contained in the present Charter shall authorize the United Nations to intervene in matters which are essentially within the domestic jurisdiction of any state or shall require the Members to submit such matters to settlement under the present Charter; but this principle shall not prejudice the application of enforcement measures under Chapter VII.'

Ironically, Article 2(7), now frequently cited by post-colonial states in defence of their newly won sovereignty and in condemnation of any intervention without consent, has a colonial origin. Some of the pressure for the wording of Article 2(7) came from Britain, which was nervous about the strong pressures to dismantle the British Empire, and feared that the Charter might reinforce them. British diplomats, having failed to achieve collective British Commonwealth representation (with appropriate titanic status) in the new organization, fought a long battle to limit the powers of the new organization so far as the Empire was concerned. In particular, Britain worked hard and successfully to introduce wording into the 1944 Dumbarton Oaks proposals that the provisions for the pacific settlement of disputes 'should not apply to situations or disputes arising out of matters which by international law are solely within the domestic jurisdiction of the State concerned'.[4] This provision was the precursor of Article 2(7) of the Charter.

Notwithstanding the strong presumption against the use of force against a state on account of its treatment of its inhabitants, the Charter leaves some scope for humanitarian intervention in two main ways.

The first arises from the references to fundamental human rights, which are proclaimed to be central purposes of the UN in the Preamble and in Article 1. These references, and all that flowed from them, did much to establish that the UN was no mere trade union of states, as the League had often seemed to be, but was rather a body which could have some real appeal to individuals. The UN includes in its purposes, in Article 1(2): 'To develop friendly relations among nations based on respect for the principle of equal rights and self-determination of peoples, and to take other appropriate measures to strengthen universal peace'; and in Article 1(3): 'To achieve international co-operation in solving international problems of an economic, social, cultural or humanitarian character, and in promoting and encouraging respect for human rights and for fundamental freedoms for all without distinction as to race, sex, language or religion'. Article 55 further specifies that the UN shall promote 'universal respect for, and observance of, human rights and fundamental freedoms for all'. These provisions inevitably raise the question, not addressed directly in the Charter, of what should be done if these fundamental human rights are openly flouted within a state.

The second way in which the Charter may leave scope for humanitarian intervention concerns the possibility of such intervention under UN Security Council auspices. In Article 2(7), cited above, the final phrase allows for enforcement measures within states under chapter VII of the Charter. Chapter VII itself is much less restrictive than had been the equivalent provisions of the Covenant of the League of Nations (1919) about the circumstances in which international military action may be authorized. Under Article 39 the Security Council can take action in cases deemed to constitute a 'threat to the peace, breach of the peace, or act of aggression': in practice, humanitarian crises within states can encompass or coincide with any or all of these. Articles 42 and 51 leave the Security Council a wide range of discretion as regards the type of military action that it can take.

In the drafting process, these two aspects of the UN Charter, which later became significant in considerations of humanitarian intervention, were seen as important but not particularly controversial. The United States and United Kingdom, in particular, favoured both the statement of purposes and principles, and the more specific provisions giving the Security Council notably broad powers. The British, who are often assumed to have been state-centric in their approach, in fact consistently favoured the inclusion of reference to social security and human rights in numerous wartime documents about international organization, from the Declaration by United Nations of 1 January 1942 to the British drafts of the UN Charter preamble in 1945.[5] This was partly because they wanted a strong Security Council, free to act in a variety of situations. However, the inclusion of these two aspects was not due solely to the USA and UK, but was the result of pressure from many states, including the Soviet Union (Russell 1958: 777–9).

Authoritative legal expositions of the UN Charter have reached different conclusions on humanitarian intervention. The commentary edited by Bruno Simma contains an entry by Karl Doehring who, after stating that in the past 'the overwhelming view in international law inclined towards a rejection of humanitarian intervention', goes on to take a sympathetic view of the lawfulness under the Charter of humanitarian intervention, especially in cases where the right of self-determination is involved.[6] However, in the same volume Albrecht Randelzhofer appears to take a more absolutist view, stating: 'Under the UN Charter, forcible humanitarian intervention can no longer, therefore, be considered lawful.'[7]

5.2   Parallel streams: human rights law and the laws of war

Since 1945 there have been many political and legal developments that have made the actions of governments subject to international scrutiny and, ultimately, to certain forms of international pressure. In fields ranging from arms control to the environment there are international standards by which the conduct of states can be evaluated. In particular, the powers of states over those under their control have been significantly limited. Two separate but roughly parallel streams of international law, both of which relate to the treatment of individuals by governments, have been of particular significance in this regard: (1) *Human Rights Law*, including especially the law relating to torture and unlawful killing; and (2) *The Laws of War* (also called international humanitarian law applicable in armed conflict), especially those aspects that address the protection of civilians.

The key concept of 'crimes against humanity' spans both these streams. It not only defines certain extreme crimes as internationally punishable, but also encompasses the proposition that even a government's actions against its own citizens may be the subject of international action. This long-standing concept was given prominence in the 1945 Nuremberg and 1946 Tokyo charters, and in the Nuremberg and Tokyo judgments of 1946 and 1948 respectively, all of which referred specifically to crimes against humanity. The first multilateral treaty explicitly prohibiting a crime against humanity is the 1948 UN Genocide Convention, which establishes that genocide, even if carried out entirely within the borders of a state, is a matter of international concern. It specifies that any contracting state 'may call upon the competent organs of the United Nations to take such action under the Charter of the United Nations as they consider appropriate for the prevention and suppression of acts of genocide...'.[8] In the 1990s, with renewed focus at the UN on the implementation of international humanitarian norms, the concepts of 'genocide' and 'crimes against humanity' were the subject of articles in the 1993 Statute of the International Criminal Tribunal for the former Yugoslavia, the 1994 Statute of the International Criminal Tribunal for Rwanda, and the 1998 Rome Statute of the International Criminal Court.[9]

The impressive body of human rights law first emerged in the period of effective Western dominance of the UN, but it acquired a momentum of its own. The first landmark, adopted by the General Assembly in 1948, was the Universal Declaration of Human Rights.[10] Although not a treaty, and technically no more than a non-binding declaration, it gave substance and specificity to some of the Charter's general references to human rights, and came to be seen as an authoritative interpretation of them (Simma (ed.) 2002: 926). At the time, it was criticized by the Soviet Union and certain other states as an infringement of sovereignty. After eighteen years of bargaining in a much-changed UN came the two 1966 human rights covenants, respectively, on Economic, Social, and Cultural Rights, and on Civil and Political Rights, both of which were legally binding, entering into force in 1976. There was also a range of treaties on such matters as refugees (1951), elimination of racial discrimination (1965), equal status of women (1979), torture (1984), and rights of the child (1989).[11]

A particular issue within human rights law that has major implications for intervention is the right of self-determination. Article 1 of both of the 1966

UN Human Rights Covenants declares: 'All peoples have the right of self-determination. By virtue of that right they freely determine their political status and freely pursue their economic, social and cultural development.' This reassertion of the Charter principle of 'self-determination of peoples' is open to interpretation as at least potentially implying a right to intervene in a territory if the rights of a people within it are being massively denied.

The large body of human rights agreements concluded under UN auspices had profound implications, not just for the relations between citizen and state, but also for the conduct of international relations. For good or ill, they strongly reinforced the view that a government's treatment of its citizens was a matter of legitimate international concern. They also provided mechanisms whereby a range of human rights issues could be pursued. The 1984 UN Convention on Torture gives a state jurisdiction if the victim is a national of that state (1984 UN Convention on Torture, Article 5). This was the basis of the judgment of the House of Lords on 24 March 1999 in the Pinochet case, that in principle the former Chilean President could stand trial in Spain. However limited its practical outcome, the decision marked a recognition that human rights standards are beginning to make inroads into the rival principle of sovereign immunity.

If such a development now seems to have been inevitable, that is not how it appeared to a majority of states at the time when many of these agreements were concluded. On the contrary, in that period the UN General Assembly also adopted numerous declarations of a general character that strongly reasserted the fundamental importance of the principle of non-intervention. A typical example is the 1965 'Declaration on the Inadmissibility of Intervention in the Domestic Affairs of States', which stated unequivocally: 'No State has the right to intervene, directly or indirectly, for any reason whatever, in the internal or external affairs of any other State.'[12]

The laws of war (otherwise known as international humanitarian law applicable in armed conflict) similarly provide some possible bases for intervention in a way that was not evident to all at the time of their adoption. In the decades after 1945, in marked contrast to much international human rights law, the laws of war mainly developed outside a UN framework. The UN was reluctant to become involved since its role was seen as the elimination of war, not the mere mitigation of its effects. As the law developed, the UN gradually became more involved in aspects of its implementation, and in the negotiation of new agreements.

Certain provisions of the main post-1945 treaties on the laws of war can be interpreted as giving some basis for humanitarian intervention. Common Article 1 of the four 1949 Geneva Conventions states: 'The High Contracting Parties undertake to respect and to ensure respect for the present Convention in all circumstances.' This wording is reiterated in Article 1(1) of 1977 Geneva Protocol I, on international armed conflicts, which additionally provides, in

Article 89: 'In situations of serious violations of the Conventions or of this Protocol, the High Contracting Parties undertake to act, jointly or individually, in co-operation with the United Nations and in conformity with the United Nations Charter.' Some have taken the view that these provisions constitute a basis for a wide range of actions against those who systematically violate the basic rules of the conventions.[13] Others, while not denying that a right of involvement may have emerged, have taken a more sceptical view of the original meaning of common Article 1.[14]

The laws of war as they have developed since 1945 contain some provisions which could infringe on the powers of states. For example, a common article in each of the 1949 Geneva Conventions provides for a system of what is widely (and perhaps confusingly) called 'universal jurisdiction' when it specifies that states parties are 'under the obligation to search for persons alleged to have committed...grave breaches, and shall bring such persons, regardless of their nationality, before its own courts. It may also... hand such persons over for trial to another High Contracting Party...'[15] However, this had only limited effects. It did not turn out to be a general licence to states to issue international arrest warrants for foreigners suspected of war crimes.[16]

The laws of war, by no means, point unambiguously in the direction of a right of intervention to stop violations. A number of agreements in the fields of international humanitarian law and humanitarian assistance contain provisions that appear to exclude the idea that such agreements could provide a basis for military intervention. These provisions are to be found mainly in international humanitarian law treaties and in resolutions of the UN General Assembly on humanitarian assistance.

Since the question of humanitarian intervention arises primarily in connection with situations that are internal to a particular state, the most relevant part of international humanitarian law is that which relates to non-international armed conflicts. Yet, this part of international law offers little support for interventionism. In the 1977 Geneva Protocol II—the main agreement on non-international armed conflict—Article 3, entitled 'Non-intervention', states (in full):

1. Nothing in this Protocol shall be invoked for the purpose of affecting the sovereignty of a State or the responsibility of the government, by all legitimate means, to maintain or re-establish law and order in the State or to defend the national unity and territorial integrity of the State.
2. Nothing in this Protocol shall be invoked as a justification for intervening, directly or indirectly, for any reason whatever, in the armed conflict or in the internal or external affairs of the High Contracting Party in the territory of which that conflict occurs.

Treaties applicable in international armed conflicts contain some comparable wording. A preambular clause in 1977 Geneva Protocol I states 'that nothing in this Protocol or in the Geneva Conventions of 12 August 1949 can be construed as legitimizing or authorizing any act of aggression or any other use of force inconsistent with the Charter of the United Nations'. Similar non-interventionist language can be found in the Preamble of the 1998 Rome Statute of the International Criminal Court and in Article 22 of the 1999 Second Hague Protocol on Cultural Property. The states negotiating these agreements may well have spotted the risk that the laws of war, like human rights law, might be used in order to justify some acts of intervention. The non-interventionist clauses that they inserted are a plea to major powers not to interpret these treaties as a ground for intervention.

5.3   The United Nations and interventions: 1945–90

In the cold war years, most members of the UN had good reason to be suspicious of any doctrine or practice of humanitarian intervention. Interventions and proposals for interventions by either of the superpowers or their allies were viewed as suspect on both legal and prudential grounds. Already, in 1946 the question of possible action against General Franco's rule in Spain proved extremely difficult, and highlighted the variety of possible interpretations of the Charter (Hamilton 1995: 46–63). From the mid-1960s onwards the new post-colonial members of the UN were not about to tolerate a reversion to interventionist doctrines, which they associated with the era of colonialism. The response of UN bodies to military interventions, while by no means entirely consistent, was in general to condemn them, including those with purportedly humanitarian justifications.

Security Council records are not the best place to look for an examination of the views of states on interventions during the cold war. Many issues were never discussed at all in the Security Council; and even when they were, many draft resolutions condemning particular interventions were vetoed, usually by the USSR or the USA.[17] The main focus here is on the General Assembly's stance, since that provides a fuller record, and an indication of the views of the membership as a whole.

The General Assembly almost routinely condemned a number of military interventions, including the Anglo-French intervention in Suez (1956), the Soviet intervention in Hungary (1956), the Indonesian intervention in East Timor (1975), the Moroccan intervention in Western Sahara (1975), the Vietnamese intervention in Cambodia (1978), the Soviet intervention in Afghanistan (1979), and the US-led interventions in Grenada (1983) and Panama (1989). However, not all interventions were condemned. For example, the General Assembly failed to criticize the Indian intervention in Goa (1962), partly because of sympathy with the principle of retrocession of colonial enclaves; and it did not condemn the Soviet-led intervention in Czechoslovakia (1968), because the Czechoslovak government, acting under duress, asked that the matter not be discussed.

During the cold war, the most interesting conflict of opinion within the UN on questions relating to humanitarian intervention was in connection with the India–Pakistan War of 1971. On 3 December 1971 Indian forces invaded the eastern part of Pakistan, following extreme cruelties perpetrated there by Pakistani forces in the preceding months. India justified its actions in terms which, apart from encompassing an element of self-defence, referred repeatedly to the urgency of responding to a situation that had resulted in ten million refugees fleeing from East Pakistan to India. On 4 December 1971, in a discussion in the UN Security Council on the Indian military action which had just commenced, the Indian representative said: 'We are glad that we have on this particular occasion nothing but the purest of motives and the purest of intentions: to rescue the people of East Bengal from what they are suffering.' India's policy was supported by the Soviet Union, but opposed by a majority subscribing to the language of non-interventionism. The US representative condemned the Indian action: 'The time is past when any of us could justifiably resort to war to bring about change in a neighbouring country that might better suit our national interests as we see them.' At the Council's meetings, three resolutions, which India strongly opposed, calling for a withdrawal of forces and a ceasefire were defeated only because of the Soviet veto.[18] After the Security Council decided on 6 December to refer the matter to the General Assembly under the 'Uniting for Peace' procedure, the General Assembly passed a ceasefire resolution almost identical to the one vetoed earlier in the Security Council.[19] The war only ended on 16 December, with the surrender of Pakistani forces in East Pakistan.

There were notable exceptions to the thrust of the UN's general pronouncements and resolutions opposing any kind of intervention or interference in states. The Security Council determined that two particular situations that were largely internal (in both of which a critical issue was racial domination by a white minority population) constituted threats to international peace and security: Rhodesia (1966) and South Africa (1977). In both cases it initiated sanctions under chapter VII of the Charter.[20] In neither case did the Security Council view the situation as one of acute emergency; nor did it authorize direct external military intervention within the state concerned. Thus, the Council did not support humanitarian intervention in these cases. However, it did appear to accept that domination by a racial minority, and refusal to take into account the wishes of the majority population, were factors that helped to justify taking measures under chapter VII.

None of this implied any more general challenge to the principle of sovereignty, which continued to be emphasized in UN General Assembly resolutions on many subjects. For example, resolutions on the question of aid to victims of emergency situations at one and the same time asserted the primary importance of such aid, and the continuing validity of the principle of state sovereignty, a typical example being a resolution adopted after the 1988 earthquake in Armenia that reaffirmed both 'the importance of humanitarian assistance for the victims of natural disasters and similar emergency situations' and 'the sovereignty of affected States'.[21] Some have viewed this and subsequent General Assembly resolutions as evidence of an emerging 'right to humanitarian assistance', or even a basis for a right of humanitarian intervention.[22] However, it is wishful thinking to read the provisions of these resolutions as moving even one inch beyond the sovereignty-respecting position of inviting, appealing to, and urging states to facilitate the work of inter-governmental and non-governmental humanitarian organizations.

The pre-1990 writings of many scholars in international law and relations addressing the question of humanitarian intervention classically defined often had little to say about the UN's actual and potential roles in this area. In particular, writers who were opposed to recognition of a right of such intervention, emphasizing its incompatibility with Article 2(4) of the UN Charter, paid relatively little attention to the possibility that such intervention might be authorized by the UN Security Council.[23] On the other hand, a minority of writers suggested that humanitarian intervention was compatible with the existence, legal principles, and developing role of the United Nations.[24] In 1984, Hedley Bull suggested that an era characterized by increased attention to human rights, and by an increased focus on the UN, was bound to see a revival of doctrines of humanitarian intervention.

If unilateralism could be avoided and intervention was seen as expressing 'the collective will of the society of states', Bull argued, the harmony and stability on international society could be maintained.   (Bull 1984b: 195).

What conclusions can be drawn from UN doctrine and practice in matters relating to humanitarian intervention during the cold war years? The non-intervention rule continued to be widely seen as fundamental. However, there were some conflicting trends and disjointed moves which pointed, often ambiguously and always controversially, in the direction of accepting the legitimacy of intervention in support of an oppressed and threatened population, especially where it was seen as a victim of colonial rule. These trends related more to intervention to support self-determination struggles than to humanitarian intervention as traditionally conceived. In addition, some writers glimpsed the possibility that the UN Security Council itself might authorize interventions on humanitarian grounds.

5.4   The United Nations and interventions: 1991–2000

After the end of the cold war, the UN became involved in the practice and doctrine of humanitarian intervention in an extraordinary variety of circumstances. The problem of whether forcible military intervention in another state to protect the lives of its inhabitants can ever be justified became politically sensitive due to the conjunction of a large number of factors, many of which were discussed in Chapter 1. The most significant new factor was the changed nature of great power relationships within the Security Council. From the late 1980s onwards, with the decline and fall of the communist system in the Soviet Union, the Permanent Five were more disposed than before to work together on issues of peace and security. Moreover, there was a greater willingness to view internal conflicts as potential threats to international stability, and therefore a matter for Security Council action. At the same time, serious tensions between major powers remained, often hampering agreement on military action; and many UN members continued to be nervous that major powers, whether or not acting in a UN framework, might intrude into what they still saw as their internal affairs.

5.4.1   Nine cases

During the period 1991–2000 the question of whether external institutions should, on partly or wholly humanitarian grounds, organize or authorize military action within a state arose frequently. Within the UN Security Council, it did so most sharply in nine cases. In each case there was, sooner or later, a humanitarian intervention of some kind, whether or not it was with explicit UN authorization and host-state consent (years of the relevant Security Council resolutions are in brackets): Northern Iraq (1991), Bosnia and Herzegovina (1992–5), Somalia (1992–3), Rwanda (1994), Haiti (1994), Albania (1997), Sierra Leone (1997–2000), Kosovo (1998–9), and East Timor (1999).

These nine cases, while indicating how deeply the UN has become involved in humanitarian intervention, also reinforce doubts about the extent to which 'humanitarian intervention' is a separate legal or conceptual category. With the possible exceptions of the French-led operation in Rwanda in 1994 and the Italian-led operation in Albania in 1997,[25] neither the UN Security Council, nor states acting independently, have cited humanitarian considerations alone as a basis for intervention. They have generally, and justifiably, referred to other considerations as well, especially considerations of international peace and security. This is not only for the obvious procedural reason that such reference is a *sine qua non* for any action by the Security Council, but also because different issues do overlap in practice.

In all nine cases the circumstances were such as to justify a serious international response. There had been massive social disruption and violence, with large numbers of people becoming internationally displaced persons or refugees. The causes of the disruption varied greatly: in some cases the key factor was the collapse of state institutions and the emergence of widespread disorder, while in others it was the brutality of an over-powerful state. Whether every single case really constituted a 'threat to international peace and security' is less sure, but any quibbles on this did not prevent the UN Security Council, in all but one of these cases, from explicitly referring to chapter VII of the UN Charter. Even with respect to the exception, northern Iraq in 1991, the Security Council made a veiled allusion to chapter VII by referring to threats to international peace and security.

The results of these interventions were mixed. In most if not all of them, intervention, even if too little or too late, did help to restore conditions in which people could return to their homes. The number of refugees and displaced persons who have returned, and the much more limited scale of any new outflows, is perhaps the most important single measure of the effectiveness of these interventions. However, the interventions have not had an especially impressive record of achieving a stable political order. For example, neither in Somalia following the intervention in 1992, nor in Haiti following the intervention in 1994, has there been a fundamental departure from long-established patterns of fractured and violent politics. In northern Iraq and Kosovo, interventions on humanitarian grounds did not, and perhaps could not, resolve issues of ethnic rivalry and disputes over political status.

The fact that there was much intervention with humanitarian purposes can easily distract attention from the many failures of the UN to act effectively, or even at all, in certain cases of extreme violence against civilian populations. In Rwanda in April 1994, and at Srebrenica in Bosnia in July 1995, the presence of UN peacekeeping forces did not save the victims of slaughter. In both cases the UN did subsequently authorize a use of force with a protective mandate, and in 1999 it issued the results of inquiries into the failure to act effectively at the time of these atrocities.[26] The reasons for the failure to protect endangered civilians included concern about the capacity, and safety, of the UN peacekeeping forces on the spot, lack of military preparedness for a combat role, reluctance of outside powers to risk the lives of their forces in a humanitarian cause, administrative delay and muddle, and a commitment to UN values of impartiality and non-use of force in situations where they had ceased to be appropriate. As Michael Barnett has written in his inside account of US and UN decision-making over Rwanda, what the UN did was 'all theater and public relations', but its failure to respond forcefully was also 'the *only* available choice given the reality on the ground, what member states were willing to do, the rules of peacekeeping, and the all-too-clear limits of the UN. Rwanda was beyond those limits.' He emphasized that, however questionable it was, the UN's failure to act was 'grounded in ethical considerations'.[27]

The role of individual states and alliances in the military aspects of these interventions is noteworthy. When force had to be used in a situation where military resistance was anticipated, it was generally deployed, not by the UN as such, but by a state or a coalition. The United States assumed the lead in all four cases of intervention without consent, and also in the episodes of

NATO military action in Bosnia in 1993–5. Other states took lead roles in the other four cases: France in Rwanda, Italy in Albania, the United Kingdom in Sierra Leone, and Australia in East Timor. Thus, these cases of humanitarian intervention have confirmed the more general truth that when force has to be used in support of UN purposes, its use does not follow those provisions of the Charter that envisage direct UN management of force. States, it appears, are still indispensable as mechanisms for the effective use of force.

5.4.2   Host-state consent

The nine cases demonstrate that the distinction between coercive intervention and intervention by consent has been much more blurred in practice than it ever was in theory. Of the nine cases, only four (northern Iraq, Somalia, Haiti, and Kosovo) involved a clear decision to engage in anything like a 'humanitarian intervention' in the classical sense—that is, without consent of the host state. However, even in these four cases elements of consent to the international presence did sooner or later play some part. In the case of Haiti, reluctant consent was finally given while the invading force was airborne.

In the remaining five cases (Bosnia, Rwanda, Albania, Sierra Leone, and East Timor) the international presence for the most part had a degree of host government consent. Again, in many of these cases—particularly Indonesia's acceptance of the operation in East Timor—host-state consent was given only reluctantly, and might not have been given at all if the proposed intervention had not had a degree of UN authorization and control. In all five of these interventions with host-state consent certain actions were taken which did not have such consent. Even in government-held areas intervening forces which operated on the basis of consent sometimes took particular actions without the agreement of the authorities of the country concerned; and there was an implication in many Security Council resolutions that the international activity in the territory might continue even if host-state consent were to lapse.

In all cases, the fact that there might be some degree of consent from the central authorities did not mean that there was a general situation of consent. Intervening forces, even with full consent of the host state, often had to operate in parts of the territories concerned that were under hostile—for example, rebel—control. The degree of consent could vary greatly from one place to another, and from one moment to the next.

5.4.3   International authorization

In all nine cases in 1991–2000 the UN Security Council passed resolutions calling for the observance of humanitarian norms by a particular target state or by parties to a particular war; and in seven of the nine cases it explicitly authorized an intervention, whether by the forces of a state or coalition, or by UN peacekeeping forces, or a combination of the two. This is a record of activity going far beyond anything in the first forty-five years of the UN's existence, and it suggests that decision-making regarding humanitarian intervention, though not a monopoly of the Security Council, has become one of its key functions.

Of the seven cases in which the Security Council authorized an intervention, five for the most part had the advantage of host government consent (Bosnia, Rwanda, Albania, Sierra Leone, and East Timor). Thus, at least in legal terms the international action taken in these cases was relatively unproblematic. The two authorizations without host-state consent (Somalia and Haiti) represent a more remarkable development of the Security Council's powers. The fact that the Security Council authorized these two 'classical' humanitarian interventions, and that its right to do so was not contested by the UN membership generally, suggests that the Council is seen as being within its powers in authorizing humanitarian interventions without host-state consent. However, as Nick Wheeler suggests in his chapter, any such right is not absolute. In both cases the Security Council used language emphasizing the uniqueness of the particular situation addressed. The key resolution on Somalia, passed in 1992, said in the preamble: 'Recognizing the unique character of the present situation in Somalia and mindful of its deteriorating, complex and extraordinary nature, requiring an immediate and exceptional response.' Two years later, almost identical wording was used in the equivalent resolution on Haiti.[28] It appears that these phrases were inserted at the insistence of members of the Council who were apprehensive about creating precedents for interventions. Thus, the Council's approval of particular instances of humanitarian intervention has stopped well short of general doctrinal endorsement.

The remaining two of the 'classical' humanitarian interventions, northern Iraq and Kosovo, did *not* have explicit Security Council authorization. In both cases, it was evident that such authorization was not likely to be obtained, and so it was not formally requested. Military action was initiated by groups of states with the stated purpose of achieving the UN Security Council's objectives, but without its authorization; and it was only after such initial non-UN military action that a UN-authorized presence was established and deployed, benefiting from the consent (albeit belated) of the host state. Of these two, the Kosovo operation was much the most controversial, because it involved war, and because in the short term it increased the threat to the very people supposedly being protected. The Kosovo crisis raised the difficult question of the legality of an intervention in a case in which the Security Council had agreed on the seriousness of a problem, and had identified it as a threat to international peace and security, but had not been able to agree on military action.

Although the desirability of UN Security Council authorization for any intervention is widely accepted, even by many who would otherwise challenge the existence of any right of intervention, there are difficulties about viewing such authorization as absolutely essential. Such a conclusion would mean accepting that five states each have a veto on interventions, with the effect that any government able to count on the support of any one of them at the UN could engage in mass killings with a degree of impunity. It would also mean that the views of states in the region concerned counted for little or nothing. The International Commission on Intervention and State Sovereignty (ICISS) was right to say in its 2001 report that the UN Security Council could not have an absolute monopoly on the authorization of interventions for human protection purposes (ICISS 2001a: 53–5).

The difficulties that have been experienced in securing authorization from UN bodies mean that some scope has remained for action by individual states and groups of states, and for authorization by regional bodies. In many of the nine cases listed above, regional bodies had a significant role in issues relating to humanitarian intervention, and in some cases authorized it. Such authorization is politically and legally less convincing than that of the UN, with the result that it is difficult to arrive at a clear answer regarding the legality of interventions on humanitarian grounds, such as that in Kosovo in March–June 1999, not based on UN Security Council authorization.[29] There is bound to be pressure to bring an operation that did not initially have UN blessing back under the authority of the Security Council or of the UN more generally, as happened regarding both Kosovo and (in much more limited form) northern Iraq.

Authorization of an action by the UN or a regional body, while highly influential, is not the only possible source of legitimacy. Judgements about the legitimacy of an action depend not only on which international bodies give it formal approval, but also, quite properly, on perceptions of the facts on the ground. Some interventions may have a strong legal basis in the form of explicit UN Security Council approval, and yet quickly lose their legitimacy owing to a failure to achieve their humanitarian objectives or to adhere to humanitarian norms. The unravelling of the UN Operation in Somalia II (UNOSOM II) in 1994–5, following its losses in violent incidents and its involvement in killings of Somalis, is the clearest example.

Within the UN, is there an alternative to the Security Council as a source of authorization? One theoretical possibility is that, in cases where the Security Council is unable to act, the matter should be addressed by the General Assembly under its 'Uniting for Peace' procedure.[30] This requires a two-thirds majority of the Assembly.[31] In certain long-running crises there might appear to be a certain logic in pursuing this procedure. However, the permanent members of the Security Council show no sign of transferring their key powers to the General Assembly. There are, in any case, two serious difficulties with this procedure. First, getting a two-thirds majority is likely to be a time-consuming process—a luxury in a situation of extreme urgency in which large numbers of people are at risk of being killed. Second, the General Assembly has power only to make recommendations on such matters, not decisions with binding force. Despite these difficulties, the possibility that the General Assembly might embark on such a course might be 'an important additional form of leverage on the Security Council to encourage it to act decisively and appropriately' (ICISS 2001a: 53).

5.5   Issues and controversies at the United Nations

The international community's repeated involvement in interventions with a humanitarian dimension has deeply affected the UN. It has imposed new tasks and expectations, and has required changes in the way the organization works and thinks. It has also reinforced the view that the organization (particularly the Security Council) needs to be reformed. It has elicited opposing views from states, and has significantly changed the images of the UN held by governments and their subjects. Most remarkably, it has led Secretary-General Kofi Annan to take a strong personal stance on a controversial issue.

5.5.1   Kofi Annan's stance

In a succession of speeches and papers Kofi Annan has reminded states that there can be a need for intervention in cases of urgent humanitarian necessity. His first major contribution on this subject was in a speech at Ditchley Park, Oxfordshire, in June 1998, in which he stated that the UN Charter 'was never meant as a licence for governments to trample on human rights and human dignity'. In this and subsequent statements, along with most proponents of humanitarian intervention, he suggested certain criteria which should be met if such intervention were to be justifiable. At the beginning of the NATO bombing campaign over Kosovo in March 1999, he issued a statement which recognized that there were occasions when force might be necessary, but also referred to the importance of Security Council authorization. He pursued the theme in a report on protection of civilians in war dated 8 September 1999, and in his address to the UN General Assembly later that month.[32] In the 1999 UN General Assembly debate following Kofi Annan's address, only eight states supported the position he took on the 'developing norm in favour of intervention to protect civilians from wholesale slaughter'. The great majority of states addressing this matter were opposed.[33] In addition, the UN's Office of Legal Affairs has remained extremely circumspect about any purported legal doctrine of humanitarian intervention.

Annan's speeches on intervention have chimed with two significant long-term changes in how the state is viewed. First, there is a tendency to see the state as subject to certain international institutions, decisions and norms—a point that had already been emphasized by his predecessor Boutros-Ghali in his *Agenda for Peace* in 1992 in which he wrote: 'The time of absolute and exclusive sovereignty, however, has passed; its theory was never matched by reality.'[34] Second, there is an emerging view that the state should be understood to be the servant of the people, not its master. Some UN General Assembly resolutions have pointed in the same direction.[35] A stronger variant of this view is that state sovereignty is vested in the people, not in the government. Neither of these changes in how the state is viewed constitutes in itself a general justification of humanitarian intervention. An argument for intervention based on the presumed failure of a government to represent the majority of a population would not be relevant in a case, such as Rwanda in 1994, in which a government engaging in crimes (in this case genocide) against a minority could at least claim to represent a majority of the population. However, such an argument can help to justify humanitarian intervention in cases, such as Haiti, in which an armed minority has seized power in a state, overthrowing a democratically elected government, and continues to defy international efforts to restore an elected government.[36]

Annan's campaign has been more than a personal and institutional act of atonement for the failures to act in Rwanda and at Srebrenica. Most importantly, it has contributed to a subtle change in the terms of international debate. While there is no agreement on a new norm, there is now more awareness than before that intervention for humanitarian purposes cannot be completely excluded. Intervention can no longer be defined, as it often was in the past, as 'dictatorial interference': it is now associated with democracy and human rights. There is also more awareness that in peacekeeping or other operations under UN auspices there may be a need to use force, not least to protect threatened communities. Annan's campaign should be interpreted as a partially successful attempt to change the terms of international debate, rather than as a call for any specific change in international law.

Annan's approach received support in December 2001 in the shape of the ICISS report. The principal contribution of the report is implied in its title. It seeks to divert the international debate away from a single-minded obsession with military intervention, and to focus instead on the 'responsibility to protect'.[37] This is a responsibility of all governments, first and foremost in their own territories. The essence of the Commission's argument is that only if governments fail in this duty, and if preventive measures also fail, may coercive actions be needed. These 'may include political, economic or judicial measures, and in extreme cases—but only extreme cases—they may also include military action'. While Kofi Annan has supported the ICISS approach, it remains to be seen whether it will help to overcome states' suspicions of doctrines of humanitarian intervention.

5.5.2 Opposition of states and the General Assembly

Large numbers of post-colonial states, particularly in Africa and Asia, have opposed, and continue to oppose, the principle of humanitarian intervention. Many such states see themselves as vulnerable to foreign intervention, and are understandably sensitive about threats to their sovereignty. In some cases other and less creditable considerations are involved: many an oppressive regime would like to stop the emergence of a new norm that could upset its monopoly of power within the state.

In the UN, as in other fora, representatives of states have put forward numerous justifications for a sceptical stance towards 'humanitarian intervention'. The very term raises a daunting number of questions. Many suspect that the label 'humanitarian' conceals a range of other motives for, interests in, and outcomes of an action. In developing countries there is a strong fear that the Western powers have forgotten the economic and social agenda because of an obsession with the peace and security agenda. Behind such doubts there is often a degree of scepticism verging on hostility in regard to the actions of the United States. Even if a US-led intervention has its origins in genuine concern about atrocities, it may be perceived by other states as an act of expansionism and a strategic threat. Russia's views at the outset of NATO's 1999 war over Kosovo reflected such considerations, which were reinforced by Russia's sense of slight caused by the recent accession to NATO of three former allies, Poland, the Czech Republic, and Hungary. In addition, any practice of humanitarian intervention is inevitably selective, leading to unavoidable accusations of double standards or worse. The United States, and with it the UN, are accused of being willing to stop ethnic cleansing of the Albanian majority in Kosovo, but failing to act in Rwanda, the West Bank, Tibet, and Chechnya. Humanitarian intervention can easily be seen as just one part of a supposedly systematic pattern of US dominance of the UN. Whether such objections have real substance, they suggest that humanitarian intervention offers no quick escape from the jealousy and political warfare that has always accompanied power politics. The General Assembly's opposition, based on such considerations, is not absolute. It is directed much more against any formal doctrine of humanitarian intervention (especially in its classical sense) than it is to the occasional practice of intervention as it developed in the 1990s. The General Assembly never explicitly condemned NATO's war over Kosovo, or any of the other cases in the 1990s of military action for humanitarian purposes. The perception of some observers that states speak with different voices in the General Assembly and in the Security Council reflects the fact that in the former states frequently deal with general issues, whereas in the latter they almost always deal with concrete and current cases.

A notable feature of the debates at the UN is the way in which humanitarian intervention has been widely viewed as a separate issue from intervention in support of self-determination struggles. Some states (mainly Western, in the 1990s) have supported the first, some (mainly third world, in the 1970s and after) the second. Viewing these two categories of intervention as distinct and unrelated, and not discussing them together, is understandable. While humanitarian issues are widely (though not universally) viewed as 'non-political', and not directed at achieving a specific permanent change in the status of a territory, self-determination is clearly a political goal. Yet human-itarian and self-determination issues do, in actual fact, overlap. It could be useful, not least in reducing the emotional temperature of the issues in inter-national diplomacy, to recognize that humanitarian intervention is not a tidy category on its own, but part of a larger legal and political debate about very exceptional circumstances in which certain uses of force may be justified or at least tolerated.

If the General Assembly will not accept any doctrine of humanitarian intervention, will it support a more modest commitment, as proposed by the ICISS, in favour of a 'responsibility to protect'? A draft resolution has been circulating at the UN, but any substantive document embodying this principle is likely to require a lengthy and difficult process of negotiation, which has been made more difficult by the emergence of the 'Bush Doctrine' which many states see, rightly or wrongly, as representing a general interventionist threat of such a kind as to make them respond by renewing their commit-ment to non-intervention.

Indeed, the interventionism of the years since 1990 has not been confined to intervention on humanitarian grounds. Any world in which there is a dominant major power that is skilled at managing coalitions, and in which there are also numerous international agreements and principles that need some measure of enforcement, is bound to see a considerable interest in interventionism. In these circumstances, it is not surprising that some, such as Michael Glennon, have argued that a completely new world has emerged in which the whole UN Charter-based body of law seeking to outlaw inter-state violence is fundamentally out of date, and needs to be replaced by a new interventionist regime.[38] The idea that existing international law on the *jus ad bellum* can be ignored, or needs to be completely revised, has special appeal in the United States. The reasons are numerous: the simple fact of the USA's preponderance of military power is one, but not the only one. The special difficulties of some of the challenges that the USA has faced since 1990, and the frustrations of tackling them in a multilateral framework, have also been factors. Furthermore, the USA has inherited from its revolutionary origins and its early history certain revolutionary traditions of thought about international relations that are suspicious of old-fashioned inter-state relations and all their diplomatic, legal, and military accompaniments.

In September 2002 President Bush announced a new 'National Security Strategy' that is bound to affect debates on the right of states to use force.

Although the word 'intervention' is never used, the document is implicitly interventionist on eclectic grounds that include fighting rogue states, tyrants, and terrorists, and acting against certain threats before they are fully formed. The document is no pure unilateralist manifesto: in two short passages it recognizes the value of acting through multilateral institutions, including the UN.[39] However, the 'Bush Doctrine' has caused anxiety because, in this initial version at least, it conveys little sense of the continuing importance of the non-intervention rule. It has had the effect of reinforcing fears both of US dominance and of the chaos that could ensue if what is sauce for the US goose were to become sauce for many other would-be interventionist ganders. One probable result of the enunciation of interventionist doctrines by the United States will be to make states even more circumspect than before about accepting any doctrine, including on humanitarian intervention or on the responsibility to protect, that could be seen as opening the door to a general pattern of interventionism.

Paradoxically, another probable result may be to move the focus of decision-making about the use of force more towards the UN Security Council. This is because interventions on preventive grounds, or to topple dictatorial governments, usually pose problems about whether they conform to international law, and whether they will have the effect of worsening international tensions. One way around such problems, and also around domestic political doubts, is to seek international approval through an authoritative body. Other things being equal, a fundamental distinction is still drawn between intervention with Security Council approval, which tends to be tolerated, and intervention without it, which is often viewed internationally with suspicion.

5.5.3   Changes in Security Council powers, composition, and decision-making

The facts that the Security Council has the power to authorize interventions, and has often done so since 1990, have contributed to a sense that the Security Council actually matters. Questions have been raised about its powers, its composition, and its manner of reaching decisions on life and death issues.

The considerable legal powers of the Security Council have been the subject of much discussion and analysis in the post-cold war era. The exercise of these powers, not least in cases of intervention, has confirmed the breadth of the discretion conferred on the Council to proclaim a situation a 'threat to peace and security'—the essential legal preliminary to its taking action on a matter. Furthermore, the Council has remarkable powers under Article 25 of the Charter to require UN member states 'to accept and carry out the decisions of the Security Council in accordance with the present Charter'. There are legal limits on the Council's powers, but they are modest (Gowlland-Debbas 2000: 301–11; Nolte 2000: 315–26; Simma (ed.) 2002: 442–64, 701–16).

In reality, the Council's powers are limited more by nature than by specific legal provisions. They are limited by the fact that states still maintain a strong capacity for independent decision-making: powers so extensive that the Security Council has never dared to do what it is technically entitled to do under Article 25, namely, to require all states to take part in a military action. Furthermore, even operations that have support from the Security Council frequently run into practical difficulties, one of the most serious of which is the dismal fact that states participating in an action are often prepared to put only minimal resources into it. When such states are primarily concerned with limiting their losses, and with exit strategies, they almost invite opponents to attack them. The disillusion in the United States about the UN, however artificial, ill-informed, and Washington-based it may be, is evidence of the reluctance of great powers to get heavily committed to supporting the operations of an organization they do not entirely control.

The long-standing question of the Security Council's composition has also been affected by its practice of intervention. There have been accusations that there has been selectivity in decisions about intervention due to the preoccupations of the Permanent Five. Yet expansion of the Security Council would not be simple. It has sometimes proved difficult to reach decisions in a Security Council with fifteen members, five armed with the veto. True, this difficulty should not be exaggerated: the real obstacle to getting prompt and effective action in Bosnia in 1992–5 and in Rwanda in 1994 was not so much lack of capacity of the Security Council to reach decisions, but the lack of willingness of states (including members of the Council) to implement such decisions as were reached. Nonetheless, it is likely that it would be harder to achieve results in an enlarged Security Council. This suggests that if the much-needed expansion of the Security Council does take place, it will have to be accompanied by other changes to improve its capacity, and that of its member states, for taking and implementing decisions promptly.

The process by which decisions are made to intervene, or not to intervene, has been undergoing significant scrutiny and change. In an age of instant communications, such decisions are taken against a background of widespread but often superficial awareness of the human dimension of humanitarian crises. Improvements in decision-making procedures, especially any that improve first-hand knowledge of the situation in the territory concerned, are needed in their own right. They can also help to overcome perceptions of humanitarian intervention as exclusively reflecting the interests and preoccupations of Western states.

There have been three specific changes in recent years in how Security Council decision-making regarding intervention is conducted and then examined at the UN:

1. *Permitting certain non-state bodies to give testimony to the Council.* Regarding Kosovo, UNHCR gave such testimony on 10 September 1998. This had a

major impact on the deliberations of the Council, was followed by some tough resolutions, and is an interesting case of one part of the UN system effectively lobbying another part into taking action.

2. *Sending delegations from the Security Council to investigate particular situations on the ground.* This was done in September 1999 in respect of East Timor, before the Australian-led force was authorized. In October 2000 eleven members of the UN Security Council visited Sierra Leone and other states in the region to examine the UN role.

3. *Conducting serious retrospective examinations of humanitarian crises involving the Council.* Two important examples are the detailed account of the establishment, maintenance, and fall of the 'safe area' of Srebrenica in Bosnia in 1993–5, and related events; and the survey of genocide in Rwanda in 1994 and the failure both of the UN and its member states to act.[40]

Among the hard problems that remain is the acceleration of the Security Council's decision-making process. The three changes outlined above may on occasion help with expediting the decision-making process, but even this cannot be guaranteed. The first two in particular could be used as a delaying tactic. By definition, cases of extreme humanitarian emergency are urgent; and the spectacle of UN inaction in crises is damaging. Yet the UN, including the Security Council, has often been seen by states as an institution on which insoluble problems can be dumped, sometimes with the unstated but detectable purpose of avoiding decisive action. Another delayed or inadequate response, as in Rwanda or Bosnia, remains a distinct possibility.

5.5.4   Use of force distinct from peacekeeping and enforcement

In many crises during the 1990s, the absence of preparedness to use force in a manner appropriate to extreme humanitarian crises was at least as serious an obstacle to intervention as was the lack of an agreed legal doctrine of humanitarian intervention. A key issue is for the UN and its member states to develop a conception of the use of armed force that is distinct from the familiar forms of peacekeeping and enforcement. Such a conception has been needed, not just in cases where a humanitarian intervention into a country is being contemplated, but also in cases where UN peacekeeping forces are already in place and, in a deteriorating situation, witness atrocities or cease-fire violations. In such cases, the notions of neutrality, impartiality, and the non-use of force (all of which have been associated with peacekeeping) are not necessarily appropriate.

The purposes for which force can be used in humanitarian operations include the following: defending safe areas, protecting threatened populations, opposing and even trying to remove a regime, protecting humanitarian relief, protecting international observers, and rescuing hostages. The performance of such tasks requires armed forces that are configured, trained, and equipped for action in a hostile environment, and have an effective system of command and control, whether UN-based or delegated to a state or international body. Such action may also require the withdrawal of UN peacekeeping forces and related personnel from places where they are vulnerable to reprisals and hostage-taking. In some cases, a peacekeeping force might need to be so armed from the start that it can adopt a forceful protective or combat role. In other cases, it might metamorphose into a body with such capacity: the transformation of UNPROFOR in Bosnia in May–August 1995, and then the further post-Dayton transformation into IFOR and SFOR, being such cases.

The UN has begun to address the use of force in UN operations. In its report issued in 2000, the Panel on UN Peace Operations chaired by Lakhdar Brahimi took some limited steps in this direction. It stated, for example:

United Nations peacekeepers—troops or police—who witness violence against civilians should be presumed to be authorized to stop it, within their means, in support of basic United Nations principles. However, operations given a broad and explicit mandate for civilian protection must be given the specific resources needed to carry out that mandate.[41]

It was symptomatic of the state of the debate in the UN that the Brahimi panel was able to make progress by entirely avoiding the question of humanitarian intervention as such. A glance at the panel's composition, which reflected real divisions on this issue in the world generally, indicates that there would have been no prospect of agreement on the principle of humanitarian intervention. The Brahimi report avoided certain other matters as well: it did not address squarely the systems of military support, control, and deployment that would be necessary for such missions to be conducted effectively. However, the report was a step in the direction of getting more serious about the use of force. A key remaining question concerns the extent to which UN member states generally will prepare their armed forces for coercive operations under UN auspices: failure to do so will merely perpetuate the unhealthy reliance on a very few states—principally the USA, UK, and France—to do the UN's military work.

The various UN-related efforts to protect vulnerable populations since 1991 suggest some uncomfortable lessons about how force should be organized and used. Two stand out. *First*, it is no accident that the Security Council has shown a marked tendency to rely on the armed forces of states and coalitions, as distinct from under UN command and control, not merely for enforcement actions against international aggression, but also for operations with human protection purposes. Many reports, including Brahimi and ICISS, have failed to note how consistent this pattern is. The reasons for it include not just the greater military resources of states, but also their greater capacity for strategic planning and fast decision-making. *Second*, it is often impossible to provide protection on a neutral and impartial basis, simply responding to attacks and threats. Instead, there is a need to recognize the principal threat and adopt a robust policy towards it, an approach that may on occasion require something close to an alliance with one or another party to a conflict. This is a plausible interpretation of how policy eventually developed in Bosnia in 1995, East Timor in 1999, and Sierra Leone in 2000. In all these cases such an approach helped to bring a phase of armed conflict to an end. These are difficult lessons for various UN bodies and agencies to absorb. In particular, they suggest that even more radical departures from the traditional doctrines associated with UN peacekeeping may sometimes be called for than the modest changes accepted in the Brahimi and ICISS reports (*Report of the Panel on United Nations Peace Operations* 2000: 48–55; ICISS 2001a: 57–67).

5.5.5   International administration

A principal cause and consequence of many interventions for humanitarian purposes is the need for some form of international administration of the territory concerned. Even in cases in which the UN Security Council did not authorize the original intervention, it may find itself having to handle the resulting situation. Many of the interventions of the 1990s led to the establishment of some form of international administration, or at least administrative assistance, in the territory concerned. In 1999, in both Kosovo and East Timor, the UN assumed direct although temporary responsibility for the territory. There were also many cases in which the UN had some more modest administrative role. In Bosnia and Herzegovina from December 1995 onwards, when the Office of the High Representative was established under European Union auspices with a powerful supervisory function, the UN Mission in Bosnia and Herzegovina (UNMIBH) was jointly involved with it in many aspects of administrative assistance. There were also elements of such assistance in Haiti, Albania, and Sierra Leone. These various exercises in latter-day enlightened colonialism have been marked by a commendable degree of flexibility. Instead of following certain standard concepts of trusteeship, as the League of Nations did, the UN has adopted a wide variety of forms of international administrative assistance, sometimes in cooperation with regional bodies.[42]

The United Nations' involvement in the administration of territories poses some difficult, even threatening, problems. It puts UN officials in a peculiar position, in which they have both to uphold the interests of the territory they administer, and the impartiality of the UN *vis-à-vis* its member states. It requires a high degree of competence in the management of a range of administrative matters with which the UN does not ordinarily deal, and often depends on relatively young and inexperienced people to do much of the work—hence the accusations of 'gap-year colonialism'. Although by no means all these efforts have been successful, there are some solid achievements. A common feature of these 'variable geometry' systems of administrative assistance has been the emphasis on multi-party elections as one mechanism to facilitate both the resolution of conflicts and the transfer to self-government.

5.5.6 Alternatives to intervention: prevention and protection

Some have concluded from the enduring problems and mixed results of interventions in the 1990s that it would be better to concentrate on prevention of man-made catastrophe, not intervention once it has happened; and on a broad range of protection efforts rather than just those embodied in military interventions. There has been much support for this general approach, with particular attention being paid to preventive diplomacy. In 2000, both the UN General Assembly and the Security Council adopted resolutions on the vital role of conflict prevention. In 2001, the ICISS report particularly favoured protection and prevention as means of reducing the need to rely on military intervention (ICISS 2001a: 11–27).

However, viewing intervention and preventive diplomacy as two different topics, even as alternatives, may be mistaken. Serious efforts to resolve a conflict situation often, quite naturally, threaten the prospects of one or more belligerent parties, and lead them to engage in acts of violence. Thus, it was after serious efforts at preventive diplomacy in East Timor in 1999 that events reached a crisis requiring international intervention. The same was true of negotiated agreements on the wars in Rwanda in 1993 and Sierra Leone in 1999. ICISS is on strong ground in calling for a wide range of protective measures, but in this connection it explicitly accepts that this does not resolve the difficult questions about the circumstances in which the responsibility to protect should be exercised through intervention.

In many cases, the alternative to intervention is to allow politics to take their course. Processes of political change, peaceful struggle, or even civil war, do sometimes in the end yield outcomes that lead a society back towards international standards. There are grounds for scepticism about the assumption that the use of force from outside can always cure a difficult situation. Foreign military interventions to save lives of the subjects of dictatorships of the Right or Left, in Spain or the Soviet Union, might well have failed, led to prolonged war, and reinforced the regimes they would have been intended to remove. There is something to be said for letting some dictatorial systems die from their own inner defects, and for the proposition that self-liberation leads to more enduring results than external assistance. The existence of alternatives to intervention needs to be more fully accepted in UN debates, but offers no escape from the dilemma in which the UN is repeatedly placed: some situations can be of such gravity and urgency as to make intervention seem justified as a first rather than last resort.

5.6   Conclusion

The subject of humanitarian intervention is unavoidable for the UN because of its dual role both as an upholder of international standards in human rights and humanitarian law, and as the global body with responsibilities regarding the use of force. However, the subject is as difficult for the UN as it is unavoidable, and could even pose a threat to the organization.

In principle, humanitarian intervention is one important means of addressing a fundamental problem of international organization: the relation between law and power. If there is no effective means of implementing international law, it may be discredited, and the UN would be discredited with it. The old dictum that law without power is no law retains its meaning, and can reinforce the case for humanitarian intervention to stop flagrant and repeated violations of basic norms. Although lawyers sometimes see law as gradually replacing power politics, in reality law and power have to operate in harness together; and humanitarian intervention may be one way in which they can do so.

However, in practice, if law and power are to operate in harness, law may get tied too closely to the most powerful state, with potentially damaging results. The potential threat to the UN arises partly because the subject of humanitarian intervention has the capacity to worsen the always crucial and at the same time tangled relationship between the UN and the United States. The United States, which is usually expected to be the principal intervener in humanitarian causes, has shown every sign of impatience with tying its military might and reputation to this difficult role. Humanitarian intervention threatens to exacerbate an already strong American sense that the UN is a body that lures the United States into traps in such places as Somalia. The associated emphasis on humanitarian norms and procedures is seen as placing burdensome constraints on US actions, with such baneful results as the strong US opposition to the International Criminal Court.

There are other ways in which humanitarian intervention could be an issue to weaken, even destroy, the UN. This is because of six worrying developments arising from the practice of intervention since 1991: (1) the great majority of member states, having long seen the UN as an institution in which their sovereignty can be protected, are worried about any doctrine or practice that would challenge that vital UN function; (2) states may augment their national armaments to reduce their vulnerability to intervention, and trust the UN system as a source of protection even less than before; (3) there is a risk of the UN building up expectations of its capacity to protect threatened civilians, only to preside once again over another Rwanda or Srebrenica, leading to disillusion and cynicism about the organization; (4) actual cases of humanitarian intervention leave the UN having to manage a series of difficult territories, some of which may fall prey to violence and chaos; (5) different states and different parts of the UN system often have opposing views either on the issue in general, or on particular cases, adding to the mutual suspicion among states; and (6) the governments of many developing countries suspect that the Western powers have down-played the economic and social agenda (and have provided very limited resources for aid programmes) because of their preoccupation with the peace and security agenda in general and military interventions in particular.

In reality, any damage to the UN caused by the idea and practice of humanitarian intervention is likely to be more limited than this catalogue of problems suggests. This is because of two key considerations on which this chapter has focused. First, ever since the inception of the Charter the UN has been based on a delicate and logically insoluble tension between the rights of peoples and the rights of states; and it has been part of the success of the UN that it has not rested on exclusively statist pillars. Second, the phenomenon of humanitarian intervention, thanks to its costs and inherent fragilities, is likely to be self-limiting. Already, in the early 1990s, it was widely recognized that there would be limits to the new interventionism, and in particular to the UN's capacity to manage complex crises in collapsing states.[43] What has been happening at the United Nations is a gradual and incremental change in the interpretation of the Charter rules and the UN's responsibilities, particularly as regards the balance between the rights of individual sovereign states and the rights of the community—whether the latter be defined as individual human beings or the entire community of states. These trends will doubtless continue, more through precedent and improvisation than by any legal or doctrinal revolution. The UN will continue to be involved occasionally in proclaiming policy objectives which lead to calls for intervention on humanitarian as well as other grounds; authorizing such intervention; and picking up the pieces of interventions by others. If the UN presides over just enough humanitarian intervention to make cruel dictators and criminal warlords lose sleep, and to enable failed states to begin the path to recovery, but not enough to make rulers generally fear collapse of the non-intervention norm, a tolerable point of balance will have been struck.

6

Humanitarian Intervention in the Balkans

Nicholas Morris*

6.1 Introduction

Two components of the international responses to conflict in the former Yugoslavia were described as humanitarian, but there are fundamental differences between a humanitarian intervention and a humanitarian operation or action. The former is defined in this volume as coercive (military) interference in internal affairs of a state with the purpose of addressing massive human rights violations or relieving widespread human suffering.[1] The latter covers non-coercive action to deliver relief supplies and essential services to, and to try and safeguard the human rights of, those in need. Meeting such needs is the responsibility of the state or occupying—or intervening—power; international humanitarian action may be necessary if this responsibility is not fulfilled.

Humanitarian action was a major component of the response of the international community to the break-up of the former Yugoslavia and to large-scale violations of basic human rights there. The lead agency for the United Nations was the Office of the UN High Commissioner for Refugees (UNHCR). UNHCR's mandate is to ensure protection and help provide assistance to persons forced to flee their country. Assistance is generally delivered through non-governmental organizations (NGOs) or local authorities. Increasingly, UNHCR has become involved with persons displaced within their own country. In the Balkans, UNHCR's traditional role was significantly expanded, as it sought to provide relief and protection to many who were in need but not displaced. This chapter examines the conflicts and humanitarian interventions in Bosnia and Herzegovina (hereafter Bosnia) and the then Federal Republic of Yugoslavia (Serbia and Montenegro—hereafter FRY) from the viewpoint

---

*Former staff member of the Office of the United Nations High Commissioner for Refugees (UNHCR). The views expressed are those of the author and are not necessarily shared by the United Nations or UNHCR.

of a participant in that humanitarian action, an operation which itself increasingly became a factor in the political considerations of the parties to the conflict and of the international community.

It is argued that the humanitarian interventions in Bosnia and Kosovo were at least as much the consequences of events and circumstance as they were demonstrations of the commitment of the international community to address massive violations of human rights. Although there was significant military involvement in Bosnia by the UN (from 1992) and NATO (the North Atlantic Treaty Organization) (from 1993), the coercive action in 1995 occurred over four years after the start of conflicts that brought widespread suffering and death. Its result was an agreement that effectively sanctioned ethnic partition. The NATO air action against the FRY in the spring of 1999 was begun some nine months after there was clear evidence of widespread suffering and mounting deaths in Kosovo, and as a last resort to achieve a political goal. Its initially declared purpose was to force the FRY to accept the terms of a peace agreement.

6.1.1 Humanitarian action

The delivery of humanitarian aid amidst conflict has, for well over a century, been predicated on respect for certain basic principles.[2] These require that humanitarian aid be provided impartially by civilians to civilians on the criterion of need, without distinction as to origins or beliefs. In addition, such aid should not contribute to the military effort of any party to a conflict. Humanitarian action requires the consent of the parties to a conflict, and that they respect the principles. Such respect was lacking in the Balkans, as it often is, particularly in intra-state conflicts. In such circumstance, the humanitarian action may not be seen as impartial.

The association of military forces with a humanitarian operation conducted in accordance with these principles can create problems for both humanitarian organizations and intervening forces. From 1992 onwards, UN and later NATO-led military forces were closely involved with the humanitarian operation in the Balkans. When such involvement takes place within the framework of the implementation of an internationally agreed solution to the underlying political problems (as, for example, in Cambodia, East Timor, and Namibia), it should not create problems for the humanitarian actors on the ground: agencies of the UN system; the International Red Cross; and NGOs. Problems arise when there has not been an accepted peace settlement. They are likely to be most acute where the political and military involvement is seeking to contain the conflict rather than address its causes. While it supported much of the population of Bosnia through three hard years of conflict, and helped keep many alive, the humanitarian action was also variously seen as fuelling the war, aiding the wrong side, and a poor substitute for justice.

6.1.2   Perceptions and expectations

A combatant's perception of a humanitarian operation during conflict has, in a sense, become the practical measure of its impartiality, and therefore, of the safety of humanitarian aid workers. All sides in Bosnia saw the humanitarian operation as directly helping their opponents. With mobilization and local militias, the distinction between male civilians and combatants was often meaningless. The Bosnian Serb Army (BSA) and for a time the Bosnian Croat forces surrounded enclaves controlled by the Bosnian government. They saw the humanitarian operation as undermining their military efforts by breaking the siege and as helping prevent a solution to the conflict on their terms. For the Bosnian government, the humanitarian operation was a means for the international community to evade its responsibilities to halt aggression (the government strongly objected to being equated with the Bosnian Serbs as a 'party to the conflict' when Security Council resolutions identified the latter as the aggressor). The humanitarian operation in Kosovo that ended with the NATO military intervention was perceived by the Serb authorities as helping 'the terrorists'. This was inevitable, given the attitude of those authorities towards the Kosovo Albanians, who comprised the great majority of the beneficiaries of the operation.

All sides in such conflicts are likely to seek to use humanitarian relief for political ends and to feed their military forces. There was little alternative for Bosnian government forces besieged in the enclaves and Sarajevo. The provision of fuel in Bosnia for priority humanitarian needs in hospitals and elsewhere effectively released other fuel for the combatants. Thus, the Bosnian government accused UNHCR of fuelling Serb offensives, and its opponents blocked access for UNHCR fuel to government-controlled areas, maintaining that it would be used against them. The BSA frequently obstructed access for food and other relief supplies.

Frequently, both the beneficiaries and the international community have or promote unrealistic expectations of what a humanitarian operation that is not accompanied by political action to address the causes of the crisis can and should achieve. These expectations may influence decisions on a subsequent humanitarian intervention. Outside governments whose response to a crisis does not halt large-scale violation of human rights do not like to be reminded that, however well supported, humanitarian action cannot substitute for the necessary political action. European politicians opposed to humanitarian intervention or the lifting of an arms embargo that had seriously inhibited the Bosnian government's ability to counter aggression, and to a lesser extent that of the Croatian government, cited the adverse effects on the humanitarian action as a reason not to take more resolute steps. For the beneficiaries and victims, as for the parties to the conflict, false expectations are often the result of wishful thinking, and sometimes reflect a genuine misunderstanding of the limits of humanitarian action. Unrealistic expectations can fuel the perception that the humanitarian action itself is not—or should not strive to be—impartial and neutral.[3]

In Bosnia from 1992 until the 1995 Dayton agreement,[4] the UN Protection Force, UNPROFOR, bore the brunt of the burden of these false expectations, which began with its name. At least through 1994, Western leaders who were questioned on their response to the unfolding tragedy tended in reply to give prominence to their country's support for the humanitarian action. The humanitarian action was presented as successful, and was well supported financially. After the Dayton agreement, the NATO-led intervention force (IFOR, later SFOR) was also presented as successful, which it was within goals that were more modest relative to means than those expected of the much-criticized UNPROFOR.

Many of the more serious problems after Dayton were inherent in the non-military provisions of that agreement, which stopped the conflict but did not resolve and has still not resolved its causes. With no significant change in the circumstances that drove people from their homes, and no removal of the political constraints, some governments and NATO military leaders, never-theless, looked to the international administrators and UNHCR to deliver what the military intervention and political process had failed to achieve: the reversal of ethnic cleansing. As another example, from late 1999 UNHCR was expected to be able to assist East Timorese in West Timor to escape the control of the militia and repatriate even though the political efforts of the Security Council, the United States, and others to achieve the disbandment and disar-mament of the militia had demonstrably failed.

6.1.3   The break-up of Yugoslavia

The break-up of the former Yugoslavia has been extensively documented;[5] only a summary of the main events is necessary here. Croatia and Slovenia proclaimed their sovereignty and independence from the Socialist Federal Republic of Yugoslavia (SFRY) on 25 June 1991. Two days later, the Federal Yugoslav Army (JNA) moved into Slovenia and parts of Croatia. The war in Slovenia ended after ten days and the JNA withdrew, but conflict in Croatia intensified. A ceasefire was agreed between the Croatian forces and the JNA on 2 January 1992, leaving Croatian Serbs in control of three areas with a significant population of ethnic Serbs,[6] one bordering Serbia and two bordering Bosnia. These were later declared UN Protected Areas. The European Community (EC) recognized Croatia and Slovenia as independent states on 15 January 1992, and called on the Bosnian government to hold a referendum on independence.

This referendum was held at the end of February 1992, against a back-ground of rising violence from those opposed to independence: most ethnic Serbs boycotted the vote. Of a turnout of 63 per cent, 93 per cent voted for independence. On 6 April 1992, the EC recognized Bosnia and violence intensified, spreading to Sarajevo. By the end of April, many of the non-Serb inhabitants had been driven from large areas of eastern Bosnia by local Serbs with support from Serbian paramilitaries and the JNA. Ethnic cleansing and conflict extended throughout Bosnia and the siege of Sarajevo by the JNA-equipped BSA began. In the spring of 1993, serious fighting began in central and western Bosnia between the Bosnian Croats, supported by the new Croatian army, and the Bosniaks.[7] This was formally ended by the agreement on a Bosniak/Croat federation signed in Washington on 18 March 1994.

There were few major lasting changes to the confrontation lines in either Bosnia or Croatia until early May 1995, when the Croatian army expelled local Serb forces from Western Slavonia. The enclave of Srebrenica fell to the BSA on 11 July. Over the following days thousands of Bosniak men and boys from the enclave were summarily executed.[8] In early August, the Croatian army took the remainder of Serb-occupied territory in Croatia, with the exception of a strip in Eastern Slavonia, on the border with Serbia. A campaign of air strikes by the NATO against Bosnian Serb targets began on 30 August. Croatian and Bosnian forces made significant advances against the BSA. The war in Bosnia formally ended in mid-October 1995, and a peace agreement was reached in Dayton on 21 November.

The UN civilian leadership and force were replaced by a High Representative and a NATO-led force. A new UN operation oversaw the re-establishment of Croatian control in Eastern Slavonia.[9] There was no new conflict in the former Yugoslavia until early 1998, when the uneasy relative calm in Kosovo finally broke. The developments thereafter that led up to the NATO military intervention in March 1999 are covered later in this chapter.

These events caused much human suffering and loss of life. The forcible displacement of civilians was a key objective, rather than a consequence of the conflicts. The conflicts were a major preoccupation of the Security Council,[10] and also brought a new level of involvement by the Council in the humanitarian aspects of the response. Regional political and military organizations were closely engaged at the highest level, as were *ad hoc* groupings, most notably the Contact Group.[11] The conflicts also posed new challenges to the coordination of the humanitarian, political, and military elements of the international community's response. Lessons were learnt that are likely to be relevant in future crises, whether or not the international response involves military intervention.

6.2   1991–5: Croatia and Bosnia and Herzegovina

The efforts of the EC to stop the fighting in Croatia that had begun in June 1991 were not successful. Only when this was obvious did the UN become involved. Adopting Security Council Resolution (SC Res) 713 on 25 September 1991, which imposed a 'general and complete embargo on all deliveries of weapons and military equipment to Yugoslavia', the Security Council invited Secretary-General Pérez de Cuéllar to offer his assistance. The UN's initial aim was to deploy a peacekeeping operation (PKO) to create the necessary conditions for the pursuit of political negotiations for a peaceful settlement. The Yugoslav government formally requested a PKO on 26 November. In SC Res 721 of 27 November, the deployment of a PKO was made conditional on full compliance by the parties with the provisions of an agreement reached on 23 November, central to which was a ceasefire. The agreement was not respected but, on 15 February 1992, the new UN Secretary-General, Boutros Boutros-Ghali, recommended the establishment of UNPRO-FOR. He argued that the risks that further delay would lead to a breakdown of the ceasefire outweighed the danger that the PKO would fail for lack of cooperation from the parties. SC Res 743 was adopted on 21 February, establishing UNPROFOR as 'an interim arrangement to create the conditions of peace and security required for the negotiation of an overall settlement of the Yugoslav crisis'. On 7 April, in SC Res 749, the Security Council authorized UNPROFOR's earliest possible full deployment.

In early October 1991 the Yugoslav authorities requested UNHCR's assistance in responding to population displacement in Croatia. The High Commissioner consulted the Secretary-General, who replied requesting her to lend her good offices to bring relief to internally displaced people and to coordinate humanitarian action in the region. In his letter, the Secretary-General stated that he appreciated that UNHCR's ability to respond would be conditional on security (and funding). On 14 November UNHCR formally accepted the Secretary-General's request. At that time some 500,000 persons were displaced as a result of the conflict in Croatia.

Although the majority of Security Council Resolutions from 724 of 15 December 1991 onwards had made positive reference to the initiatives of the Secretary-General in the humanitarian field, and with increasing frequency called on the parties to facilitate humanitarian assistance, it was not until SC Res 752 of 15 May 1992 that reference was made to the possibility of 'protecting international humanitarian relief programmes' and of 'ensuring safe and secure access to Sarajevo airport'. This resolution was also the first to call for a halt to ethnic cleansing.

6.2.1 The element of chance

UNPROFOR was established for Croatia and not conceived either as part of a humanitarian intervention or with a role in the humanitarian assistance operation. Its headquarters were initially in Sarajevo.[12] The combination of its presence and the early and public self-confidence of Europe's leaders in their peacemaking and deterrent capacity made physically abandoning Bosnia difficult to contemplate when conflict erupted there in early April 1992. UNPROFOR's presence in Sarajevo had significant bearing on the international community's subsequent engagement in Bosnia and on the eventual humanitarian intervention.

Had UNPROFOR not already been deployed to Sarajevo, it is not evident that there would have been the international will to deploy a PKO in response to the conflict in Bosnia. By April 1992 Vukovar had been razed and Dubrovnik bombarded without any resolute international response; even with UNPROFOR in Sarajevo, no effective action was taken to stop the shelling and siege of the city. In some respects UNPROFOR's presence and the expectations it raised complicated efforts to contain the consequences of the conflict with a minimum of direct involvement, arguably the real aim of some European governments in the absence of a readiness to address the massive violations of human rights in the region.[13] The degree of UNHCR's own involvement in a role that was logically that of the International Committee of the Red Cross (ICRC), which has a specific mandate for civilians in conflict, was itself determined by the withdrawal of ICRC delegates from Bosnia for a month from late May 1992, following an attack on a Red Cross convoy that took the life of its head of delegation in Sarajevo.

Sarajevo airport quickly became a focus and measure of international resolve. SC Res 757 of 30 May 1992 included a demand that the parties establish a security zone encompassing Sarajevo and its airport. This demand was repeated in identical language in SC Res 758 of 8 June. On 5 June, UNPROFOR had negotiated an agreement for the BSA to hand over control of the airport to the UN force, but the airport only reopened for humanitarian flights with the start of the UNHCR humanitarian airlift on 3 July. The commitment to keep the airport open was in part a reaction by the international community to the unexpected flight to Sarajevo of the French President on 28 June. The Sarajevo humanitarian airlift operated within the framework of the airport agreement with the Bosnian Serbs, and required their consent, so was not a coercive intervention. Throughout the conflict the BSA retained and frequently used its ability to close the airport. While the operation to airdrop relief to besieged and isolated locations did not require explicit Bosnian Serb consent and, unlike the airlift, was a wholly military operation, airdrops did not take place where there was a perceived danger of BSA fire-control radar illuminating participating aircraft.

6.2.2   UNPROFOR and the humanitarian operation

By the time of the adoption of SC Res 770 and 771 on 13 August 1992, greater political prominence was being given to humanitarian assistance. The former, which was adopted under chapter VII, recognized not only that the situation in Bosnia was a threat to international peace and security but also 'that the provision of humanitarian assistance in Bosnia and Herzegovina is an important element in the Council's effort to restore international peace and security in the area'. It called on States 'to take nationally or through regional agencies or arrangements all measures necessary' to facilitate the delivery of humanitarian assistance. It requested 'all States to provide appropriate support for action undertaken in pursuance of this resolution'. The latter (771) demanded respect for international humanitarian law. Therein, the Security Council decided that all concerned in the former Yugoslavia 'shall comply with the provisions of the present resolution, failing which the Council will need to take further measures under the Charter' (only this paragraph made reference to chapter VII). Successive resolutions contained similar language exhorting the parties to comply with provisions of earlier resolutions that they continued to ignore.

SC Res 770 effectively authorized military intervention in support of humanitarian assistance but did not specify that this should be within the framework of the UN PKO. However, on 10 September 1992 the Secretary-General reported to the Security Council recommending a further expansion of UNPROFOR's task and mandate in order to support UNHCR's efforts to deliver humanitarian relief throughout Bosnia and Herzegovina, and in particular, to provide protection at UNHCR's request (and support to ICRC at ICRC's request). On 14 September the Security Council adopted SC Res 776. This noted offers made by a number of States, following the adoption of SC Res 770, to make available military personnel to facilitate the delivery of humanitarian assistance in Bosnia. It authorized the enlargements of UNPROFOR's mandate and strength recommended in the Secretary-General's 10 September report. This report stated that UNPROFOR troops would follow normal peacekeeping rules of engagement, which authorize the use of force in self-defence, and indicated that this covered situations in which armed persons attempt by force to prevent UNPROFOR from carrying out its mandate. Resolution 776 made no mention of chapter VII. Thus, UNPROFOR had a coercive authority, but not one that required or authorized it to intervene to prevent widespread suffering (a task for which it was not equipped). The ambiguity and scope for raising false expectations as to UNPROFOR's role and the Security Council's intentions were compounded by subsequent resolutions.

The initial focus of the humanitarian operation was on the immediate consequences of forced displacement. In the early months, as most of the non-Serb population of Eastern Bosnia were driven from their homes, UNHCR and ICRC officials found themselves operating in the middle of ongoing ethnic cleansing and conflict, where the most pressing need was to get recently displaced civilians to relative safety. Where it could, UNHCR sought to ensure freedom of movement and access to asylum, or at least safety, even if provoking flight was the aim of the ethnic cleansers. Some criticized this as aiding ethnic cleansing.[14] The Bosnian government resolutely opposed departures from Sarajevo and the enclaves, whence many of the inhabitants would have fled if they could.

As the BSA extended its control, access to the 'new' minorities left behind became an increasing concern, and securing consent for this access and to cross front lines became and remained a major preoccupation. With the exception of Sarajevo and specific events, such as the engagement of UNPROFOR's Bosnia Commander, General Morillon, in Srebrenica in April 1993, UNHCR had little close involvement with UNPROFOR for much of the first year of the conflict. UNPROFOR was initially not mandated to support UNHCR, and focused on deploying and trying to negotiate a halt to the fighting, while UNHCR had misgivings at too close an identification of the humanitarian operation with a military force that could be perceived as a party to the conflict. Until May 1993, when Thorvald Stoltenberg was appointed Special Representative of the Secretary-General (SRSG),[15] there was no structure within the Balkans that brought the humanitarian, political and military sides together under one authority: the UNHCR Special Envoy[16] had reported only to the High Commissioner in Geneva and the UNPROFOR Commander to UN Headquarters in New York.

UNPROFOR faced huge difficulties in deploying and operating. The report approved by SC Res 776 foresaw UNPROFOR deployment throughout Bosnia, with four or five new zones (in addition to Sarajevo) and an infantry battalion group in each with a headquarters including staff for liaison with UNHCR. With the exception of unarmed military observers, UNPROFOR was never able to deploy on territory controlled by the BSA. Over 30,000 UN troops were eventually deployed in large part to assist the humanitarian operation, but that operation was without UNPROFOR support, and the victims of the conflict without an UNPROFOR presence, over the majority of the territory of Bosnia.

6.2.3   The political framework

Initial expectations were that the intensive efforts of various negotiators would soon yield the results promised. A humanitarian intervention would therefore be unnecessary, and humanitarian aid could quickly be phased down. UNHCR sought to address immediate needs and prevent further displacement, hoping that within weeks the conflict would be over. Immediate action on the ground was complemented by forceful interventions with the leaders and an increasingly high profile in the media, particularly from the first UNHCR Special Envoy, José-María Mendiluce, who on several occasions witnessed large-scale ethnic cleansing and killings, and from UNHCR in Sarajevo.

As time passed, and different peace plans, conferences, deadlines, and ultimata came and went, it became clearer that the international community was not going to bring an early end to the war. As the front lines stabilized, large-scale displacements became rarer, with people either trapped in the enclaves and Sarajevo or the subject of smaller-scale and more targeted ethnic cleansing. The focus of the humanitarian operation became the regular delivery of relief supplies and whatever efforts were possible to prevent, mitigate, or at least draw attention to the ongoing forced evictions of remaining minorities.

From mid-1993 onwards, UNHCR greatly increased its practical interaction with UNPROFOR. With the SRSG's arrival, the UNHCR Special Envoy became an integral member of his senior management team. Coordination became close and effective, as it was between UNHCR and ICRC, which sought to preserve its distinct identity and kept its distance from UNPROFOR. UNHCR's misgivings had not been allayed: UNPROFOR was increasingly seen as a party to the conflict, and the humanitarian operation increasingly became a political factor. Nonetheless, UNHCR's operation would have been severely restricted without the assistance of UNPROFOR. This fact did not necessarily mean that maintaining the humanitarian operation was or should have been a higher priority than a humanitarian intervention.

While the parties were reluctant to agree on anything in the political and military negotiations, agreement was often reached in the humanitarian negotiations. For example, at a meeting convened by UNHCR in Geneva on 18 November 1993, the three Bosnian leaders signed a joint commitment to ensure the delivery of humanitarian assistance by suspending hostilities and allowing free and unconditional access by the most effective land routes. They also committed themselves to allow UNHCR and ICRC to determine, without any conditionality or linkages, the content of humanitarian assistance. Such agreements, at whatever level they were reached, were ignored in practice by the Bosnian Croat and Serb forces in the field; their leaders blamed violations on 'rogue elements'.

6.2.4   NATO air power and the use of force

As the prospects for peace dimmed and the constraints on UNPROFOR became more evident, attention was given to the possible use of NATO air power. The US government was the driving force behind this initiative; NATO governments with troops in UNPROFOR were understandably more cautious in their approach. The Security Council had banned local military flights in Bosnian airspace in October 1992 (SC Res 781). This ban was frequently violated, though not by combat activity until Serb aircraft bombed villages east of Srebrenica on 13 March 1993. In response, with the adoption of SC Res 816 on 31 March, the Security Council extended the ban to cover all unauthorized flights, and authorized 'all necessary measures' to ensure compliance. The result was a NATO-enforced 'no-fly zone'.

SC Res 836, adopted on 4 June 1993, extended UNPROFOR's mandate to the protection of designated safe areas,[17] and decided that states 'may take, under the authority of the Security Council and subject to close coordination with the Secretary-General and UNPROFOR, all necessary measures, through the use of air power, in and around the safe areas in the Republic of Bosnia and Herzegovina, to support UNPROFOR in the performance of its mandate set out in paragraphs 5 and 9 above'. Paragraph 5 covered the extension of the mandate 'to deter attacks against the safe areas... in addition to participating in the delivery of humanitarian relief'. Paragraph 9 authorized, in carrying out the paragraph 5 mandate but with the qualification 'acting in self-defence', the use of force in reply to attacks on the safe areas or deliberate obstruction of UNPROFOR's freedom of movement in and around them, and that 'of protected humanitarian convoys'. The fundamental contradiction between these two paragraphs well illustrated the gap between declared intent and reality in the international community's approach to intervention. This resolution gave rise to the false expectation that UNPROFOR could and would defend the safe areas.[18]

The question of whether, if it is an option, humanitarian relief should be delivered by force is likely to arise as consent becomes more difficult to obtain.[19] International humanitarian law imposes on the parties to a conflict the obligation to accept humanitarian aid, but does not confer on others the right to impose it. There is general agreement that such use of force changes the nature of a humanitarian operation from one that respects and demands respect for the principles of humanitarian action to a military operation with a humanitarian objective. It is unlikely that such force, even if successful initially, would be sustainable in the longer term. And there is the basic question of whether, if the will to use force and accept casualties exists, this would not be better applied to a humanitarian intervention to end the conflict and the abuses that make humanitarian relief necessary.

From the start of UNPROFOR's involvement, UNHCR considered that the use of force to deliver relief would be counter-productive. While there was some discussion of the possibility, it is doubtful that it was ever a real option. UNPROFOR only rarely threatened credible force to ensure its own freedom of movement, though to do so would have been less contentious to an obstructing party than the coercive delivery of relief to its 'enemy'. However, the involvement of NATO airpower and the lack of a clear distinction between UNPROFOR and the humanitarian operation in the minds of the combatants markedly increased the risks to the humanitarian actors. These risks—for example, crossing active front lines in soft-skinned vehicles and the vulnerability of the relief convoys—were already significantly greater than those that troop-contributing nations were prepared to accept for their contingents.

The North Atlantic Council held a special meeting on 2 August 1993 to discuss the situation in Bosnia. A press statement by the NATO Secretary General after the meeting described the humanitarian situation as unacceptable and warned the parties of the determination of the Allies to take effective action in support of UN Security Council decisions. Noting that the Alliance was already ready to provide 'protective air power' for UNPROFOR on the basis of SC Res 836, the statement announced that the Alliance had 'now decided to make immediate preparations for undertaking, in the event that the strangulation of Sarajevo and other areas continues, including wide-scale interference with humanitarian assistance, stronger measures including air strikes against those responsible'. These measures were to be in support of and in full coordination with UNPROFOR, and in consultation with UNHCR. In the statement, the Allies stressed 'the limited humanitarian purposes of the military measures envisaged'. The humanitarian operation was now formally identified with the threat of coercive action.

In addition to the threat and rare use of close air support (protective air power) in defence of UNPROFOR, there were several threats of air strikes with limited objectives. The first threat, in February 1994, demanded and achieved the withdrawal of BSA heavy weapons from the Sarajevo exclusion zone. It was initiated by a letter on 6 February from the UN Secretary-General to his NATO counterpart, following the deadly shelling of the Sarajevo market the previous day. Only in the summer of 1995 was a threat seriously implemented. The military intervention then appeared motivated at least as much by the failure of other policies and the prospect of an opposed withdrawal of UNPROFOR as it was by humanitarian considerations.

While the international community finally took military action against the Bosnian Serbs, the maintenance of the arms embargo established by SC Res 713 (1991) had much greater effect on the Bosnian government's forces than on the BSA, which received weapons from the Yugoslav army and Serbia. The Bosnian government maintained that the embargo was grossly unfair, arguing that if the international community was not ready to intervene to deter aggression, then it should not deny the recognized government the means to defend itself.[20] It may also be noted in this context that the Bosnian and Croatian forces made major advances at the expense of the BSA in the autumn of 1995, and were poised to extend the government's territorial control (and thus, the territorial integrity of Bosnia, to which many Security Council resolutions made reference) well beyond the percentages foreseen by the Contact Group and earlier negotiators. At that point, international pressure was exerted to halt these advances.

Like every peace proposal from the Lisbon Agreement in March 1992 onwards, the terms of the Dayton agreement effectively left those responsible for ethnic cleansing in power. It entrenched ethnic division: explicitly in its constitutional arrangements and in reality for those unable to exercise their right of return to their former homes. The IFOR mandate did not require coercive action against those who continued ethnic cleansing or obstructed return. Hopes that the force would, nevertheless, respond robustly evaporated immediately, with the forced displacement of 60,000 Serbs from Sarajevo in full view of but without action from IFOR. Extremists on all sides took comfort. Of fundamental importance in the context of what followed in Kosovo was the fact that not only did the Dayton agreement not address the Kosovo problem, dashing the expectations of Kosovo Albanians, but it also reinforced the position of President Milošević, who had played a major role in bringing conflict to Slovenia, Croatia, and Bosnia and was to bring it to Kosovo.

6.3   1998–9: Kosovo

On 28 February 1998 the Serb security forces began a series of actions against Kosovo Albanians accused of being supporters of the separatist Kosovo Liberation Army (KLA). These left civilians dead and forced the flight of others. On 31 March the Security Council, acting under chapter VII, adopted SC Res 1160. This condemned the use of excessive force against civilians by the security forces and acts of terrorism by the KLA. Among other provisions, it established an arms embargo, 'for the purposes of fostering peace and stability in Kosovo' and set conditions for reconsidering it, including confirmation of the withdrawal of special police units and that the security forces had ceased action affecting the civilian population.

On 21 April 1998, briefing the Security Council on return from a mission to the region that included Kosovo, the UN High Commissioner for Refugees shared her concerns at developments there. By June it was clear that the province was sliding into serious conflict and that a much expanded humanitarian operation would be needed. It had long been accepted that conflict in Kosovo would have far-reaching implications. Within a few months, hundreds of thousands of the majority Kosovo Albanian population were affected by the actions of the Yugoslav security forces and paramilitaries, with large-scale internal forced displacement. Relatively few became refugees in neighbouring countries but some 100,000 sought asylum outside the region in the twelve months preceding the start of NATO military action on 24 March 1999.[21] A number of Kosovo Serb civilians were themselves victims of the actions of the KLA. The Serb security forces justified their actions as legitimate reaction to KLA terrorism. The longer the abuses of the security forces continued, the more of their victims supported the political aims, if not the more ruthless methods, of the KLA.

There was general agreement that resolution of this conflict would be even more difficult than it had been in Bosnia. There was a declared international consensus that independence was not a solution, but the principal demand of the Contact Group and the Security Council—the withdrawal of the security forces repressing the civilian population—left control of much of the province to the KLA, aggressive champions of an independence sought by the overwhelming majority of the inhabitants of the province. Whatever the negotiated solution, it required the agreement of President Milošević, who was responsible for the continuing problems that any solution had to address.

6.3.1 Déjà vu?

For the humanitarian actors, there were some strong echoes of the Bosnian conflict. An internal UNHCR report noted in early August 1998 that

an international community that two months ago was saying that Kosovo would not be allowed to become another Bosnia seems to be at a loss as to how to prevent very similar human suffering ... We are seeing many of the familiar problems and dilemmas too: abductions; armed civilians; humanitarian symbols being misused; the perception that our efforts are helping the enemy; access being obstructed, and the like.

Humanitarian personnel were again witness to, but powerless to prevent, forced displacement and killings. There were also parallels in the practical conduct of the relief operation, with front lines to be crossed and eventually a need for international convoy teams, though neither side deliberately targeted the convoys and aid vehicles, as all sides had done in Bosnia.

The overriding need of the Kosovo Albanians was for security, not material assistance. During the war in Bosnia, many civilians could flee if necessary to somewhere where they felt relatively safe, whether behind their own front-lines—though there was not necessarily actual safety in numbers—or elsewhere. The same was true for Serb and most other non-Albanian residents of Kosovo. But once the conflict escalated, few Kosovo Albanians had any option but to flee relatively short distances within Kosovo: away from the immediate threat at that time. Many were displaced more than once within Kosovo; unlike in Bosnia, the great majority sought to return home as soon as the immediate threat appeared to have lessened.

There was no senior UN political presence within the province or elsewhere in Serbia. This was a serious omission; it was clear from mid-1998 that such a presence was needed. With the UN having been heavily criticized over its performance before the Dayton agreement, Secretary-General Annan and his senior advisers appeared unwilling to run the risks inherent in such exposure. One result was that the Secretary-General's monthly political reports to the Security Council were known by all parties to have as a primary input information from UN civilians on the ground with the humanitarian operation. These reports were important in the adoption of key resolutions, and used by some to justify threats of military intervention. This allowed the Serb authorities and their media to present the humanitarian actors as anti-Serb. The UN was formally absent from political involvement in the negotiating process within the region and later in France, though the negotiators informally briefed UNHCR and tried to take account of its concerns, some of which were informed by the difficulties encountered in implementing the Dayton agreement.

In June 1998 Belgrade agreed under pressure to the deployment of the Kosovo Diplomatic Observer Mission (KDOM). KDOM comprised unarmed Russian, United States, and European observers, some of the latter redeployed from the European Community Monitoring Mission elsewhere in the Balkans*. Most were newly (and with delays) accredited to their embassies in Belgrade and detached to Kosovo. By August there were some hundred such observers. KDOM significantly increased the international presence in Kosovo but suffered from its 'just tolerated' status with the authorities, a fragmented structure and the lack of a clear mandate and single authoritative reporting channel.

The humanitarian operation inside Kosovo was much less a political component of the international response, and less a focus of international attention, than that during the war in Bosnia. Nevertheless, while it was also less subject to obstruction, both Belgrade and the Kosovo Serbs quickly perceived it as partial. This was not just because the great majority of its beneficiaries were Kosovo Albanians. UNHCR and others were drawing attention to the consequences for civilians of unchecked massive abuses of human rights. Belgrade denied that these abuses were anything more than legitimate anti-terrorist actions (with all able-bodied male Kosovo Albanians considered potential terrorists).

6.3.2 NATO threats

NATO's response to the deteriorating situation in Kosovo gave priority to the threat of air strikes to stop the escalating abuses of human rights. Its first manifestation was on 16 June 1998, when some hundred NATO aircraft conducted an exercise close to Serbia's borders, within Albanian and Macedonian airspace. This was intended to demonstrate NATO's resolve and capacity to mobilize quickly, and thereby to deter President Milošević. The same day in Moscow, Presidents Milošević and Yeltsin issued a joint statement that sought to address and defuse Western demands and criticism.[22] In July the Serb forces began a large-scale operation against the KLA, which by then controlled substantial areas of the province. This led to significant new civilian suffering and forced displacement.

Media and international attention to the implications of events on the ground increased.[23] At the request of the Security Council, UNHCR gave a first-hand briefing at closed consultations on 10 September 1998. After intensive negotiations, the Council adopted SC Res 1199 on 23 September. Among other provisions, this demanded a halt to hostilities, that the Yugoslav authorities and Kosovo Albanian leadership 'take immediate steps to improve the humanitarian situation and to avert the impending humanitarian catastrophe', and that the Yugoslav government 'cease all action by the security

* After November 1993, when the Maastricht Treaty came into force, the European Community (EC) was referred to as the European Union (EU).

forces affecting the civilian population and order the withdrawal of security units used for civilian repression'.

Although adopted under chapter VII, this resolution did not authorize the use of force. Rather, the Security Council decided, should the measures demanded therein and in SC Res 1160 'not be taken, to consider further action and additional measures to maintain or restore peace and stability in the region'. NATO used SC Res 1199 to advance its internal planning for air strikes,[24] and made public its threat to President Milošević. When the UN High Commissioner for Refugees met him in Belgrade on 24 September, the President began the meeting by complaining that the international community had used UNHCR reports and its exaggerated numbers of displaced persons in Kosovo in order to adopt SC Res 1199. In that sense, he held UNHCR indirectly responsible for the NATO threats.[25] The President maintained, as his Minister of Foreign Affairs had told the Belgrade diplomatic corps on 14 September, that the situation was almost back to normal. On 28 September, the Serbian Prime Minister told parliament that peace now reigned in Kosovo and life was back to normal.[26]

6.3.3 The OSCE verification mission

In early October 1998, as NATO intensified planning for air action, US Envoy Richard Holbrooke travelled to Belgrade and eventually secured a Serb statement agreeing to the withdrawal of the additional security forces, the deployment of an unarmed OSCE verification mission (the KVM), a complementary NATO air verification mission, and early progress towards a political settlement. To ensure that these commitments were implemented, on 12 October NATO gave authority for air strikes, an authority that was to be effective after ninety-six hours (extended to ten days as negotiations continued, and then suspended). Agreements for the verification missions were signed with NATO and OSCE in Belgrade on 15 and 16 October and endorsed by SC Res 1203 on 24 October, which also demanded the full and prompt implementation of these agreements. The resolution was adopted acting under chapter VII, with thirteen votes in favour and China and the Russian Federation abstaining.

The deployment of the KVM and the limited withdrawal of the security forces raised the confidence of the Kosovo Albanians in their security and allowed a significant return of those displaced within Kosovo. Clarity on and respect of the authorized levels and locations of Serb security forces was clearly critical to decisions on return. It soon became apparent that the agreement on specific security force levels reached with NATO in Belgrade on 25 October, while it accelerated withdrawal, did not provide sufficient details. NATO also appears to have accepted Serb force levels in Kosovo higher than those before the conflict. No copy of the agreement was released. UNHCR and the KVM were thus unable to inform displaced persons considering return as to how many Serb security personnel should be where in their home areas.

This lack of precision also meant that the KVM had no clear baseline against which to monitor one of the key demands of the Security Council. As expected, the KLA moved to take control of areas from which the Serb security forces did withdraw. It was generally accepted that the agreements had bought limited time for political negotiations to succeed and that if these failed, as appeared likely given the diametrically opposing demands, it was probable that NATO would use its air power. With the precedent of UNPROFOR hostages during the first NATO air strikes in Bosnia in 1995, it was evident that the KVM would have to be withdrawn in advance of any NATO action, or risk being taken hostage.

The KVM presence throughout the province provided significant help to the humanitarian operation, including with security, at least for the humanitarian actors themselves. The fact that many KVM personnel were serving or retired military officers from NATO member states fuelled Serb suspicions that the KVM and by association UNHCR were not neutral and impartial. After the KVM was withdrawn, some personnel did shift straight to NATO duties. Just as the KDOM's creation reflected the fact that an OSCE mission was not then an option, so the choice of KVM rather than a more robust approach reflected the fact that US military participation, even in an operation by consent, was not an option that Ambassador Holbrooke was authorized to negotiate. Whether, if it had been, Belgrade would have accepted, was moot, but the option would have strengthened Holbrooke's hand.

6.3.4 End of the humanitarian operation in Kosovo

By the end of 1998 the ceasefire was collapsing, Serb security forces were on the offensive, and forced displacement was again on the increase. As the humanitarian crisis deepened, some saw the need for NATO air action as linked to the challenges faced by the humanitarian operation within Kosovo. The involvement of NATO with Kosovo prior to the start of the air campaign was, however, much less directly linked to the humanitarian operation than had been the case in Bosnia. Nevertheless, aerials were ripped off UNHCR vehicles and from office roofs in Belgrade and elsewhere once the bombing started, with the explanation that they would otherwise guide NATO aircraft. As in Bosnia, local perceptions and propaganda determined the level of risk to the humanitarian actors.

The situation inside Kosovo stabilized somewhat during the peace negotiations at Rambouillet, France, in February 1999 but deteriorated rapidly thereafter. An 8 March 1999 UNHCR briefing note, prepared for the EU Special Envoy for Kosovo on the occasion of the visit to Belgrade of the President of the EU Council of Ministers (the German Foreign Minister), recorded that since the breakdown of peace negotiations on 23 February, some 28,000 persons had fled their homes. The note assessed generalized fear among the

Kosovo Albanians as being as great or higher than before the international community's intervention in October 1998. While affecting many fewer persons than the actions of the Serb forces, violence and intimidation by the KLA was increasing and forcing more Serbs to leave their homes. The note concluded: 'Kosovo is a political problem, with devastating humanitarian consequences, for which there is only a political solution. That solution is vital. Without it and with Kosovo therefore sliding into disaster, even the most determined and effective humanitarian action would very soon be unable to keep pace with the ever greater humanitarian needs.'

The UN humanitarian operation in Kosovo ended with some 250,000 Kosovo Albanians displaced within the province. Some 200,000 others had sought safety outside the province over the previous twelve months.[27] As the last UNHCR and World Food Programme international staff withdrew from Kosovo on 23 March 1999, they turned over relief supplies and equipment to ICRC, in the hope that ICRC would be able to continue distribution. ICRC soon found itself having to operate in unacceptable conditions and suspended its operations, withdrawing its delegates from Kosovo. In late May, the UN Secretary-General sent a humanitarian assessment mission to Serbia, including Kosovo. This mission appears to have been in part motivated by a need to be seen to be doing something. A fully objective needs assessment was not possible in the prevailing circumstances, and there was no possibility of restarting UN humanitarian assistance within Kosovo during the NATO air action.

There were other external humanitarian initiatives for Kosovo during the war. The Greek chapter of the NGO Médécins du Monde organized several humanitarian convoys into Kosovo from Macedonia, arguing that the need for assistance outweighed the fact that its use could not be monitored, and that it was unlikely that much would reach Kosovo Albanians. A Greek, Russian, and Swiss initiative (FOCUS) sought to deliver humanitarian assistance to the province, including by air, but never received NATO clearance. Near the end of the war, the International Rescue Committee (an American NGO) organized several airdrops of relief to internally displaced Kosovo Albanians. Others concluded that, with even the ICRC unable to operate, the minimum conditions for humanitarian assistance within Kosovo could not be met while the war continued.

Every effort was made to continue the humanitarian assistance programme within Serbia for the 500,000 ethnic Serb refugees from the earlier conflicts in Croatia and Bosnia. Belgrade had insisted on placing 14,000 of them in Kosovo, and resisted UNHCR's efforts to have them relocated for their own safety once the clashes there began, but most had left by the time the war started. UNHCR maintained an international presence in Belgrade throughout the war, but only very limited assistance was possible. UNHCR temporarily withdrew its international presence in Montenegro just before the start of the air campaign, but re-established and reinforced it after a few days. Montenegro was effectively a country of asylum where, although not technically refugees, most displaced Kosovo Albanians found a guarded welcome, and where the humanitarian actors enjoyed good cooperation with the beleaguered authorities.

6.4 Lessons from the Balkans

The political, military, and humanitarian strands of the international community's response to such complex situations are likely to remain closely interwoven. Some of the lessons of the Balkans experience have wider relevance. This remains so despite the shift of focus away from threats to human security posed by internal human rights abuses and towards threats to state security posed by international terrorism.

6.4.1 Act early and credibly

The passage of time can make the acceptance of a humanitarian intervention politically easier or leave states with no option but to act, if the consequences of inaction have become politically unacceptable (as was the case in both the interventions considered here). However, as time passes effective intervention is likely to become much more difficult. This suggests that early and principled action is in the national interests of states, and not just of those whose widespread suffering and death it could prevent. If the best efforts at non-coercive prevention have failed, the necessary early action may appear significantly more risky than any single stage of an incremental and short-term reactive approach. But finally having to deal with the cumulative consequences and dangers of the latter approach will be more risky still, as the very close-run outcomes of both of NATO's military interventions in the Balkans demonstrate.

Whatever form the response of the international community takes, its intent must be clear and credible if it is to be effective in deterring and stopping gross violations. This was not the case during the conflict in Bosnia. Various Security Council resolutions were ambiguous in real intent, authorized action that was unlikely to be possible with the resources available, raised false expectations, and revealed an increasingly clear gap between demands—many made under chapter VII and repeated almost routinely—and commitment to ensure their respect. As a result of these and other indications of lack of purpose and disarray in the international community, those committing the violations felt emboldened, not inhibited. The credibility and resolve of the Security Council must be made evident to all.

6.4.2 Address causes

The Balkans experience shows that an international response whose primary purpose is to relieve human suffering is unlikely to be sustainable in conflicts involving serious violations of human rights and will lose legitimacy the longer it continues without effective action to prevent suffering. Loss of legitimacy is likely to be most marked in situations where the creation of such suffering is a war aim, as it was in the Balkans, rather than a consequence of conflict. Humanitarian assistance should not be delivered by force. If there is the will for coercive military threats or action, a humanitarian intervention should have prevention and an end to the causes of suffering, not relief of that suffering, as its primary purpose.

Civilian humanitarian operations may need to be suspended during such an intervention. At every stage of the conflict in the Balkans—and no doubt elsewhere—those whose human rights were being violated saw action to stop this as much more important than action to maintain humanitarian relief. They have more right than outsiders to judge the priority to be accorded to maintaining a humanitarian operation in such circumstances. If there is not the will to prevent suffering and bring a just resolution to the conflict, then there may be circumstances when the delivery of humanitarian relief in conflict is better limited to the role of the ICRC under international humanitarian law.

6.4.3 End impunity

One element of the necessary early and principled action (and credibility) must be to end the impunity of those who orchestrate and commit mass violations of human rights and crimes against humanity. In the Balkans this would have been possible: SC Res 827 of 25 May 1993, adopted unanimously, established an international tribunal covering crimes committed in the territory of the former Yugoslavia from 1 January 1991 onwards. On deployment in Bosnia at the end of 1995, the NATO-led force (IFOR) failed to take the resolute and swift action against indicted war criminals that many within and outside the region expected. To have done so would have been a significant contribution to international and individual security. Eight years later Karadžić and Mladić remained at large. The International Tribunal finally first indicted President Milošević in 1999 for events in Kosovo. Those governments that could have helped the prosecutors with evidence to support an earlier indictment for events during the wars in Croatia and Bosnia appear to have given this low priority until the Kosovo crisis.

6.4.4 Engage the United Nations

From 1994 onwards, the UN was increasingly excluded from the key negotiating processes in the Balkans. In the future, the UN Secretary-General and Secretariat should be substantively involved in any such negotiations. Not only would this bring a wider legitimacy and perhaps greater coherence to that process itself, whether successful or not, but it would help ensure that the desired negotiated solution met international standards. There is also a need to ensure that the views and experience of the relevant humanitarian organizations are taken into account in the formulation of a peace plan. This is of particular importance with regard to the security of returning refugees and of minorities.

Negotiations are generally expected to have broken down before the use of force, though once force is threatened, credibility becomes a factor in the timing, as NATO's credibility was in Bosnia and Kosovo. If negotiations fail and military intervention is contemplated, the earlier involvement of the UN may help build a consensus that intervention is indeed unavoidable. East Timor, not the Balkans, should be the precedent.

There should be a senior UN official within the affected region, normally a special representative of the Secretary-General. This official should have overall responsibility for all including military aspects of the international community's response (if this involves coercive military action, other arrangements may be necessary for its duration). This has not been the case in post-conflict Bosnia and Kosovo.

6.4.5 Preserve the identity of the humanitarian operation

Humanitarian action in conflict cannot be isolated from its political context, and the political, military, and humanitarian components of the international response must be closely coordinated. At the same time, the separate identity and nature of the humanitarian operation should be respected.[28] This will be easier if that operation itself is well coordinated, coherent in its aims, and consistent in respect of its principles.

One specific structure helped the humanitarian operation in the Balkans to keep a separate identity from the political and military components of the international community's response. At the meeting of the Conference on Yugoslavia in London in July 1992, the UN High Commissioner for Refugees agreed to chair the Humanitarian Issues Working Group (HIWG), one of several working groups established by the Conference on issues related to the break up of the former Yugoslavia. The HIWG allowed humanitarian concerns to be examined with less political polarization than was evident in other fora.[29] It provided the humanitarian operation with a means of highlighting humanitarian concerns directly to governments, and continued to serve a useful purpose after the Dayton agreement and throughout the Kosovo crisis. There is likely to be value for both governments and humanitarian organizations in having such a framework; how it is best created will depend on the circumstances.

Humanitarian action is a concern of the Security Council to an extent that surely neither it nor the humanitarian organizations who now brief the Council could have imagined in 1991. The benefits of ensuring that humanitarian considerations and a first-hand picture of conditions on the ground are put directly before the Council well outweigh the risks of politicization of the humanitarian action.

6.5 Conclusions

Conflicts in the Balkans and elsewhere have focused attention on the circumstances in which a humanitarian intervention might be warranted and on the standards that should be met. The report of the International Commission on Intervention and State Sovereignty set the arguments out clearly.[30] Its proposals appear convincing and realistic, if necessarily challenging for the international community. Measuring the humanitarian interventions examined in this chapter against the principles elaborated by the Commission suggests that in both Bosnia and Kosovo the 'just cause' threshold was met, and that the former intervention broadly respected the other principles while the latter only respected some of them.

The humanitarian intervention in Bosnia in 1995 was almost too late. It stopped the fighting, but the passage of time without effective action to address years of massive violations of human rights meant that only a seriously flawed settlement was achieved, and that only at the last hour of negotiations. The position of President Milošević as the key interlocutor in any international search for solutions was consolidated for more than three years. The Kosovo problem was not addressed at Dayton, despite the earlier understandings given to the Kosovo Albanians, and the EU's link of recognition of FRY to progress in Kosovo was abandoned.

There is evidence that, from the spring of 1998, the NATO leadership and some governments saw the dangers in Kosovo and were more ready to take resolute action than in Croatia in 1991 and Bosnia in 1992. But the challenge of Kosovo was greater, and earlier inaction had foreclosed all but bad and worse options. In a sense, NATO's humanitarian intervention in 1999, like that in 1995, came about as much by default as design. Its public justification changed from obtaining FRY agreement to the Rambouillet accord, to ending the expulsions and abuses that followed the coercive NATO action, to ensuring the complete withdrawal of Serb security forces and the return of refugees. The fact that it was explicitly limited to the use of airpower reduced its effectiveness, raised concerns as to its proportionality, and may have prolonged the intervention.

Humanitarian interventions are, and are likely to remain, very rare. Most large-scale violations of human rights and international humanitarian law attract little of the attention, concern, and resources focused on the Balkans since 1991. Even when they do, for many of the victims it is too late. It is in the interests of all that international attention to massive abuses of human rights is not selective but timely, principled, and consistent. This is a requirement for prevention, and for the credibility of any humanitarian intervention should prevention fail.

7

Humanitarian Intervention and International Society: Lessons from Africa

James Mayall

Africa was the last part of the world to be enclosed by European imperialism, and amongst the last to acquire independence. Perhaps, for this reason, African countries have always had a special relationship with the UN. Looking back on the often heated debates of the 1950s and early 1960s about decolonization, it seems to me that at the time many on the left saw the continent (absurdly as it turned out) as a kind of blank slate on which to inscribe the new constitution of liberation and social justice; those on the right insisted on the contrary that, with the withdrawal of European power, anarchy would reassert itself and that African traditional cultures were inherently resistant to modernization. No doubt this is a caricature, but it catches something of the incomprehension with which liberal internationalists and latter day imperialists viewed one another when they were both caught off guard by the speed of imperial withdrawal. Robert Jackson has provided a more sober assessment of Africa's predicament. In an influential book, he argued that many African states possessed only 'juridical' sovereignty, and that their entry into international society on this basis, virtually as its wards, represented a new and problematic development in world affairs.[1]

In Africa itself, after an initial period of political quarrelling over the concept of unity, African governments emerged as the most enthusiastic supporters of the 'pluralist' conception of international society—that is, a society of sovereign states.[2] Their theoretical commitment to territorial integrity and non-interference in domestic affairs was buttressed by the Organization of African Unity's (OAU's) adoption in 1964 of the principle of *uti possidetis, ita possideatis*: 'as you possess so you may possess'. This principle originated in nineteenth century Latin America, but was revived by African states in the twentieth and later accepted by the international community as a whole in their efforts to confine self-determination to European decolonization and to deny the legitimacy of secession (Jackson 2000: 325–8).

Having played a defining role in the attempt to freeze the political map after the transfer of power, it was not surprising that after the cold war Africa was seen, in the West if not in Africa itself, as a testing ground for the argument that international society was evolving in a solidarist direction—that is, towards a society of peoples in which sovereignty would not be regarded as absolute and where, when necessary, the international community would intervene for humanitarian reasons and to protect the victims of massive and sustained human rights abuse.[3] The experience of the last decade initially seemed to support the optimists on this issue, but then confirmed the views of the pessimists. The jury is still out on whether a more balanced and realistic set of expectations about the prospects for honest government and the protection of human rights is now emerging. This chapter will seek to answer two questions. First, to what extent are the problems that have confronted the international community in Africa a result of the contradictions inherent in the concept of humanitarian intervention itself, and to what extent of the particular complexity of African conflicts? Second, are there specific lessons to be learned from African experience about the prospects for, and limitations of, humanitarian intervention?

7.1   Debates about humanitarian intervention: 1945–90

The idea that force can or should be used for humanitarian purposes raises difficult questions of definition, since action intended for other purposes may turn out to have humanitarian consequences, and vice versa. For the purposes of the present discussion, I shall adopt the definition employed by other authors in this volume, namely that humanitarian intervention consists of coercive (military) interference in the internal affairs of a state with the purpose of addressing massive human rights violations or relieving widespread human suffering.

It is helpful to start by sketching how African governments viewed the subject before the end of the cold war. It is no exaggeration to say that they were vehemently opposed to military intervention in independent Africa under any guise. They would have supported military intervention to overthrow white minority rule in the Portuguese colonies, Rhodesia (Zimbabwe), Namibia, and South Africa, but since all attempts to persuade the Security Council to take effective action against these regimes were vetoed by one or more of the Western powers, they knew that this was not a realistic option. When the Security Council eventually imposed comprehensive mandatory sanctions against Rhodesia, following Ian Smith's Unilateral Declaration of Independence in 1965, it was at Britain's request and the sanctions were deliberately adopted as an alternative to force, not as a preliminary to enforcement action. In the case of South Africa, the Western powers resisted the imposition of comprehensive sanctions to the end, arguing that the only way to bring about change was through quiet diplomacy.

It is not surprising, therefore, that many first generation African leaders viewed all forms of intervention with deep suspicion. The exceptions were the Francophone leaders, most of whom came to power having signed defence agreements with France, which in some cases allowed France to maintain troops in their countries on a permanent basis. But even they did not challenge Kwame Nkrumah's assertion that Africa would not be secure until the continent as a whole was freed from colonialism. Nor did they initially oppose Patrice Lumumbas's triple approach to the UN Secretary-General and the US and Soviet governments, after the Congolese army had mutinied three weeks after independence in 1960 and the Belgian government had sent in troops to cover the evacuation of Belgian citizens. Almost simultaneously, the British were persuaded to abrogate their defence treaty with newly independent Nigeria after the opposition had used this aspect of the independence settlement to accuse the Nigerian government of putting the country's independence at risk with a neo-colonial agreement. Independence was seen as an end in itself; it was, therefore, self-evident that African rights would be better protected under indigenous than under alien and/or racist rule. Indeed, one of the main reasons for establishing the OAU in 1963 was to reduce the vulnerability of African states to external intervention. In the rhetoric of the early independence period, inter-African conflicts were invariably a product of external interference.[4] African nationalists believed that, left to themselves, Pan-African solidarity would enable them to create a *Pax Africana* under which appropriate African solutions would be sought to African problems.

The reality was rather different. In most cases, constitutional government and democratic institutions were grafted onto authoritarian patterns of colonial rule very late in the day. The problems that this would pose were not immediately apparent as ethnic, religious, and other political divisions had mostly been subordinated to the common anti-colonial struggle. Everything changed after independence, when most African governments regarded opposition as treason. Those who lost out in the competition to control the post-colonial state—and who found themselves stigmatized in this way— sensibly went into exile in neighbouring countries in order to avoid persecution at home. Since many ethnic groups straddled the political boundaries between states that had been drawn during the nineteenth-century scramble for Africa, they frequently found a ready-made political constituency, which could be mobilized against the exile politician's own state. The result of this 'export–import business' in opposition politicians was widespread political instability, an environment in which governments were vulnerable to externally organized subversion, regardless of their formal ideological commitments. It was to overcome this locally generated insecurity that, under the OAU Charter, African leaders proscribed interference in the domestic affairs of other states, subversion, and political assassination.

For a time, what the press called the 'spirit of Addis Ababa' appeared to constrain the internecine conflicts that had flared up in many parts of the continent in the early 1960s. It did so, however, at the price of insulating African leaders from international criticism. The OAU was regarded by its critics as little more than a trade union for African leaders. By this, they meant that it provided equal protection for rulers who had seized power by force, or who had established single party states and had themselves declared 'President for Life', as it did for those who had led their countries to independence and whose rule rested on a solid basis of domestic support. As the years passed, the list of those in the former category rose precipitately. Their leaders justified the establishment of one party states on the grounds that, for countries in need of rapid economic development, inter-party competition was a wasteful distraction. Whenever it seized power, the military claimed that as the only genuinely national institution, it was uniquely well placed to purge government of the corruption and ethnic rivalry that had become the trademark of civilian governments throughout the continent. In no case did the new rulers pay much attention to protecting the individual freedoms of the people. Even in countries whose governments were genuinely committed to improving their welfare such as Tanzania the security forces could be a law unto themselves, frequently arresting people on suspicion and imprisoning them without trial.[5] The non-interference principle inscribed in the OAU Charter ensured that African governments refrained from criticizing each other's domestic policies. And until the mid-1980s, Western governments were similarly cautious, accepting the argument that to attach political conditions to foreign aid would amount to an infringement of sovereignty.

The OAU may have been more concerned to buttress the external authority of governments than to protect the rights of African peoples, but it was not totally immune from internal criticism on its humanitarian record. On three occasions, Julius Nyerere, the first President of Tanzania, challenged the Organization over its refusal to impose criteria for membership. The first was over its refusal to expel Malawi, after President Hastings Banda had recognized South Africa and established a diplomatic mission in Pretoria in 1967. Opposition to apartheid was a constitutive principle of the Organization. Nyerere argued that since its members had committed themselves to a policy of economic and military confrontation with South Africa and the other white minority regimes in the region, Malawi was in breach of the Charter. During the Nigerian civil war (1967–70) Tanzania itself breached the Charter by recognizing the breakaway state of Biafra. In 1969, Nyerere circulated a memorandum to his fellow OAU Heads of State arguing that since a substantial proportion of the Nigerian population believed itself to be threatened by genocide, the contract between government and people had lapsed.[6] Although he had himself proposed the 1964 resolution, under which African governments accepted the boundaries inherited at independence, on this occasion he maintained Pan-African solidarity required that the interests of the Ibo population of Biafra have priority over those of the Nigerian Federal Government. Nyerere again pressed for the expulsion of an OAU member state in the 1970s—this time Idi Amin's Uganda—in opposition to his expulsion of the Ugandan Asian community and murderous persecution of his Ugandan opponents. He argued that Africans could not consistently call for the over-throw of the South African government, on account of its racist ideology and denial of rights to the African majority, while simultaneously tolerating a fascist regime within the OAU.

Nyerere failed in his attempt to establish an 'ethical' foundation for the OAU. Malawi was allowed to continue its membership; although Zambia, Ivory Coast, and Gabon joined Tanzania in recognizing Biafra, the Lagos government won the diplomatic battle within the OAU and there were no further defections; and after a year's delay, Idi Amin was allowed to host the OAU summit and serve his term as its Chairman. It is unlikely, however, that Tanzania's policy had no impact at all. Malawi, although not formally expelled, was not a member of the frontline states (an informal cooperative arrangement of the group of states most actively involved in providing sanctuary and other support to the Southern African liberation movements) and was ostracized within African diplomatic circles. Tanzania's policy in the Nigerian civil war reinforced humanitarian pressure on the Lagos government from outside Africa, notably though the Commonwealth. Consequently, while Nigeria recovered from its early reverses in the propaganda war and was able to insist that no third party could have contact with Biafra, unless they first accepted the principle of Nigerian unity, it was forced to concede the legitimacy of outside concern about the humanitarian aspects of the conflict. In Uganda, when finally the Tanzanians responded to a border incursion by Amin's forces, not merely by hot pursuit in the border area but by allowing the Tanzanian army to take Kampala and overthrow the regime, the action was formally condemned by the OAU but greeted with considerable relief in private. The principle of sovereignty may have been upheld, but the policies of several OAU member states had been exposed to unprecedented public scrutiny.

How exceptional was Africa in this regard? Not very, it seems. The particular civil conflicts that led to international debate and, from some quarters, calls for humanitarian intervention, were unique, but in resisting them, African governments were upholding accepted international norms and standards. The international political landscape of the late 1970s contained a number of confusing features. On the one hand, US President Jimmy Carter had attempted to base American foreign policy on the promotion and protection of human rights. On the other, the collapse of Portugal's African empire led to an intensification of cold war competition in Southern Africa and the Horn in particular. African governments welcomed the Carter human rights policy since they believed that it implied a more active US engagement in attempts to resolve the outstanding problems of white minority rule in Rhodesia, South Africa's continued control of Namibia in defiance of the United Nations, and above all, apartheid itself. In response to the policy, they also adopted the African Charter of Human Rights. At the same time, the emergence of a group of states—Angola, Ethiopia, and Mozambique—that were linked to the Soviet Union by treaty, and of another—Kenya, Somalia, and Sudan—that provided the United States with facilities for the Rapid Deployment Force created in response to the Soviet occupation of Afghanistan, meant that African states were increasingly drawn into a cold war pattern of patron client relationships.

The intensification of regional conflicts in the Horn and Southern Africa resulted in a massive increase in the number of refugees and internally displaced persons, a development to which African host countries, with the help of the UNHCR, generally responded positively. The late 1970s also witnessed an increase in the scale of NGO activity in bringing relief to communities caught in the crossfire. Unlike governments, NGOs could negotiate access with the local authorities without infringing the non-interference principle. Indeed, for this reason their work was often supported unofficially by Western governments, which were already vulnerable to public demands that 'something must be done' whenever famines and other humanitarian catastrophes caught the attention of the media. One example of this approach was Ethiopia in the famine-stricken years after the Revolution and during the long civil war with Eritrea.

With hindsight, it is clear that the groundwork for the humanitarian interventions of the 1990s was prepared well before the cold war ended. In particular, reliance on NGOs was probably unsustainable as a long-term policy, and certainly ineffective. Not only are these organizations, unlike governments, not accountable, but also they will do whatever is necessary for them to operate, even if this means, as in Somalia, buying protection and so feeding the conflict that led eventually to the collapse of the state and its accompanying humanitarian catastrophe. But, as Adam Roberts argues in Chapter 5, these trends were not confined to Africa. Tanzania could have argued for a right of humanitarian intervention in justification for its invasion of Uganda, but did not. Nor did Vietnam in overthrowing Pol Pot in Cambodia or India in intervening in East Pakistan to defeat the Pakistani army and help decisively in the creation of Bangladesh. Throughout the cold war period, in other words, the salience of human rights and humanitarian issues rose in international politics, but no government, within Africa or elsewhere, was prepared to contemplate a general right of humanitarian intervention in the sense of the definition offered earlier. Nor, so long as the cold war persisted, did the UN contemplate intervening in civil conflicts for humanitarian purposes but without asserting such a right. In Cambodia, East Pakistan, and Uganda, the three cases that are normally cited as precedents for humanitarian intervention, the intervening state had a clear objective, which it defined in other terms and which it achieved. These cases are of limited use, therefore, in answering the first question posed at the beginning of this chapter, namely whether the problems faced by the international community in the humanitarian interventions of the 1990s were a result of the contradictions inherent in the concept itself, or arose from circumstances peculiar to Africa. The cold war evidence would seem to rule against African exceptionalism.

The case for humanitarian intervention, like the case for universal human rights that underpins it, is not in principle culture- or region-specific. Nor are the problems posed by such intervention. The arguments for and against humanitarian intervention are general. If there is a case against intervention, it rests on general principles of international law and diplomatic practice: respect for sovereignty and territorial integrity; of prudence, that is, doubts about whether intervention is likely to be successful; and of incoherence since the decision to use force necessarily involves political and strategic calculations that may cut across humanitarian objectives. By contrast, as the authors in Part One of this book argue, if despite these objections, such a case is to be made, it can only rest on the assertion that humanitarian catastrophes demand an exceptional response; or that there are definable circumstances under which sovereignty can be said to have lapsed and the international community to have acquired a duty to intervene. Chapter VII of the UN Charter provides a basis on which intervention can be sanctioned but only if the Security Council determines that a threat to international peace and security exists. It is significant that in his report to the Security Council—*The causes of conflict and the promotion of durable peace and sustainable development in Africa*—Secretary-General Kofi Annan repeatedly refers to the problems of humanitarian intervention and peacekeeping in broad international terms (Secretary-General's Report to the Security Council, 16 April 1998).

7.2 The African context in the post-cold war era

The case against African exceptionalism is persuasive. There are, nonetheless, four reasons why Africa has been—and seems likely to continue to be—the testing ground for the theory and practice of humanitarian intervention. Let us consider them in turn. The first is the sheer scale of Africa's humanitarian crisis. The Secretary-General's report opens with some melancholy statistics:

Since 1970, more than 30 wars have been fought in Africa, the vast majority of them intra-state in origin. In 1996 alone, 14 of the 53 countries of Africa were afflicted by armed conflicts, accounting for more than half of all war-related deaths world wide and resulting in more than 8 million refugees, returnees and displaced persons. The consequences of these conflicts have seriously undermined Africa's efforts to ensure long-term stability, prosperity and peace for its peoples (para 4).

The HIV/Aids pandemic, along with the long-term consequences of post conflict traumatization and of the employment of child soldiers in several countries, merely reinforces his conclusion. It would be possible to deny the relevance of these facts and figures to the issue of intervention. Traditional international society was a self-help system: governments were entitled to defend their own interests and might therefore be expected to take steps to prevent the consequences of a nearby conflict spilling over their own frontiers, for example, through an uninvited influx of refugees. But, on this view, there is no broader obligation to assist the welfare and development of foreign countries (cf. Jackson 2000: 169–75).

It is still possible to argue in this way, but given the interdependence of the modern world economy and the impressive array of international agreements that governments have entered into since 1945—both within the UN and outside it—it is difficult. These agreements are based on the assumption of the desirability of international cooperation in pursuit of common objectives, if not of international solidarity. From the start, the UN was deeply influenced by the values of the Western democracies, and, in particular, by their insistence on the importance of entrenched human rights. The strategic imperatives of the cold war often pushed such considerations into the shadows—and certainly provided ammunition for their critics, who argued that the West was both selective in the assistance it offered to the rest of the world and hypocritical in its attitude towards the human rights policies of many of its strategic clients.

After 1989, however, the 'model' of plural democracy was unchallenged at the international level. There were two consequences of this apparent triumph. One was that the resurgence of ethnic and other conflicts in Africa and elsewhere was widely viewed as an impediment to the transition to democracy, even if the attempted transition was sometimes amongst the causes of conflict. The other was that, in the absence of any obvious strategic danger, the governments of the industrial democracies found it increasingly hard to resist demands for remedial action.

The second reason for Africa's prominence in debates about the legitimacy of humanitarian intervention is that, in many parts of the continent, the state itself is in crisis. Most African states are extremely fragile, partly because control of state institutions is regarded as a prize in a ferocious competition, where the stakes are high and the players employ ruthless methods. Traditionally, African politics have been characterized by 'winner takes all' assumptions, and in few cases has democratization made much difference. It might reasonably be argued that humanitarian intervention will deny the state time to consolidate itself and to develop a political culture that reflects local rather than imported values.[7] It is true that the imposition of structural adjustment programmes, at the insistence of the IMF and World Bank from the early 1980s onwards, was aimed at reducing the size of bureaucracies that had often become grotesquely inflated. But rolling back the state in circumstances where politics were essentially patrimonial in character, threatened to roll it out of existence altogether. In some countries, such as Somalia, the state itself is an exotic import that has failed to strike roots. In others, such as Liberia and Sierra Leone, local warlords have regarded it as dispensable. The trouble with arguments that plead for time is that the damage has already been done. Perhaps, left to themselves, some African countries would in time develop viable systems that respect both the individual and collective rights of their citizens. This was the case successfully advanced by President Museveni of Uganda against Western pressure that he should replace his system of no-party democracy with multi-party competition. But, on the evidence of Angola, Liberia, and Sierra Leone since the end of the cold war, the Ugandan case looks more like the exception than the rule. When the state fails, it not only creates the preconditions for recurrent humanitarian catastrophes—and hence the demand for international action—but also compounds the difficulties of intervention because of the lack of a stable and/or legitimate interlocutor for the international community.

Third, there is a disturbing absence of fit between Western interests and African needs. With the end of the cold war, no sub-Saharan African country figures prominently in the geo-strategic priorities of any of the major powers, even though their governments regularly argue in favour of policies aimed at promoting the conditions of international stability generally, and have become increasingly concerned at the prospect of state failure as a potential breeding ground for international terrorism. Local powers do have a strong interest in containing the spillover of local conflicts. Indeed, in the Charter of the African Union two new principles were added to those taken over from the OAU, which it replaced in July 2000. Article 4(h) allows the Union to intervene 'in respect of grave crises namely: war crimes, genocide and crimes against humanity', and Article 4(j) gives the member states the 'right to request intervention from the Union in order to restore peace and stability'. Nonetheless, while one purpose of the new Union is to promote self-reliance (Article 4(k)), they mostly lack the capacity to intervene effectively without outside support.

This mismatch of interest and need is the primary explanation of the double standards of which Africans complain in relation to the international response to international crises in other parts of the world. The International Commission on Intervention and State Sovereignty (ICISS) has attempted to establish a set of political criteria for establishing 'a responsibility to react to situations of compelling need for human protection' (ICISS 2001a: 29). The Report is both admirably clear and judicious in its recommendations. We do not yet know, however, how generally they will be followed. Meanwhile, in most of the recent cases of international enforcement, a lead country or organization identified a major political interest to drive the military action forward—NATO in Kosovo, Australia in East Timor, and the United States in Afghanistan. The intervention in Kosovo confirmed the worst fears of many African and Asian countries about Western motives in seeking to impose their hegemony under cover of humanitarian concern.[8] At the same time, after the failure of the UN-sanctioned American intervention in Somalia (see pp. 132–5) it became increasingly clear that without a strong political interest it would be difficult to generate decisive external support for peace enforcement operations in Africa.

The Somali intervention also revealed the extent of African schizophrenia on the subject of humanitarian intervention. In 1991 Zimbabwe and India as non-permanent members of the Security Council were opposed to western enforcement of safe areas for the Iraqi Kurds and Shiites. Following the NATO intervention in Kosovo, the Non-Aligned Movement (NAM), to which all OAU members belong, issued a public statement in April 2000, reaffirming 'the distinction between humanitarian action and UN peacekeeping and peace enforcement operations'. They also rejected 'the so called "right" of humanitarian intervention which has no legal basis in the UN Charter or in the general principles of international law'.[9] On the other hand, African states had previously accepted that the total collapse of the Somali state had created a crisis that called for an exceptional response; and after the failure of the Somali operation, in 1993 the OAU itself established a Mechanism for Conflict Prevention, Management, and Resolution.[10] The Declaration under which the mechanism was established does not refer to humanitarian intervention, but while placing the emphasis firmly on the need to address the socio-economic concerns of African peoples, it does concede that no single internal factor has contributed more to these problems 'than the scourge of conflicts within and between our countries. Conflicts have forced millions of our people into a drifting life as refugees and internally displaced persons, deprived of their means of livelihood, human dignity and hope' (para 9). The Declaration echoes the determination of the Founding Fathers of the OAU to 'promote understanding between the African peoples and cooperation among the African States, and to rekindle the aspirations of the African people for brotherhood and solidarity in a larger unity transcending linguistic, ideological, ethnic and national differences' (para 1). In the spirit of African solidarity—and recognizing the chronic resource constraints under which African governments operate—the Heads of State emphasized conflict prevention. They recognized, however, that in some cases conflicts might degenerate to a point where they required international intervention and policing. In these cases, 'the assistance or where necessary the services of the United Nations will be sought under the general terms of the Charter' (para 16), with the African states themselves considering how best they might contribute to effective UN peacekeeping. By reasserting the principle of continental self-help, the African Union has arguably attempted to soften official African opposition to humanitarian intervention, providing it is instigated by the Union and remains under African control. In practice, capacity constraints mean that African countries will not easily be able to escape the dilemmas of dependence on the outside world.

The final reason why Africa seems likely to remain the testing ground for the evolving theory and practice of humanitarian intervention is that, in the absence of strong external interests, the running is likely to be left to the UN and regional organizations such as the Economic Community of West African States (ECOWAS) and the Southern African Development Conference (SADC). The continuing if residual interest of the former imperial powers, Britain and France, at first sight might seem to contradict this proposition, but both have been anxious to justify their continued permanent membership of the Security Council and both are at the centre of post-colonial international organizations, the Commonwealth and La Francophonie, respectively. The French were not prepared to act in Rwanda without the blessing of the Security Council and although Britain has remained outside the UN operation in Sierra Leone, British Ministers have repeatedly insisted that they are acting in support of the world body. On the African side, the significance of the 1993 Declaration establishing the new Mechanism is the care it took to establish the continuity rather than the change in African policy. The Mechanism was not only firmly based on the OAU Charter and its bedrock principles of sovereignty, non-interference, and territorial integrity, but intervention was only to be contemplated in association with the UN.

African governments have always looked to the UN as the guarantor of their independence. Nor have they always been unsuccessful in attracting its support. The 1990s opened with the Somali intervention, the largest deployment of UN peacekeepers up to that time, and in 2002, the largest operation was again in Africa, this time in Sierra Leone. From the mid 1990s, the Americans, British, and French all took initiatives aimed at strengthening African capacities to take the lead in local peace-building as a way of reducing pressures on themselves for direct intervention. These programmes have been generally although not universally welcomed. Several African countries, for example Botswana, Ghana, and Senegal, have had extensive experience of participating in traditional UN peacekeeping operations under chapter VI of the Charter. After taking part in a US-led training exercise, the Senegalese army complained that the US military had less experience of the kind of operations likely to arise in Africa than they did themselves. The South African government was also extremely critical of the original US African Crisis Response Initiative, which they regarded as a clumsy effort to co-opt African governments to promote Western policies.

There is some justice in these criticisms. The Western powers had, after all, refused to be drawn into the murderous Liberian civil war in 1990, and showed similar reluctance to get involved in 2003. Despite their historic links with Monrovia, the Americans limited their intervention in 1990 to lifting off US citizens from an off-shore aircraft carrier. In the end, it was left to ECOWAS, under Nigerian leadership, to organize the intervention (and the accompanying diplomacy) that eventually brought the war to an end in 1997. Strictly speaking, the regional body was in breach of the UN Charter, which provides for cooperation with regional organizations under chapter VIII, but in the case of peace enforcement measures only with the prior authorization of the Security Council. In this case, Council approval was obtained in 1992, *ex post facto*, further evidence, if it was needed, of Africa's marginalization in world politics (SC Res 788 1992). Humanitarian considerations were, no doubt, amongst the ECOWAS motives for intervention, but they were not the only or even the central ones. Moreover, although ECOWAS was eventually successful in negotiating an end to the war, this was only on the basis of first arranging a share of power for Charles Taylor and his rebel forces and then orchestrating his victory in Presidential elections. This was certainly an African solution to an African problem, and, in the short run may also have helped to stabilize the region. In the longer run, it contributed to further destabilization through leaving Taylor free to continue his support of the rebel RUF in Sierra Leone. Admittedly, lacking the resources of a major UN peacekeeping operation, ECOWAS had few options; nonetheless, transforming the chief poacher into the leading gamekeeper seems a perverse response to a humanitarian crisis. At the end of the 1990s the UN had resumed the lead in the international effort to bring a measure of order and stability to one of the most chaotic regions in the world. It is difficult to foresee the likely reaction to future African crises, but the pattern does suggest that it is most likely to be led by the UN, in line with the 1993 OAU Declaration, although in collaboration with regional organizations. It also suggests that if there is an emergent international norm of humanitarian intervention (or even as some have claimed a new principle of customary international law) it is most likely to reveal itself in Africa.

An answer to the second question asked at the beginning of this chapter—namely, whether there are lessons to be learned from African experience about the prospects for and limitations of humanitarian intervention—requires a distinction between international engagement in African conflict resolution and intervention, humanitarian or otherwise. A number of African conflicts have been more or less satisfactorily resolved or contained with UN and/or international assistance under the rubric of peacekeeping.[11] These operations have certainly helped to relieve human suffering and to stabilize the countries involved, but they do not seriously challenge the existing theory or practice of international society. UN peacekeeping operations are not explicitly provided for in the Charter, but their evolution during the cold war was assumed to fall under chapter VI covering the peaceful resolution of disputes. Moreover, host-state consent and UN impartiality were prerequisites of these operations. With the emergence of expanded peacekeeping as a response to the numerous complex emergencies since the end of the cold war, there has been an increasing and understandable tendency to blur the distinction between engagement and intervention, to see them as end points along a continuum.

Such engagements may fail with disastrous consequences as in Angola and pre-genocide Rwanda, but they do not cross the line between chapters VI and VII of the Charter. It is when these conditions do not apply, or apply fully, that both practical and theoretical questions arise. The practical question is what, if anything, is to be done and by whom? The theoretical question is with what justification, and under what authority?

What are the answers to these questions from Africa? My general conclusion is that Africa does *not* provide support for the proposition that there is a new norm of humanitarian intervention. The Security Council continues to insist on the political principle of treating each case on its merits. Nonetheless, African experience does suggest that there has been an evolution of international society to a point where state collapse and/or humanitarian catastrophe are more likely to lead to intervention than previously. And there is some evidence of lessons learned in relation to expectation and capacity. I shall attempt to support this conclusion primarily in relation to three cases— Somalia, Rwanda, and Sierra Leone.

7.2.1 Somalia: a new norm asserted, then abandoned

It was unfortunate that the first major test for the UN's new policy of using chapter VII for humanitarian purposes should have come in Somalia, a country whose political culture, while highly sophisticated in its own terms, was out of step with the rest of Africa, let alone the wider society of states. Built around a shifting pattern of alliances and rivalries between families, clans, and sub-clans, Somali politics would make perfect sense in the world of Thucydides' Melian dialogue, but is much harder to interpret on Western liberal assumptions. When the USA eventually intervened with the unanimous support of the Security Council, the competing Somalia warlords— respectful of power above all else—welcomed them with open arms. The idea of impartiality, however, plays little part in Somali culture and the operation began to go wrong, when the UN was perceived to be taking sides.

The point that is usually made about Operation Restore Hope and UNOSOM II is that they failed. This is not wholly true with respect to the provision of humanitarian relief, but it is true if political rehabilitation and reconstruction are considered preconditions for preventing a recurrence and hence the underlying justification for the initial intervention. The argument that humanitarian intervention can only be ethically justified if it addresses not only the immediate symptoms of the crisis but its underlying causes, sets the bar very high, possibly impossibly so in a country like Somalia.[12] Apart from other considerations, it assumes that these causes can be clearly identified and rectified by external intervention. Poverty is the most frequently quoted underlying cause of civil conflict. That adequate resources make most problems easier to deal with is not in doubt, but one has only to reflect on how many civil conflicts occur against a background of rapid social and economic change to question how deep this analysis goes. It remains true that while the Somali famine had receded by 1994, when the UN finally pulled out, nothing had been done to restore either political authority or the most basic human security.

The UN operation in Somalia, nonetheless, had fateful consequences, not all of which were negative. On the positive side, the legitimacy of the operation was not in doubt: UNITAF established that chapter VII enforcement for humanitarian purposes is possible within existing legal and institutional arrangements, providing the Council so chooses. The establishment of safe-havens for Kurds and Shia Moslems in Iraq had proved controversial because it was regarded by some states as constituting an attack not on Iraq's act of aggression but on its sovereignty. No such reservations stood in the way of the Somali operation, even though there was no Somali government to invite the UN in. Once it chose to act, the Security Council had no difficulty in calling a humanitarian catastrophe a threat to international peace and security (SC Res 794, 3 December 1992). If the Council could redefine what constituted a threat in this case, there was no reason why it should not do it in others. Given the almost certain impossibility of revising the Charter to include a formal right of humanitarian intervention under chapter VII, there are obvious practical advantages in its ability to interpret its responsibilities flexibly.

The practical lessons to be derived from the operation—that is, how is intervention to be carried out and by whom—are more problematic. The intervention was spearheaded by the United States, which led the coalition of the willing that constituted UNITAF, and remained a leading participant once responsibility was passed to UNOSOM II. This would not have caused difficulties had the USA been more committed either to the success of the operation regardless of the risks, or to building up the UN's own peacekeeping and peace enforcement capacities. Neither was the case. With the end of the cold war, the Horn of Africa lost its relevance in terms of US foreign policy priorities. So long as President Bush Sr. was contending for re-election, his Administration refused to contemplate intervention. It was only after he had lost the Presidential election to Bill Clinton that the supporters of intervention were given access to the President. Perhaps because he was now interested in securing his historical reputation, Bush reversed his previous policy of non-involvement (Mayall (ed.) 1996: 107–16). There were subsequently serious errors of judgement that contributed to the US reassessment of UN operations, in general, and the speed of its own disengagement from Somalia. Singling out and going after Aideed was the gravest of these. That he was guilty of organizing the skirmishes in which first some Pakistani UN soldiers and then some US Rangers lost their lives, matters less than the fact that by putting a price on the head of just one warlord in a warlord culture, the Americans allowed Aideed to represent himself as an heroic figure who had single-handedly exposed the duplicity of US imperialism. Not only was the United States forced to climb down and negotiate directly with Aideed, but his defiance led directly to their retreat from the internationalist policy they had nervously adopted by putting US forces under UN command. From now on their cooperation with UN security operations would be strictly on a limited liability basis, only when US interests were directly involved and only with an exit strategy decided at the outset. Politically this reaction was understandable, since US interests in Somalia were negligible, but it effectively buried the idea of disinterested humanitarian intervention and the expanded role of the UN in international security that the P-5 had endorsed at their Security Council summit in 1992.

The political lessons of the Somali debacle cannot so easily be generalized, although so deep was the quagmire into which the UN found itself drawn that it undoubtedly had wider political ramifications than it deserved. To paraphrase George Bernard Shaw, international society has a deeply middle-class morality. The idea of statelessness is shocking, undermining the comfortable assumption that the world rests on solid foundations and that there is a 'proper' way of doing things. The UN Charter also gives states primary responsibility for protecting human rights. The major failure in Somalia was of imagination and realism. Neither the USA nor the UN could cope with a society that had disintegrated, not merely because after a horrific civil war there was no trust—that was true—but because Somali society was more accustomed to statelessness than statehood. And when Somaliland, the one part of the country of which this was not unambiguously the case, declared independence, *uti possidetis* prevented (and continues to prevent) its recognition.

The wrong lessons were learned from Somalia because although all interventions in civil conflicts face comparably intractable problems, very few—Afghanistan and Kurdistan are two possible exceptions—are faced not merely with the corruption of central authority but by its total disappearance combined with powerful structural obstacles to its reconstruction. Failure in Somalia did not have to mean that any external intervention was bound to fail elsewhere in Africa, but that was how it was interpreted. If such interventions were doomed to fail, it was not because African conflicts have special characteristics that are general to them all, but as suggested earlier, because of contradictions in the concept of humanitarian intervention itself. It follows that replacing great power involvement by peace enforcement operations organized on a regional basis must be expected to face similar problems. The replacement may be politically expedient, but it does not represent a conceptual solution.

7.2.2 Rwanda: the duty to intervene denied

Support for this conclusion can be found in even the most cursory review of international reactions to the Rwandan genocide. The immediate consequence of disengagement from Somalia was the Western denial that genocide had occurred in Rwanda. The two cases were not similar in that while the Hutus and Tutsis of Rwanda had a history of conflict over the ownership of the state, unlike the Somalis they did not question its necessity, nor had it collapsed. But they were similar in being marginal in terms of Western, particularly US, interests.

Rwanda played a pivotal (although ambiguous) role in the evolution of the theory and practice of humanitarian intervention and peacekeeping. With regard to the question of legitimacy, we have already seen that Somalia had established that the Security Council had wide discretion in interpreting the Charter—if it wanted it could invoke chapter VII in any circumstances; but it did not have to. On this occasion, it deliberately chose to interpret the threat posed to international peace and security in a narrow and traditional way, even though it quickly became clear that the catastrophe had dangerously destabilized the Great Lakes region as a whole. Further, key states also deliberately refrained from calling the genocide by its proper name. Had the Genocide Convention been invoked in April 1994, it would have been much more difficult to avoid intervention. So they resisted the classification until the killing was over. As Bruce Jones concludes in his comprehensive study *Peacemaking in Rwanda: The Dynamics of Failure*, 'it is evident that UN Secretary-General Boutros Boutros-Ghali failed to provide leadership within the UN Secretariat and Security Council at this critical juncture.' Nor did what Michael Barnett called 'the politics of indifference' stop there (Barnett 2002). One senior peacekeeping official later admitted to Jones 'that it was only after the outbreak of the genocide that he learned of the Genocide Convention and of the United Nations' legal capacity and moral obligation to respond to genocide' (Jones 2001: 121). Why this display of moral turpitude?

There were extenuating circumstances: the UN itself was overstretched; throughout 1993 they were still mired in Somalia and Bosnia, had unfinished business in Cambodia, and were under pressure from the United States and the Organization of American States to establish an operation in Haiti and from Russia to do the same in Georgia. With a vastly increased workload and their inexperience in dealing with political intelligence, it is, perhaps, not surprising that the Department of Peacekeeping Operations failed to make proper use of the early warnings that reached New York well ahead of the impending catastrophe (Jones 2001: 103–33). However, the UN was also severely constrained in what it could do by the lack of enthusiasm amongst the major powers, particularly the United States. In the aftermath of Somalia, the Americans had no stomach for another open-ended African adventure. The result was that UNAMIR I, the chapter VI peacekeeping operation that was eventually put together to monitor the implementation of the 1993 Arusha peace agreement, was deeply flawed. As Jones concluded, 'whatever the explanation or reason, the fact is that the United Nations sent a small, poorly equipped, reactive mission possibly capable of monitoring a generally accepted peace to a country in which the peace deal was a source of aggravated disagreement' (Jones 2001: 110). When the genocide was launched on 6 April 1994 UNAMIR—and its Belgian contingent in particular—was amongst its first targets. The aim of the *génocidaires* to force the withdrawal of the UN force was effectively accomplished when the Security Council passed Resolution 912 reducing its strength to symbolic levels. There were no contingency plans in place to cover the breakdown of the negotiations, with the result that the Security Council believed it had no alternative than to reduce the size of General Dallaire's force to a point where it could barely defend itself, let alone intervene in the genocide for which it, in any case, lacked a mandate. Had the crisis occurred either earlier or later, it is possible that different and wiser, or at least more honourable counsels might have prevailed in New York.

When we turn to the practical aspects of the international response to the Rwanda crisis we find that, in Jones's graphic phrase, the failure lay in 'actions taken, not failure to take action'. In many ways, the pre-genocide Rwanda peace process was exemplary. It was multilayered; conducted at a leisurely pace with ample opportunity for consultation with the parties on the ground; involved cooperation from an early stage between the OAU and the UN; and aimed to establish a power sharing democracy that would reassure the major players that their fundamental interests would be protected. Yet, it failed, because the Hutu extremists, the one group that had no interest in a settlement, had not been immobilized. In retrospect, it seems that President Habyarimina's participation in the peace process, like his agreement under French pressure to embark on political reform in 1990, was largely cosmetic, designed to buy time and to mollify the Western donors, whose support had become more than usually critical following the collapse of the international coffee price in 1987. The most damaging criticism of both the OAU and UN's sponsored peacemaking effort was that it was based on a best-case scenario. Much as one may deplore the intrusion of such practical issues as timing and the impossibility of putting together an effective coalition of the willing into a decision of great moral urgency, it is hard to deny their relevance. Nonetheless, if there are any events when international action is required regardless of calculations of national interest—and this is what the existence of the Genocide Convention implies—Rwanda was surely such a case. The explanation, one suspects, is that the major powers do not accept this proposition. And, the underlying reason for this non-acceptance is their refusal to accept the imperial implications of humanitarian intervention, a point to which I will return in my conclusion.

The failure to take effective action in Rwanda helped to create multiple threats to regional peace and security, to which at the time of writing, no credible solution is in sight. The Security Council eventually authorized France to intervene under chapter VII of the Charter on 22 June 1994. The stated purpose of *Opération Turquoise* was humanitarian and lives (most estimates put it at around 10,000) were saved. But it is also widely accepted that the operation was fatally flawed. This was partly because France was so identified with the previous government that its impartiality was not accepted by the RPF, but mainly because the French failed to separate the refugees from the leaders of the genocide, who were, thus, able to control the camps in Tanzania and eastern Zaïre, and because they effectively provided cover under which units of the FAR (the Rwandan army) and Interhamwe (the militia that had played a major role in the genocide) were able to escape. Their presence in Zaïre—and the threat they posed to the new RPF regime in Kigali—led first to the Security Council decision to intervene in Eastern Zaïre in November 1996 (Resolution 1080) and then to the RPF decision to repatriate the refugees themselves. Although the Canadian government agreed to lead the new force (and had an advance party on the ground when the RPF seized the initiative) it was unclear what they were meant to do. The RPF decision to intervene, which was clearly political and strategic rather than humanitarian, saved the international community from embarrassment, and set the stage for the overthrow of President Mobutu of Zaïre and the prolonged DRC crisis under the two Kybilas.

The DRC crisis lies beyond the scope of this chapter. It has been accompanied by multiple interventions, all of them African and none humanitarian in motivation. The attempt to find an African solution to the problem led eventually to the Lusaka peace agreement and the re-entry of the UN in a monitoring and facilitating role. According to the latest Secretary-General's report, there has been some progress in containing the conflict, and in securing the withdrawal of some foreign troops. The situation remains precarious, however, with regular outbreaks of fighting between government and externally assisted rebel forces in the east of the country, and major violations of human rights in areas controlled by both the government and rebels. Diplomatic progress has not been accompanied, moreover, by equal progress towards the re-establishment of a countrywide administration.[13]

7.2.3 Sierra Leone: retrieval?

During the 1990s there was a sustained, although highly selective, attempt to de-legitimize non-democratic governments and to build democratization into reconstruction programmes established in the wake of humanitarian interventions. In Haiti, the Security Council eventually authorized the United States to reinstall the democratically elected President who had been ousted from power in a military coup. No such action followed the ousting of Sierra Leone's President Kabbah, in 1997. He was eventually reinstated by ECOWAS under Nigerian leadership more than a year later. The coup was not recognized by the UN or the Commonwealth, which insisted on the importance of democratic government as a basis for conflict resolution. It was doubly ironic, therefore, that the restoration of the elected government was brought about by a Nigerian military regime, which had itself been suspended from the Commonwealth because of its judicial murder of Ngoni activists in 1995. The death of Abacha, the Nigerian military dictator, and the return to civilian rule in Nigeria, led to the scaling down of ECOWAS's involvement and the resumption by the UN of the lead role. The ensuing crisis threatened to demonstrate yet again the international community's inability to deal with a humanitarian and political crisis in the absence of a compelling interest.

At the time of writing, the situation remains precarious but at present, there does seem a chance that UNAMSIL will be able to retrieve the UN's reputation for humanitarian intervention. In requesting a further six-month extension for the operation in September 2001, Secretary-General Kofi Annan reported that 'the continued progress, in particular in the disarmament, demobilisation and reintegration programme and the deployment of UNAMSIL eastward, gives grounds for cautious optimism regarding the consolidation of the peace process in Sierra Leone'. In March 2002, the operation was again extended for six months and, on this occasion, Annan was able to report that both the disarmament process and the registration of voters for Presidential and General Elections, scheduled for May 2002, had been successfully completed. The elections passed off without major incident and returned President Kabbah to power. By September 2002, the security situation had improved sufficiently for the Secretary-General to submit detailed proposals for the gradual draw-down of the mission. Reading between the lines, it is clear that he believes that the situation remains precarious, not least because of the continuing conflict in Liberia that has a tendency to attract former Sierra Leone combatants and to destabilize the entire region. In successfully seeking a further extension of UNAMSIL's mandate to 30 March 2003, he emphasized the scale of the continuing reconstruction. 'In order to safeguard its large investment in Sierra Leone, the international community must stay the course, provide the resources needed to complete the reintegration of the ex-combatants, enhance the capacity of the Sierra Leone police, ensure the effective functioning of the Truth and Reconciliation Commission, and support the transition to peace-building, and thereby grasp the success that lies within reach.'[14]

It is worth asking if this apparent progress towards the resolution of a conflict whose humanitarian consequences were as horrific as those to be found anywhere in the world, is the result of good fortune or evidence that the Council is at last applying the practical lessons it has learned from earlier failures. No doubt, the answer is a combination. In the face of the Nigerian desire to reduce its presence in Sierra Leone, the international community welcomed the Lomé Agreement in July 1999. The agreement not only granted an unconditional pardon to all those in the RUF rebel movement but included their leader, Fodoy Sankoh, and his principal lieutenants in the government. In October, the Council established UNAMSIL with an initial deployment of 6,000 'to ensure the security of movement of its personnel, and within its capabilities and areas of deployment, to afford protection under immediate threat of violence, taking into account the responsibilities of the Sierra Leone government and ECOMOG'. Although this mandate was under chapter VII, the last phrase seriously constrained what the UN could do, particularly given the modest resources that had been committed, since the RUF was now part of the government. The UN was saved partly because Sankoh miscalculated the consequences of preventing their deployment into the diamond producing Eastern provinces which he controlled and partly because the British came to the aid of the government and UNAMSIL, while nonetheless, remaining outside it. British motives in providing crucial support to the more robust UN policy, while remaining at arm's length from UNAMSIL, are not entirely clear. It is difficult to avoid the conclusion that the UK wishes to claim credit for playing a constructive role (which on the whole it has) while being able to walk away if the political situation deteriorates. The RUF not only captured UN equipment and armour but also took UN peacekeepers hostage, thus provoking a showdown with the UN that would have been difficult for them to avoid. The Security Council subsequently took the action that was necessary to rein in the RUF, embargoing conflict diamonds and bringing pressure to bear on Charles Taylor, the President of Liberia, to end his support for the rebels.[15] With Sankoh in custody and the UN force increased to 7,500, serious reconstruction work at last got under way.

7.3 Conclusion

It, thus, seems that the western P-5 states (Russia and China can sometimes be persuaded to go along with them, but generally take an even more sceptical position towards such operations) have concluded that the theoretical problem of finding a middle position between peacekeeping and enforcement is insoluble. The central difficulty turns on the issue of consent. Peacekeeping requires the consent of the parties to the conflict, which will only be forthcoming if the peacekeepers are perceived to be impartial. Enforcement requires the attribution of responsibility to one side or the other. Even if the rules of engagement are administered in a scrupulously impartial fashion from the point of view of the peacekeepers themselves, this is unlikely to be the perception of those against whom action is taken. It follows that it is better to engage in pragmatic humanitarianism—doing what is politically possible in particular circumstances and accepting that success, defined as the resolution or at least containment of the conflict, will not always be possible and that it may be necessary, therefore, for the UN and individual intervening countries to cut their losses. This position is sensible, if decidedly unheroic. If it is accepted, the imperial implications of humanitarian intervention can be avoided, although not without risking dangerous destabilization. The UN, which is regarded by most of its member states as a strongly anti-imperial organization, would certainly reject this elision of humanitarianism with imperialism, as would most NGOs. I should conclude, therefore, by explaining what I mean.

Consider the contrast between the international response to natural disasters—famines, floods, earthquakes, volcanic eruptions, and so on—and to those caused by communal, ethnic, religious, or any other form of civil conflict. Even during the cold war, natural disasters provoked a surprisingly generous and bipartisan response, providing evidence that, even in a pluralist society of states, trace elements of human solidarity can be found. Governments have no difficulty, it seems, in accepting that natural disaster can strike anywhere and tax the resources of even the most powerful to cope by themselves. External assistance is tied to the immediate crisis and has no necessary long-term consequences.

It is different with war, which is no longer accepted, as it once was, as part of the natural order, something to be endured like the weather. Civil conflicts require a political response, and hence, one in which it may be difficult to avoid allocating responsibility or—as in the regional settlements in West Africa—compromising moral principles in the interests of peace. Such decisions are inherently controversial. The emerging consensus on humanitarian intervention seems to be that civil conflicts should be treated, so far as possible, as though they were natural disasters—hence, the emphasis on identifying a legitimate authority and then providing short-term support for its recovery work. The success of this strategy depends on the survival of the basic infrastructure of the state and its institutions. Blankets can be given to the destitute; security requires at the very least a legitimate justice system and policing. If these no longer exist, they cannot be flown in from outside and expected to function overnight. They not only require resources but also need to be tailored to local circumstances and culture, a point that is implicitly recognized by ICISS, which proposes 'a constructive adaptation' of chapter XI of the Charter under which the now dormant Trusteeship Council was established. European imperialism was self-interested not humanitarian, but since the imperial powers were in the game for the long haul, they had no alternative but to create institutions to provide these goods.[16] In many contemporary crises, where the state has collapsed, leading to the systematic abuse of basic rights and/or genocide, the realistic choice is between allowing the conflict to run its course and intervening to establish a new political order from the ground up. There are perils whichever choice is made, but while the second choice seems to have been accepted, albeit reluctantly, in former Yugoslavia and East Timor, so far it has not been extended to Africa.

8

International Intervention in East Timor

*Ian Martin**

The coincidence of international military interventions in Kosovo and East Timor during the same year has led to them not infrequently being bracketed together as parallel cases of humanitarian intervention. Thus, the US human rights organization, Human Rights Watch, reported on the year 1999:

Twice in the past year, in Kosovo and East Timor, members of the international community deployed troops to halt crimes against humanity... The two instances may signal a new readiness on the part of the international community to use extraordinary resources, including troops, to address crimes against humanity that are within its power to stop   (Human Rights Watch 1999: p. xiv).

Yet, it is in fact the contrasts between the two interventions that are most instructive for thinking about the future of international intervention. In fact, as this chapter will show, the East Timor case is so particular that its lessons may be hard to generalize.

In Chapter 4 of this book, Jennifer Welsh notes that a key aspect of the legal definition of humanitarian intervention is the absence of host-state consent.[1] In this respect, the case of East Timor presents a relationship between sovereignty and intervention that is in striking contrast to the intervention in Kosovo. As regards the Federal Republic of Yugoslavia and Kosovo, NATO intervened over a claim to sovereignty that it insisted it would continue to recognize. Indonesia's claim to sovereignty over East Timor was not recognized by the United Nations (UN) and a majority of its member states, yet the international community deemed Indonesia's consent to be an essential condition for intervention. This chapter describes the background to intervention in East Timor, Indonesia's strong resistance to any international security presence in East

* Ian Martin was Special Representative of the UN Secretary-General for the East Timor Popular Consultation, May–November 1999, and head of the UN Mission in East Timor (UNAMET). The views expressed in this chapter are solely those of the author; they do not represent the official views of the UN.

Timor, and the manner in which its eventual consent to intervention was induced, before concluding with further reflections on the contrast with intervention in Kosovo.

8.1   The decades of non-intervention

It must first be said that for twenty-three years East Timor was an outstanding case of international non-intervention. Portugal, the colonial power, belatedly committed itself to decolonization after its own 'Carnation Revolution' in 1974, and withdrew from the island amid fighting between East Timorese parties in 1975. Indonesia, despite previous denials of any territorial claim to East Timor, sought to manipulate Timorese factions to bring about its incorporation, and when the pro-independence party Fretilin had established dominance in the territory, launched a full-scale invasion in December 1975. This was strongly deplored by the UN Security Council, which in December 1975 and again in April 1976 called on Indonesia to withdraw without delay all its forces from the territory, and on all states to respect the territorial integrity of East Timor and its people's right to self-determination. From then until 1981, the General Assembly passed annual resolutions reaffirming the inalienable right of the East Timorese to self-determination.

Yet, the Indonesians had invaded with reason to be confident in the complicity of key states. Recently released documentation has shed further light on the prior knowledge and acquiescence of the Australian and US governments.[2] For both, relations with a major emergent power in Asia came before self-determination for a territory of questionable viability, especially when anti-communism enabled Indonesia to project the ascendancy of the left-wing Fretilin as a threat. The then Permanent Representative of the United States to the UN, Daniel Patrick Moynihan, would record in his memoirs that thereafter: 'The Department of State desired that the UN prove utterly ineffective in whatever measures it undertook. This task was given to me and I carried it forward with no inconsiderable success' (Moynihan 1975: 247). Eager to settle the seabed border between Australia and East Timor in its interests, Australia moved rapidly beyond the *de facto* recognition of the incorporation extended by a number of governments to announce in late 1978 that it would grant *de jure* recognition to Indonesia's claimed sovereignty when talks on delineating the seabed boundary began.

The suffering of the civilian population of East Timor was extreme. Estimates of the number who died as a result of the conflict, including the famine and disease which accompanied the displacement of large parts of the population, range from tens of thousands acknowledged by Indonesia itself, to as many as 200,000. Extensive human rights violations were committed by the Indonesian armed forces against pro-independence activists and their suspected supporters. The sealing off of the territory from any independent access contributed to their receiving little attention from an indifferent international community. In 1982, when the majority for the annual resolution on East Timor had dwindled to the point at which its passage was at risk, the General Assembly gave then Secretary-General Javier Pérez de Cuéllar the mandate to begin a diplomatic effort to help find a comprehensive solution to the problem. Thereafter, while the question of East Timor remained on the agenda of the Assembly, consideration of the item was deferred each year on the basis of the progress report submitted by the Secretary-General on his good offices on the question.

There continued to be annual discussion of East Timor in the UN's Decolonization Committee, where Amnesty International and other NGOs sought to draw some attention to the humanitarian and human rights situation. In November 1991, Indonesian security forces opened fire on a pro-independence demonstration of mourners near the Santa Cruz cemetery in Dili, killing a large number of people (estimates ranged from the official 50 to well over 200). The television images and reports produced by journalists present at the scene had a major impact on international opinion, and the massacre stirred the UN Commission on Human Rights into some activity. A growing number of non-governmental and parliamentary groups in Western countries also began to influence the policies of their governments in the direction of supporting self-determination for East Timor. But the direct discussions between Indonesia and Portugal, which had begun in July 1983 under the auspices of the Secretary-General, continued to see little progress.

8.2   Towards self-determination: the role of non-coercive intervention

In late January 1999, Indonesian President B. J. Habibie (interim successor to President Suharto) decided to allow the East Timorese to choose between autonomy within Indonesia or independence. The manner in which this came about, and the decision to allow the UN to conduct the ballot, has been examined elsewhere.[3] Most relevant to the issue of international intervention is the question of whether Habibie made his decision to offer this choice—the so-called 'second option'—out of his own considerations regarding the politics of Indonesia, or as a result of international pressure to promote, at last, the right of self-determination for the East Timorese.

A new Secretary-General, Kofi Annan, had initiated a more proactive approach to the tripartite negotiations in 1997. But it was the political changes within Indonesia, with the fall of Suharto in May 1998, which opened the way for progress. Habibie began by offering 'special autonomy' to East Timor. While for Indonesia this autonomy would be the final dispensation, Portugal was only willing to consider autonomy as an interim or transitional arrangement pending the eventual exercise by the people of East Timor of their right to self-determination. The East Timorese resistance, under the leadership of Xanana Gusmão, had for some years endorsed the idea of transitional arrangements within Indonesia for an agreed period before the holding of a referendum.

Governments with some of the closest and most influential relationships with Indonesia—notably the United States and Australia, as well as the European Union—welcomed the initiatives of the Habibie government, including the release of many political prisoners and the offer of special autonomy for East Timor. But they realized that this offer, combined with Indonesia's reluctance to deal directly with the East Timorese independence leadership, would not be enough to resolve the issue. Meanwhile, they saw the situation on the ground in East Timor slipping rapidly beyond the control of the Indonesian authorities, and perhaps of responsible East Timorese leadership, as the mood of growing political freedom throughout Indonesia was reflected in increasingly open pro-independence activism.

The debate regarding a change of position was most intense in Australia. In opposition, the Australian Labour Party had reconsidered the policy it had pursued in government and had espoused East Timor's right to self-determination. Against the backdrop of the dramatic changes in Indonesia and the growing turmoil in East Timor, the government of Prime Minister John Howard began a policy review, which included a survey of the opinions of key East Timorese.[4] Its outcome was a December 1998 letter from Howard to Habibie. In it, Howard emphasized that Australia continued to maintain its long-standing position that 'the interests of Australia, Indonesia and East Timor are best served by East Timor remaining part of Indonesia'. But the issue, he urged, could be resolved only through direct negotiations between Indonesia and East Timorese leaders. A decisive element of East Timorese opinion was insisting on an act of self-determination:

It might be worth considering, therefore, a means of addressing the East Timorese desire for an act of self-determination in a manner that avoids an early and final decision on the future status of the province. One way of doing this would be to build into the autonomy package a review mechanism along the lines of the Matignon Accords in New Caledonia. The Matignon Accords have enabled a compromise political solution to be implemented while deferring a referendum on the final status of New Caledonia for many years. The successful implementation of an autonomy package with a built-in review mechanism would allow time to convince the East Timorese of the benefits of autonomy within the Indonesian Republic.[5]

This letter was not well received by Habibie, who took exception to the apparent colonial analogy with New Caledonia. But he used the letter to send his ministers the instruction to consider a new option:

If the question of East Timor becomes a burden to the struggle and image of the Indonesian people and if, after 22 years, the East Timorese people cannot feel united with the Indonesian people who proclaimed their independence 53 years ago and have a 400-year history, including 350 years under Dutch colonization, it would be reasonable and wise, if by a decision of the People's Consultative Assembly, the 27th province of East Timor can be honourably separated from the unitary nation of the Republic of Indonesia which, in fact, had the good intention to accept them in the struggle to achieve a civil society in the coming millennium.[6]

On 27 January 1999, ministers emerged from a cabinet meeting to announce that if the East Timorese decided to reject the offer of special auton-omy, the President would recommend to the People's Consultative Assembly that the July 1976 law integrating East Timor as Indonesia's 27th province should be revoked.

How crucial were the change in Australia's position and external pressure in giving rise to Habibie's new proposal? The fact that the offer of special autonomy alone would not resolve the issue was increasingly obvious from reports of the situation in East Timor, and its acknowledgement was being quietly pressed on Indonesia by Jamsheed Marker, the UN Secretary-General's Personal Representative for East Timor, and by other governments besides Australia, especially the USA and the EU. Indonesia's economic nego-tiators were anxious for a resolution of the issue that most bedeviled the country's external relations, and even within the Indonesian armed forces there was a growing desire to be rid of the problem. The possibility of East Timor's independence had become a subject of open discussion in Indonesia, with several opposition figures and non-governmental actors (and in private some civilian and military officials) foreseeing the holding of an eventual referendum. Habibie himself had no personal stake in East Timor, and some of his closest advisers from the more liberal wing of ICMI (*Ikatan Cendekiawan Muslim se-Indonesia*), the Indonesian Association of Muslim Intellectuals, were among those who questioned Indonesia's interest in retaining the territory, with its overwhelmingly Christian population. As an interim successor to Suharto whose democratic legitimacy was open to challenge, Habibie was eager to impress the international community with his commitment to democracy and human rights. He also saw a settle-ment of the long-standing issue of East Timor as a potential springboard to his election as President in his own right. All these elements meant that a further development in policy was in the logic of the Indonesian context. But the fact that Australia had been the firmest supporter of the integration of East Timor made its conversion to self-determination of special significance.

Nevertheless, the timetable for Habibie's second option, and his insistence on an immediate choice before the People's Consultative Assembly, was an alternative to the more gradual process that was being pressed upon the Indonesian government. Only the more radical campaigners in East Timor were urging an immediate decision on independence. Gusmão remained uncompromising in his demand for an eventual referendum and his objective of independence, but was prepared to be very flexible in defining an extended period of transition before a referendum, in which Indonesia would continue to play an active role. Such a transition was the maximum being advocated by any of the concerned governments, and Portugal would have endorsed such an outcome if it was acceptable to the East Timorese. The Howard letter explicitly advocated a course of action that '*avoids* an early and final decision on the future status of the province' [emphasis added].

Some critics of Australian policy have argued that too much pressure was applied to a vulnerable Indonesia in late 1998, pushing a weak interim President into a high-risk decision to bring a hasty end to the East Timor issue, from which—even after he had made it—he should have been restrained. But it was the political forces released in East Timor by change in Indonesia that led each of the actors—the UN, Australia, and ultimately Habibie—to perceive, correctly, that autonomy without self-determination would not settle the question of East Timor. The responsibility for deciding that the choice between autonomy and independence could only be an immediate one must rest with Habibie: he rejected the period of transition favoured by the international community and East Timorese leaders. Once Habibie had offered that choice, the UN and the key countries following the negotiations were well aware of the risk. But neither they nor the East Timorese could have countenanced the opposite risk, of failing to grasp an opportunity which had been closed for twenty-four years.

8.3 Security and the popular consultation: a failure of preventive intervention?

If some have criticized Australian policy for being too interventionist, many more critics of Australian and US policy, and of the UN, have been prompted by the violence which followed the ballot to make the opposite criticism: that much more pressure should have been applied to induce Indonesia to accept an international force in East Timor to maintain security during what was termed (in deference to Indonesia's objection to the term referendum) the 'popular consultation'.[7] Indonesia's insistence that it must retain respon-sibility for security before and after the ballot, and its rejection of any inter-national peacekeeping presence, was adamant, both in the tripartite negotiations and when it was put to Habibie by Howard shortly before the 5 May Agreements. The most that was acceptable to Indonesia was a small contingent of UN civilian police to advise the Indonesian police, to which was later added an even smaller contingent of military liaison officers. The UN defined its requirements for security during the consultation process as including the disarmament of paramilitary groups and militia, a substantial and verifiable reduction of the Indonesian army presence in East Timor, and the confinement of those who remained and of the Falintil independence fighters to designated areas one month before the ballot. The Indonesians, however, resisted the inclusion of these specific commitments in the vague security annex to the main Agreement.[8]

It is doubtful whether any amount of pressure could have induced Habibie and his Defence Minister, General Wiranto, to accept international peace-keepers at this juncture. Habibie was already on the defensive: the opening up of the independence option had been strongly criticized in Jakarta, including by Habibie's likely rival for the Presidency, Megawati Sukarnoputri, and by retired and serving generals. During the crucial last weeks of the negotiations, both the US and Australian governments urged the UN not to endanger an agreement by taking too strong a position on the security provisions. The Agreements stated that law and order would be maintained by the Indonesian police, advised by the UN, with both the Indonesian army and police remaining neutral as to the outcome of the consultation; a Commission on Peace and Stability, just established by Wiranto, would work towards the laying down of arms and disarmament. Even if a firmer stand by the UN and Portugal in the negotiations (backed by the USA and Australia) could have strengthened those provisions, it could only have been in the direction of the more explicit commitments that the UN was proposing, notably to disarm the militia. The UN ultimately presented these as its requirements in a memorandum from the Secretary-General to the parties; if they had been included in the Agreements themselves, it would have done little to increase the likelihood of their being respected on the ground in East Timor. The UN would still have faced the dilemma that lay ahead. Should it or should it not proceed with registration, the campaign and ballot, in security conditions which clearly breached the commitments Indonesia made in the Agreements?

Those who see the decision to proceed with the ballot in the absence of an international peacekeeping force as a failure of preventive intervention will see this failure as compounded by the UN's decisions to press ahead despite militia violence and intimidation, backed by an undiminished Indonesian army presence and largely uninhibited by the Indonesian police. Successive decisions to proceed, after two short postponements of registration, were taken in full cognizance of the forthright reporting of UNAMET,[9] the mission charged with conducting the popular consultation (which I headed). UNAMET had raised concern about the nature of militia violence and Indonesian army complicity, as well as improper Indonesian government involvement in pro-autonomy activities and severe limitations on pro-independence campaigning. The reasons not to go forward were unassailable in terms of the Agreements, and this might have seemed politically the safer course of action for the UN. The UN had been successfully manipulated by Indonesia in one betrayal of self-determination in West Irian (Irian Jaya to Indonesia, West Papua to many of its inhabitants) in 1969,[10] and it could not afford to be party to a corrupted outcome in East Timor.

The Secretary-General and his Personal Representative, Portugal, and the key member states supporting the UN through the 'Core Group' (Australia, Japan, New Zealand, the UK, and the USA) were, however, determined to maintain the momentum.[11] The political timetable in Indonesia was an important factor in their calculations. The outcome of the Indonesian elections in June made it highly uncertain that Habibie would win his own mandate when the People's Consultative Assembly voted for a new President. With Habibie himself insistent that the ballot must be held before the Assembly was scheduled to be convened at the end of August, and a successor perhaps likely to embrace any excuse to abort the process, the view that there might only be a 'window of opportunity' for self-determination in East Timor was well-founded.

For UNAMET, the decision to go ahead was a difficult one. We were responsible for analysing the extent to which Indonesia's commitments on security and a level playing field were being met, and our staff were in daily contact with the victims of violence. Since the conclusions of this analysis were overwhelmingly negative, they could hardly fail to question whether it was right to proceed. But we were strongly influenced by the immediately evident success of registration, when the East Timorese showed the strength of their own commitment to the popular consultation, and when international pressure seemed at least to limit the violence.

The UN consulted with key East Timorese throughout. The pro-independence front headed by Gusmão, the CNRT (*Conselho Nacional da Resistencia Timorense*—National Council of Timorese Resistance), could always have been the ultimate arbiter: the UN could not have proceeded if the CNRT had urged that it should not. Gusmão was clear-sighted in his understanding of the risk and his mistrust of the Indonesian army; he was also convinced that the East Timorese would defy intimidation to vote as they wanted to. He always wanted an international security force in East Timor, but he accepted the judgment that this was unattainable. The trust built up over the years between him and the UN negotiators was extended to UNAMET's decision-making on the ground. At all stages when the UN moved forward, it did so after consulting him. His judgment was vindicated when on 30 August 1999, despite an intensification of violence in the weeks preceding the ballot, 98.6 per cent of those registered turned out to vote. 78.5 per cent of them voted for independence.

8.4   Post-ballot violence: failures of prediction and planning for intervention

The announcement of the result of the ballot was the signal for violence to be unleashed across the territory, in which hundreds of people were killed, buildings destroyed on a scale without precedent, and virtually an entire population displaced, many of them by forced removal to Indonesian West Timor. It is beyond doubt that the destruction of East Timor was not merely the result of an emotional response of militia and a mutiny of East Timorese within the army, but a planned and coordinated operation under Indonesian army direction. Why was it that the UN and most diplomatic analysts failed fully to predict this, despite the warnings known to them?

We did expect substantial post-ballot violence, but we expected that Jakarta would and could act to restrain it. UNAMET was influenced by its experience over preceding months that heavy international pressure could lead the Indonesians to rein in the violence, and by apparent evidence that the pressure being applied just before the vote was making itself felt—for example, in the replacement of senior military commanders in East Timor. In retrospect, we placed too much hope in the signs that Jakarta was responsive to this pressure, and in the fact that the contending East Timorese leaderships seemed to have been allowed to plan to work together after the ballot.

Our predictions rested too, on a calculation of Indonesia's own self-interest. It seemed clear to objective observers that there would be a strong pro-independence vote, and at least some key Indonesian interlocutors appeared to have understood that autonomy would lose. The fact that the ballot was allowed to proceed, thus, seemed to imply a reluctant acceptance of this outcome. We underestimated the extent to which many Indonesians and pro-autonomy East Timorese still believed that the coercive autonomy campaign would be successful, or nearly successful. In the context of only a narrow defeat, the removal of a large proportion of the population to West Timor, coupled with loud accusations of UNAMET bias, might have been part of a serious strategy to frustrate the outcome, perhaps through its rejection by the People's Consultative Assembly. But what now appear as preparations for such a strategy—the plans for mass evacuation to West Timor—were known to UNAMET only as contingency plans, which were not improper if they were for a voluntary exodus.

This is not to excuse the inadequacy of the UN's own contingency plans. The recent review of the UN's peace and security activities chaired by Lakhdar Brahimi (the Brahimi Report) declared that 'the Secretariat must not apply best-case planning assumptions to situations where the actors have historically exhibited worst-case behaviour'.[12] In the case of East Timor, the UN's formal planning was on the basis of a best-case scenario which it was hoped could be realized with a high degree of international attention and pressure, but which was never realistic. Indonesia was promising in the negotiations that in the event of a vote for independence, it would maintain security, administration, and budgetary support to East Timor, until and beyond the vote of its Assembly to implement the outcome. The UN's planning relied on this continuing for some months, until it would be ready with a transitional administration and a peacekeeping force. Although the UN regarded a vote for independence as virtually certain, and thus, from May onwards was expecting to provide a transitional administration, almost no planning towards this was done by the UN or its agencies until the eleventh hour. This official scenario of a smooth transition was unrealistically optimistic. The most positive scenario conceivable would have been limited but serious post-ballot violence, and a faltering Indonesian effort to maintain security and administration in the face of the demoralization of their personnel. If this had occurred, the UN would have been required to move in rapidly, and its lack of preparedness for the deployment of military and civilian personnel would have been sharply exposed.

It was even more difficult for the UN to undertake contingency planning for the worst-case scenario, which became the reality. This goes to the general weakness criticized by the Brahimi Report. Unless worst-case planning is insisted upon as a matter of general practice, it is hard for the Secretariat to be known to be planning for the possibility that an important member state would violate the solemn undertakings it had given, at a time when its friends in the Security Council were insisting on praising it for its cooperation. In the absence of such general practice, and without a signal from the Security Council, contingency planning for military intervention of the kind which was anathema to Indonesia could only take place outside any formal UN framework.

The UN's formal planning beyond the ballot was, thus, within the framework of the Agreements, and assumed that Indonesia would maintain responsibility for security during the period from the ballot to the Assembly decision (termed Phase II), advised by increased numbers of UNAMET civilian police and with an expanded military liaison presence. Only after Indonesia's Assembly had acted on a pro-independence vote (Phase III) would the UN deploy a peacekeeping force. Australia discussed quietly with the UN contingency planning for a worst-case scenario in which an extraction force might be necessary to pull out UNAMET and other foreign nationals. Australia had doubled its combat-ready troop strength, putting a second brigade on readiness, and was ready to act unilaterally with the agreement of Indonesia should this be necessary; New Zealand too had placed troops on stand-by. Australia was also prepared to take the lead in the Phase III force. It was because Australia had engaged in such planning that the eventual intervention could be mounted so swiftly, but its planning assumptions had never included leading a multi-national peace-enforcement operation. And the fact that Indonesia was given no reason to believe in the possibility of rapid international intervention may have contributed to the Indonesian army feeling able to go so far down the path of post-ballot vengeance.

8.5   Intervention with induced consent

As the scale of post-ballot violence and the role of the Indonesian army became clear, those who had long been arguing for an international peace-keeping presence in East Timor redoubled their appeals. Even before the result was announced, Portugal was calling for swift action to establish an international force if the situation deteriorated, and Australia recognized the likely need for accelerated deployment. By 5 September the countries already on stand-by (Australia and New Zealand), and the permanent members of the Security Council most involved (the UK and the USA), were discussing possibilities with the Secretariat. One option was to bring forward the deployment of the UN peacekeeping force that was being planned for Phase III, but acting within the full UN procedures for mandating and assembling this would take weeks if not months. Even if a vanguard of the Phase III force could be deployed rapidly, it now appeared that its early task would be peace-enforcement rather than peacekeeping. The discussions quickly concluded that the only effective means of rapid intervention would be a 'coalition of the willing', mounted by a group of states under a Security Council mandate but outside UN procedures, pending the mobilization of a UN force ready to deploy into a more permissive environment.

As early as 4 September, Australian Foreign Minister Alexander Downer spoke publicly of Australia's willingness to lead such a coalition. With public opinion already critical of Australia's past role, the government could not stand idly by while the policy for which it had claimed credit turned into a disaster—and one which would bring fresh refugees to Australia's shores. But it was not prepared to destroy its relationship with Indonesia by acting without its consent—let alone to have to fight its way into East Timor against the Indonesian army. Nor was any other country with the necessary military capability willing to do so. The international community having acted in concert within a UN framework in mounting the popular consultation, Australia was also clear that it would act only with the international legitimacy conferred by a mandate from the UN Security Council. No country suggested following the Kosovo precedent for unauthorized intervention. In the Security Council the support of China and Russia, as well as of several non-permanent members, for such a mandate would itself depend on Indonesian acquiescence. The first diplomatic efforts continued to be aimed at inducing Indonesia to take effective action itself to end the violence in East Timor; member states varied in how quickly they reached the conclusion that this would not happen, according to the quality of their information on what was happening in East Timor and the degree of their reluctance to recognize the full reality of the behaviour of the Indonesian army. But as this conclusion was reached, the objective rapidly became to obtain Indonesian agreement to international intervention. The third objective was to assemble a coalition of countries willing to take part, which would be militarily viable, and as politically acceptable to Indonesia as could be achieved.

Secretary-General Annan and Prime Minister Howard, in continual contact with each other, took the lead in intense diplomatic efforts towards these objectives. On 5 September, after UNAMET's withdrawal from most regions had exposed the extent of the violence and had been reported to a Sunday briefing of the Security Council, the Secretary-General phoned Habibie. The President remained firmly opposed to any early deployment of international forces. But having sent Wiranto and Foreign Minister Ali Alatas to Dili and heard their report, he was planning to declare martial law, and he opened the door to accepting international assistance if this failed to control the situation: 'We will say the UN is coming in as a friend.'[13] The Secretary-General added public pressure to his private persuasion, by declaring when martial law was announced on 6 September that further measures would have to be considered if the situation did not improve within forty-eight hours.

A key initiative contributed to the dual purposes of persuading Indonesia and obtaining consensus in the Security Council. On 26 August, amid UNAMET's reports and predictions of violence, Under-Secretary-General Kieran Prendergast had proposed the sending of a Security Council mission. The proposal failed to find support then and when it was discussed again at the urging of Portugal on 1 September, but finally found general agreement when Prendergast pressed it again on 5 September. Once the decision to mount the first such mission since 1994 had been made, it was fielded with impressive speed, leaving New York on 6 September and reaching Jakarta to begin its meetings on 8 September.

The mission found Alatas firmly resistant to any foreign military presence before the Assembly had acted on the consultation result, and Wiranto insistent that the *Tentara Nasional Indonesia* (TNI—Indonesian National Military) could handle the situation. Habibie, too, stood firm: in the presence of his Ministers, he was perhaps less ready to admit the possibility of international assistance than he had already been in private discussion with the Secretary-General. It is likely that he had needed to proceed first by way of martial law, and to allow Wiranto to be convinced that this was not enough, before he could give in to international intervention. His internal situation was precarious: rumours of an impending coup were swirling around Jakarta.

The mission's determination grew, as it heard briefings from UNAMET staff and the best-informed Jakarta embassies, and received worsening news from East Timor, including the evacuation of most of UNAMET and the plight of the thousands of internally displaced persons (IDPs) who had taken refuge in UNAMET's Dili compound. In an emotional meeting with the mission in the British Embassy, where he was in temporary refuge after his release from his prison house, Gusmão appealed to them to act immediately to save lives in East Timor. The mission insisted that it must fly to Dili to assess the situation at first hand and show support for UNAMET, that Wiranto should accompany it to Dili, and that it must meet Habibie again on its return.[14]

Meanwhile, other pressures to induce UN action and Indonesian consent were growing. First, the non-governmental East Timor solidarity network had become highly effective during the 1990s, and worked closely with José Ramos-Horta as the CNRT's main external spokesperson: it now went into overdrive. Human rights organizations called for action to check the violations and hold those responsible to account. The concern of the Catholic Church deepened as news came out that priests had been killed, and that the house of Bishop Carlos Ximenes Belo, also a refuge for internally displaced persons (IDPs), had been attacked: the Pope spoke out, and Bishop Belo travelled to Rome and Lisbon. Media coverage was extraordinarily intense, with East Timor in the headlines and leading news bulletins for days, at a time when there happened to be no other major world event competing for attention. The voices and reports of the small group of journalists who remained in Dili, and of UNAMET's staff speaking from its besieged compound and from Darwin, sustained the focus on the destruction, the forced displacement of the population, and the plight and responsibility of the UN. In Portugal, there were vigils and demonstrations throughout the country demanding action, and the Prime Minister himself participated in a human chain that snaked around the Lisbon embassies of permanent members of the Security Council. Australia was second only to Portugal in the extraordinary expressions of public opinion.

A second source of pressure came from regional actors. Fortuitously, the Asia-Pacific Economic Cooperation (APEC) leaders' meeting was scheduled to take place in Auckland, New Zealand, with Foreign Ministers gathering on 9 September and Heads of Government on 12 September. APEC was strongly resistant to its agenda moving beyond strictly economic issues, but Canada proposed that there must be discussion of the East Timor crisis. New Zealand, as host country, was soon persuaded to convene a Special Ministerial Meeting to discuss events in East Timor, alongside rather than as part of the APEC meeting itself. The UK was not an APEC member, but Foreign Secretary Robin Cook flew to join the meeting with a European Union mandate, and Lloyd Axworthy of Canada, Don McKinnon of New Zealand, Madeleine Albright of the United States, Downer and Cook met to coordinate strategy. Indonesia might have expected that its Asian allies would absent themselves from such a meeting, but in the event nearly all attended, and mostly at the level of their foreign minister or most senior representative present.[15] There was no collective statement, but as Cook noted, three-quarters of the world's GDP was represented around the table, and the meeting served as a strong demonstration to Indonesia of the concern shared throughout its own region. Habibie and Alatas, who were to have represented Indonesia, had cancelled their attendance, but the senior Indonesian economic minister as well as McKinnon conveyed the message back to Jakarta.[16]

The economic minister had good reason for concern, stemming from even more crucial quarters. Since the rupiah had slumped amid the Asian economic crisis, Indonesia had become more dependent than ever on the International Monetary Fund and the World Bank. The Bank responded to the post-ballot violence by issuing what was perhaps its strongest-ever public statement regarding a political situation, referring to East Timor as 'of paramount concern to our shareholders' (World Bank Statement on East Timor, Washington, 7 September 1999). Bank President James Wolfensohn wrote to Habibie on 8 September, stating that donors had based their funding pledges on assurances the Indonesian government had given regarding its commitment to the East Timor popular consultation in July: 'For the international financial community to be able to continue its full support, it is critical that you act swiftly to restore order, and that your government carry through on its public commitment to honor the referendum outcome.' The IMF issued successive statements that it was closely watching the situation in East Timor, and on 9 September announced that it was putting on hold a planned mission to Indonesia on which the resumption of IMF lending depended. The economic consequences for Indonesia were not immediate: lending had already been suspended as a result of financial scandal at Bank Bali. But each of the statements, by institutions historically inclined to confine themselves to strictly economic criteria and reluctant to take account of political situations, was almost unprecedented; together they were a heavy warning of Indonesia's potential isolation and the eventual economic consequences.

In addition, the US government was now ratcheting up its own pressure. Its first response to the post-ballot violence was to intensify the representations it had already been making for the TNI to control the situation. But the US ability to send a strong signal on the need for international intervention was initially constrained by its limited willingness to participate in it.

From 4 September, officials in Washington were examining what involvement in an Australian-led coalition they could recommend to President Bill Clinton. The NGO lobby on East Timor in the USA had been highly effective over the years in maintaining concern in Congress and thereby constraining US military involvement with Indonesia; it now worked with its friends in Congress to press the Administration towards intervention. Australia, which wanted not just US support in the Security Council but US participation in the military coalition, applied its own pressure, not only through Howard's telephone persuasion of Clinton, but publicly too. In a series of interviews on 7 September, Downer spoke of the Pentagon's reluctance, and voiced Australia's feeling that the United States should reciprocate the contributions Australia had made as a military ally of the USA, most recently in the Gulf conflict with Iraq. Portugal was making similar claims of Clinton: how could it send troops to Kosovo if there was not an equivalent international response to parallel crimes in East Timor?

On 8 September Australia was promised some US military participation. At first only logistical support was envisaged, but this was extended to a small number of military who would assume key non-combat roles on the ground in East Timor. The public message to Indonesia became clear when Clinton gave a press conference as he departed on 9 September for the APEC meeting: if Indonesia did not end the violence, it must invite—'it *must* invite', he repeated emphatically—the international community to assist in restoring security. He threatened economic sanctions through the international financial institutions, and announced the suspension of all programmes of cooperation with the Indonesian military. He did not yet cut off commercial arms sales to Indonesia; that came two days later as he arrived in Auckland and further toughened his statements. Also on 11 September, the UK suspended sales of Hawk fighter jets to Indonesia, and the EU concluded agreement on its own arms boycott on 13 September. The weight of international pressure building up on Jakarta was well illustrated by the banner headline of the *Washington Post* of 10 September: 'US, IMF move to isolate Jakarta; Clinton cuts ties to Indonesia military; loan program suspended'.

Asian pressure was of a different style, but also significant. Japan was a member of the Core Group, coordinating diplomatic efforts in New York and Jakarta with Australia, New Zealand, the UK, the USA and the UN Secretariat. It followed the security situation in East Timor closely, having after deep debate in Tokyo sent civilian police officers to a UN mission for the first time since the killing of a Japanese policeman in Cambodia in 1993. Japan's warnings to Habibie before and after the ballot were conveyed privately, but insistently: they carried the weight of Indonesia's leading investor and trading partner.

A final source of pressure came from the UN itself. On 10 September, the Secretary-General made his strongest statement yet. Announcing that Australia, New Zealand, the Philippines, and Malaysia had indicated willingness to participate in an international force, he urged the Indonesian government to accept their offer of help without delay: 'if it refuses to do so, it cannot escape responsibility for what could amount, according to reports reaching us, to crimes against humanity' (Secretary-General Kofi Annan, Statement on East Timor, New York, 10 September 1999). The UN High Commissioner for Human Rights, Mary Robinson, flew to Darwin where she heard the accounts of those evacuated from East Timor, and began to talk publicly of the need to bring to justice those responsible for such crimes.

In New York, the Security Council was being briefed daily in informal consultations, but had not discussed East Timor in formal, public session since before the ballot. Portugal had requested such a session, and was joined by Brazil. The Council called an open meeting for Saturday, 11 September.

Before the Council met, the members of its mission had been in East Timor, viewing the destruction of Dili and the IDP camp which UNAMET's compound had become. Dili was quiet—another apparent indication of the ability of the Indonesian security forces to maintain a degree of calm when they chose to do so. But nothing could conceal the extent of destruction, or the misery of people waiting at the police station and the port before being taken to West Timor. In the course of that day, Wiranto gave the first indications to the mission—and to CNN—that he was considering a change of position regarding international assistance.

As the mission arrived back in Jakarta, the open session of the Security Council began in New York. The Secretary-General in his opening statement reiterated that what was happening in East Timor might well fall into various categories of international crimes. He urged Indonesia to agree without further delay to the deployment of an international force:

The international community is asking for Indonesia's consent to the deployment of such a force. But I hope it is clear Mr. President that it does so out of deference to Indonesia's position as a respected member of the community of states. Regrettably, that position is now being placed in jeopardy by the tragedy that has engulfed the people of East Timor (Secretary-General Kofi Annan, Statement to the Security Council on East Timor, New York, 11 September 1999).

In a session lasting nearly six hours, no less than 50 delegations took the floor—a highly unusual total, including some who rarely spoke as non-members. Most condemned the violence in East Timor in the strongest terms: not only the Portuguese-speaking and Western countries, but Latin Americans and others too. A majority of Security Council members pressed strongly the need for Indonesia to accept an international force: China and Russia stressed the need for Indonesian consent and Council authority. Only a few of the countries of the non-aligned movement displayed more concern about setting precedents for intervention than about the situation in East Timor, or supported Indonesia's contention that it was capable of bringing the situation under control. Asian countries expressed the need for understanding and encouragement during Indonesia's political transition, but the Republic of Korea and the Philippines urged Indonesia's agreement to international assistance and indicated willingness to participate. Overall, the session was a powerful demonstration of international outrage and Indonesia's growing isolation.

The session ended as the new day, 12 September, dawned in Jakarta. Habibie met with his cabinet. His promised meeting with the Security Council mission was held back until after the cabinet meeting to avoid further impression of conceding to pressure. When the delayed meeting took place, Habibie informed them that he had telephoned the Secretary-General to call for UN assistance to restore peace and security in East Timor: he had known, he said, when he met them three days before that it could not be avoided, but had needed Wiranto to visit Dili. The decision was, he said, without conditions: Alatas would fly to New York to work out the implementation. Habibie made his announcement to the Indonesian nation on television and radio—a calamitous eight days after the result of the ballot had been announced.

8.6   Mandating intervention

Indonesia's request made it certain that the Security Council would mandate a force. But the mandate, leadership, composition, and funding of an international force still had to be addressed. Indonesia was highly sensitive to the role of Australia and strongly opposed to its leadership of an international force. It was clear that Australia would provide the core of the force, but Indonesia wanted as much Asian participation as possible, and an ASEAN Force Commander. Australia was concerned about the immediate cooperation with Indonesia necessary for an effective military operation and about its long-term relationship with its largest neighbour. It had always made clear that it would act only with Indonesian consent, and sought to ensure that the language of the Security Council resolution made it possible for Indonesia to accept the help of friends, rather than have to submit to demands.[17] But it regarded it as essential that it should command the force to which it would make the major contribution, and that the force must have a robust mandate.

Among Council members, Canada, in particular, would have preferred to see a UN force with blue berets, symbolizing UN authority and control, and which would stay on with the necessary adjustments into Phase III, rather than an initial multinational force replaced by a UN peacekeeping operation. However, discussions reflected the growing consensus that UN command and control arrangements are unsuitable for military action that may need to be robust; in any event, UN procedures and the US requirement to consult Congress meant that a UN force was not compatible with the speed demanded by the situation. The possibility was raised of a multinational force authorized by the Security Council wearing blue UN berets, but it was felt that this had to be reserved to a force under UN command. It was, therefore, agreed that the initial force would be a multinational force, but that it would be replaced as soon as possible by a UN force, in which some of the same troops would come under UN command and don blue berets: of the precedents for this, the closest was Haiti in 1994–5.

The Secretary-General informed Indonesia that he was asking Australia to command the force, although the command might change for Phase III. He and Howard had, however, been working to maximize Asian participation. APEC leaders were still together in Auckland when it became clear that Indonesia would consent, and this provided a timely opportunity for discussions in the margins of the meeting about participation in the force. Thailand agreed to provide the Deputy Force Commander along with its contingent. Malaysia withdrew its willingness to participate substantially before Phase III, but the Philippines and the Republic of Korea confirmed their commitments; Singapore too would send a medical company. New Zealand had long had a battalion on stand-by. The commitment of the USA and the UK, as permanent members of the Security Council with strong ties with Indonesia, was important: although small in numbers, their contributions were militarily as well as politically significant. The USA would provide only non-combat personnel, but its 385 personnel in East Timor provided what the force commander called 'niche capabilities', including communications, intelligence, and civil affairs. Beyond this, a thousand US marines were stationed offshore, and the USA provided and absorbed the cost of the 'lift' for other participants. The British Gurkhas were the first troops to go in with Australia and New Zealand, and enhanced the force's immediate readiness for combat.[18] Portugal was willing to send up to one thousand troops, but accepted the judgement that their major participation would better await Phase III.

Australia and the United States were firm that the mandate had to be a fully robust one under chapter VII of the Charter. Indonesia's friends initially resisted this, preferring a weaker chapter VI mandate, but Alatas himself had said that the role was peace-enforcement, not peacekeeping. The resolution therefore

Authorizes the establishment of a multinational force under a unified command structure, pursuant to the request of the Government of Indonesia conveyed to the Secretary-General on 12 September 1999, with the following tasks: to restore peace and security in East Timor, to protect and support UNAMET in carrying out its tasks and, within force capabilities, to facilitate humanitarian assistance operations, and *authorizes* the States participating in the multinational force to take all necessary measures to fulfil this mandate   (SC Res 1264, 15 September 1999).

The potential for broader involvement was limited by the UN practice that the costs of participating in multinational forces are borne by the participants themselves. The resolution therefore established a trust fund, which enabled countries that supported but did not participate in the operation to contribute to the costs of others: the major contributor was Japan. In the meantime, Indonesia was still regarded as responsible for security in East Timor and the Council resolution looked forward to 'close coordination between the multinational force and the Government of Indonesia'. Indonesia sent senior army representatives to New York, and they agreed with the UN and Australia arrangements for a joint consultative security group to ensure this coordination in Dili, comprising the Force Commander of the multinational force, the Indonesian Military Commander and Chief of Police in East Timor, and UNAMET's Chief Military Liaison Officer and Police Commissioner.

The Security Council adopted the resolution authorizing Operation Stabilise on 15 September. Australia had placed its troops on formal alert on 8 September. The leading elements of the force gathered in Darwin, and on 19 September its Australian Commander, Major-General Peter Cosgrove, flew to Dili with his Thai Deputy and other heads of national contingents. He informed Indonesian army commander Major-General Kiki Syahnakri of the landings planned for the following day, and on 20 September the International Force for East Timor, INTERFET, established its presence in Dili.

8.7   International intervention in 1999: Kosovo and East Timor

The question of East Timor was a highly particular one, which had been on the UN agenda since 1975, and the moment at which it came to centre stage was initially determined by internal developments in Indonesia. However, the international response was influenced by the context of world affairs as it had come to be in mid-1999, although not in the way which is sometimes assumed, nor in a manner which supports the bracketing together of Kosovo and East Timor as parallel cases of humanitarian intervention.

The international diplomacy regarding the impending Kosovo crisis was undertaken by an array of American, European, and Russian negotiators, acting inside and outside a variety of international organizations: NATO, the European Union, the OSCE, and only occasionally the UN. In the case of East Timor, diplomacy was UN-led, and the supportive efforts of the governments with the greatest interest and influence were coordinated effectively within a UN framework.

When it came to intervention in Kosovo, international law and national sovereignty were ultimately overridden. International action regarding East Timor, on the other hand, was taken with the full legitimacy of Security Council authorization. And even in a case where national sovereignty did not apply, since the UN did not recognize Indonesia's claim to sovereignty over East Timor, the Security Council was solicitous of the need for Indonesia's consent to intervention. The discomfort of states in overriding claims of sovereignty was shown to have survived—perhaps even been strengthened by—Kosovo, and continued to set limits on norms relating to humanitarian intervention.

The Kosovo intervention left the status of the territory unresolved, and the international community, including the Security Council, bitterly divided.

Thus, when the UN inherited responsibility for a situation in Kosovo which was not of the UN's own making, it found itself handicapped by continuing uncertainty and divisions. The challenge of UN transitional administration in East Timor would, for all its difficulties, benefit from united international support, towards the clear objective of independence.

Since East Timor came back onto the agenda of the Security Council only after the Agreements had been reached, giving effect to a popular consultation which was the proposal of Indonesia's President, there was initially no reason why it should trouble even the most reluctant interventionists among Council members. The first issue the Council faced was how to respond to the Secretariat's briefings, based on UNAMET's reporting, regarding the security situation. It repeatedly expressed concern in Presidential statements, and in meetings between the Council President and Indonesia's Permanent Representative. But the statements drafted by the United Kingdom, which led for the Core Group and reflected the information of Australia and the United States as well as the concerns of the Secretariat, often had to be softened to secure the support of Indonesia's friends on the Council. Among these, Malaysia was the most influential and Bahrain the most uncompromising. As a traditional leader of the Non-Aligned Movement, Indonesia commanded support among members of the G77, who were predisposed to accept that Jakarta was doing its best to contain the violence. Sympathy for Indonesia as a state undergoing a difficult transition to democracy was not, of course, confined to the G77; US, Australian, EU and other policymakers were continuously conscious of the larger interest of a stable, democratic Indonesia.

As the issue within the Security Council moved on to the response to the post-ballot violence, and became one of possible intervention, the positions shaped by the recent Kosovo debate came into play. China and Russia, as well as the G77, were insistent that international 'assistance' should only be upon the invitation of Indonesia. But this was not a matter of dispute, since the country willing to lead the intervention, Australia, itself pre-conditioned its willingness on Indonesian consent. Conversely, behind China and Russia's general position on intervention there was no special desire to protect Indonesia: ethnic Chinese had been among the first victims of Indonesia's 1975 invasion of East Timor, and had more recently been the target of racial killings and assault in Jakarta. Partially offsetting Indonesia's support among the G77 was the solidarity of the Lusophone group with East Timor, while Portugal was constantly lobbying its EU partners to take a robust stand.

However different the two situations, intervention in Kosovo would have made a failure to intervene in East Timor all the more impossible to defend, and decision-makers had been repeatedly reminded of the shame heaped upon the UN for standing by at the massacres in Rwanda and at Srebrenica. No one was more conscious of this than Secretary-General Annan, whose personal human rights commitment led him to be more willing to advocate intervention than the governments of most member states.

Critical to the speed of intervention was the willingness of a country with a robust military capability and a clear national interest to take the lead, aided by its geographical proximity. But in view of Australia's requirement of a Security Council mandate and Indonesia's consent, rapid and effective diplomacy was also essential. It is impossible to attribute Indonesia's acquiescence to any single factor: what is remarkable is how well many factors worked together. They included the personal diplomacy of Secretary-General Annan and Prime Minister Howard; the fortuitous timing and use made of the APEC leaders' meeting; the strong warnings of the international financial institutions and of key member states, eventually including the United States; the Security Council mission and open meeting; and—helping to drive all of this—media coverage and the mobilization of a strong constituency of concern.

For those in East Timor, each day that passed while international intervention was under discussion was an agony, and some would argue from the precedent of Kosovo that a Security Council mandate need not have been awaited. Yet INTERFET was mandated only eleven days after the announcement of the result had triggered widespread violence, and began deploying just five days after that. The almost unprecedented speed of international action which this represented was nonetheless combined with consensus decision-making which favoured the success of both the military intervention and the transitional administration which followed. In the particular circumstances of East Timor, it would be hard to argue that true 'humanitarian intervention' (without consent) could have afforded a better basis for action than intervention with induced consent. Yet, the victims of violence, dead and alive, bear witness to decades of failure in the responsibility to protect.

9

Humanitarian Intervention and Afghanistan

Simon Chesterman

When the United States went to war with Al-Qaeda and the Taliban regime in Afghanistan in October 2001, the human rights of the Afghan population were not uppermost in the minds of the Bush Administration. Shocked by the terrorist attacks on New York and Washington, DC, the military action was presented—and broadly accepted—as an exercise of the right of self-defence.[1] Such an intervention, therefore, seems ill-suited to discussion in a volume on humanitarian intervention. But the operation in Afghanistan bears examination here for two reasons that reflect on the past and the future of the debates on humanitarian intervention.

First, a notable aspect of the conflict was the way in which humanitarian concerns came to be attributed to the action as it played out in Afghanistan—in part as an attempt to win the hearts and minds of the Afghans themselves, as well as to hold together an increasingly shaky international coalition. Such invocation of humanitarian concerns that were, at best, coincidental to other motives is a sobering theme that runs through the history of humanitarian intervention. Indeed, the attribution of humanitarian objectives begs the question of why nothing had been done for the Afghan population *before* 11 September 2001. Such 'inhumanitarian non-intervention' has usually been the rule in international relations; the rare cases of intervention that might plausibly be regarded as 'humanitarian' in character have tended to coincide with other motives.

Second, however, the situation in Afghanistan demonstrated that the collapse of the institutions of statehood may have consequences wider than poverty and lawlessness for a state's own population. Where a state is unable or unwilling to constrain terrorist groups within its territory, the civilian population more generally may be subject to official abuse or neglect. Though military action against the perceived terrorist threat is unlikely to be undertaken to assist that civilian population as such, a two-pronged approach that combines military action and civilian reconstruction may be necessary to achieve both the military aim of establishing a sustainable peace as well as the political end of maintaining international support for the military action. It is misleading to describe this as 'humanitarian intervention' under any definition of that term,[2] but such actions may come to form a more prominent feature on the international agenda than exceptional cases such as Kosovo.

This chapter will briefly discuss the evolving justifications for the first phase of US military operations in Afghanistan before considering these two issues in turn. It will not consider in depth the broader activities of the United Nations, the establishment of the interim administration, or the activities of the International Security Assistance Force (ISAF)—in which the United States elected not to participate—except in so far as these activities impact on the questions raised by the use of force.[3] Nevertheless, as we shall see, such stabilization and reconstruction efforts may give much needed legitimacy to a military adventure undertaken for (at best) partly humanitarian reasons.

9.1   Operation Enduring Freedom

On 11 September 2001, nineteen persons of non-US nationality hijacked four US commercial passenger jets and crashed them into the World Trade Centre in New York, the Pentagon in Washington, DC, and the Pennsylvania countryside. Approximately 3,000 people died in the incidents—the largest number of casualties experienced in the United States in a single day since the Civil War (Murphy 2002: 237). Following the terrorist attacks, there was an immediate call within the United States for a military response. President Bush swiftly stated that the United States would 'hunt down and punish those responsible for these cowardly acts',[4] a goal later amplified in the President's response to a question as to whether he wanted Osama bin Laden dead: 'I want justice. There's an old poster out west, as I recall, that said, "Wanted: Dead or Alive".'[5]

The incidents were frequently treated as comparable to a military attack.[6] The UN Security Council swiftly passed a unanimous resolution condemning the 'horrifying terrorist attacks', which it regarded as a 'threat to international peace and security'. The Council further stressed that 'those responsible for aiding, supporting or harbouring the perpetrators, organizers and sponsors of these acts will be held accountable'. This explicitly adopted the language used by President Bush to implicate the Taliban regime as at least partly responsible for the acts of its Al-Qaeda 'guests'. Finally, the Council stated its readiness to take 'all necessary steps' to respond to the attacks (SC Res 1368, 12 September 2001, paras. 1, 3, and 5).

Though the Security Council did become central to the sweeping measures intended to deny terrorists financing, support, or safe haven (see SC Res 1373, 28 September 2001), the implicit offer of a chapter VII legal umbrella for the

US military response was not pursued, apparently out of a desire to preserve the maximum flexibility in how that response might be conducted (see Byers 2002). Similarly, the USA did not seek the direct assistance of NATO, which invoked the collective self-defence provisions of Article 5 of the Washington Treaty for the first time.[7] On 18 September 2001, President Bush declared a national emergency[8] and signed into law a joint resolution of Congress that authorized him to use 'all necessary and appropriate force against those nations, organizations, or persons he determines planned, authorized, committed, or aided the terrorist attacks that occurred on September 11, 2001, or harboured such organizations or persons, in order to prevent any future acts of international terrorism against the United States by such nations, organizations or persons'.[9]

Despite having no diplomatic relations with the Taliban regime in Afghanistan, the USA communicated its demands to the Taliban through the government of Pakistan:

Deliver to United States authorities all the leaders of Al Qaida who hide in your land. Release all foreign nationals, including American citizens, you have unjustly imprisoned. Protect foreign journalists, diplomats, and aid workers in your country. Close immediately and permanently every terrorist training camp in Afghanistan, and hand over every terrorist and every person in their support structure to appropriate authorities. Give the United States full access to terrorist training camps, so we can make sure they are no longer operating. These demands are not open to negotiation or discussion. The Taliban must act and act immediately. They will hand over the terrorists, or they will share in their fate.[10]

President Bush went on to outline the broad scope of the intended action as involving 'far more than instant retaliation and isolated strikes' and warning of 'a lengthy campaign, unlike any other we have ever seen'. Crucially, this was said to be a war in which neutrality was not to be an option:

Every nation, in every region, now has a decision to make. Either you are with us, or you are with the terrorists. From this day forward, any nation that continues to harbour or support terrorism will be regarded by the United States as a hostile regime.[11]

The Taliban rejected these demands, calling for proof of Osama bin Laden's involvement in the terrorist attacks (Murphy 2002: 244), a refrain that was frequently repeated in the Muslim world and parts of the European press.

On 7 October, the United States informed the Security Council that it was exercising its right of self-defence in taking actions in Afghanistan against Al-Qaeda terrorist-training camps and Taliban military installations. The letter to the Council stated that the US government had obtained clear and compelling information that Al-Qaeda, which was supported by the Taliban regime, had a central role in the attacks: 'There is still much we do not know,' the letter continued. 'Our inquiry is in its early stages. We may find that our self-defence requires further actions with respect to other organizations and other States.' Finally, the letter described the actions that the USA was taking:

United States armed forces have initiated actions designed to prevent and deter further attacks on the United States. These actions include measures against Al-Qaeda terrorist training camps and military installations of the Taliban regime in Afghanistan. In carrying out these actions, the United States is committed to minimizing civilian casualties and damage to civilian property. In addition, the United States will continue its humanitarian efforts to alleviate the suffering of the people of Afghanistan. We are providing them with food, medicine and supplies.[12]

This was the most prominent mention of the humanitarian plight of the Afghan population, which was put at still greater risk by the conduct of the war as winter approached. US efforts to provide food were criticized by some humanitarian organizations (especially those who had long been active in Afghanistan under the Taliban) as window dressing both in terms of quantity and quality—the food supplied was sometimes more suited to US than Afghan palates, and the packaging bore an unfortunate resemblance to the explosive bomblets delivered by US cluster bombs (Deborah Zabarenko, 'US Offers Lesson on How to Tell Cluster Bombs From Food Packs', *Washington Post*, 30 October 2001; Elizabeth A. Neuffer, 'Food Drops Found to Do Little Good', *Boston Globe*, 26 March 2002). As in any military operation, collateral damage occurred. The USA seemed unusually cursed, however, when it struck the only Red Cross facility in Kabul not once but twice (Elizabeth Becker and Eric Schmitt, 'US Planes Bomb a Red Cross Site', *New York Times*, 27 October 2001).

As the conflict developed—in particular, as the likelihood of capturing Osama bin Laden 'dead or alive' diminished—a rhetorical shift became evident in the Bush Administration's war aims. Nation-building,[13] something that President Bush had long derided as inappropriate for the US military, came back onto the US agenda. (The United Kingdom had been a more enthusiastic proponent of the centrality of such reconstruction efforts to the coalition war aims. See, for example, David White, 'Britain Urges UN to Take Post-Conflict Leading Role', *Financial Times*, 23 October 2001.) And, with increasing frequency, the Taliban regime and its mistreatment of the Afghan civilian population were presented as the real evil, rather than being ancillary to the man and the organization that was alleged to have attacked the United States on 11 September.

During the course of the 2000 US presidential campaign, candidate Bush had been openly critical of the use of US military resources for 'nation-building' purposes. He reiterated this position once in office, including statements in July 2001:

You know, during the course of the campaign, I made it clear that I thought that our military should be used to fight and win war. That's what I thought the military was for. And that I was concerned about peacekeeping missions, and that we've got to be very clear about—to our friends and allies about how we use our troops for nation-building exercises, which I have rebuffed as a—basically rebuffed as a kind of a strategy for the military.[14]

This position was repeated by the President in the weeks after the attacks, when he stated that 'we're not into nation-building, we're focused on justice'.[15] Days before the United States commenced military operations in Afghanistan, however, the President's spokesman marked a slight shift in position as it became clear that international support of the US action would in part depend on the broader consequences for the Afghan people:

Well, to repeat what I've said many times, the United States is not engaged in nation-building in Afghanistan, but the United States will help those who seek a peaceful, economically-developing Afghanistan that's free from terrorism.[16]

This was elaborated by the President himself in a news conference after the military action had commenced, including a more substantial role for the UN in rebuilding Afghanistan:

I believe that the *United Nations* would—could provide the framework necessary to help meet those conditions. It would be a useful function for the United Nations to take over the so-called 'nation-building,'—I would call it the stabilization of a future government—after our military mission is complete. We'll participate; other countries will participate ... [*sic*] I've talked to many countries that are interested in making sure that the post-operations Afghanistan is one that is stable, and one that doesn't become yet again a haven for terrorist criminals.[17]

These evolving war aims, from a retributive strike to a defensive response and finally to the broader goals of ensuring the stability of post-conflict Afghanistan, were not necessarily inconsistent—as will be argued below, nation-building (invited or coerced) may form a substantial part of the on-going 'war on terror' in the future. But as the aims themselves evolved, so, with the benefit of hindsight, did the asserted motivation for US military operations in the first place. This appeared to be a carefully scripted shift, as evidenced in two important speeches by President Bush. Speaking to the United Nations in November 2001, he effectively equated the Taliban regime with the terrorists who had attacked the United States:

The Taliban are now learning this lesson—that regime and the terrorists who support it are now virtually indistinguishable. Together they promote terror abroad and impose a reign of terror on the Afghan people. Women are executed in Kabal's [*sic*] soccer stadium. They can be beaten for wearing socks that are too thin. Men are jailed for missing prayer meetings. The United States, supported by many nations, is bringing justice to the terrorists in Afghanistan.[18]

Then, in his State of the Union Address, the President sought to expand this into a more general doctrine intimating that the US action stemmed from goals somewhat loftier than self-defence:

We have no intention of imposing our culture. But America will always stand firm for the non-negotiable demands of human dignity: the rule of law; limits on the power of the state; respect for women; private property; free speech; equal justice; and religious tolerance. America will take the side of brave men and women who advocate these values around the world, including the Islamic world, because we have a greater objective than eliminating threats and containing resentment. We seek a just and peaceful world beyond the war on terror.[19]

By late 2002 it was unclear whether this was a new Bush Doctrine to supplant the more militant calls made earlier that states must either side with the USA or against it.

9.2   The humanitarian war on terror

The changing war aims articulated by the Bush Administration in the course of the operations in Afghanistan reflect a trend that runs through the history of debates on humanitarian intervention. In order to avoid the clear terms of the UN Charter, which prohibits the use of force,[20] some commentators have argued that an alternative norm allows for limited military intervention to protect a population at risk (see, for example, Reisman 1984; D'Amato 1990; Tesón 1997). This is sometimes linked to the actual *motive* a state might have—an unhelpful area of inquiry (see, for example, Wheeler 2000: 37–40). As in domestic criminal law, a more useful approach is to examine the *intention* behind an action and its probable outcome. Considering *why* something is done as a means of characterizing *what* is done conflates two distinct questions—benign motives for what is otherwise wrongful are appropriately considered after the allegedly wrongful act itself has been characterized (see Chesterman 2001: 226–32).[21] An examination of the US operation in Afghanistan within this framework is therefore instructive both for what it shows about the action itself, but also what it demonstrates about claims that other interventions might also be (or, *ex post facto*, become) 'humanitarian' in character.[22]

As noted elsewhere in this volume, the prohibition of the use of force in the Charter is tempered by only two exceptions: the 'inherent right of individual or collective self-defence' (UN Charter, Article 51) and chapter VII enforcement actions by the Security Council.[23] Both exceptions provide examples of the inexorable expansion of certain legal rights. Self-defence, for example, has been invoked in ever-wider circumstances to justify military action such as a pre-emptive strike against a country's nuclear programme, and in 'response' to a failed assassination attempt in a foreign country (Chesterman 2001: 205–6). As indicated earlier, it also provided the initial basis for the Bush Administration's extensive military action in Afghanistan beginning in October 2001. Security Council authorized actions have expanded even further, including actions such as those in Somalia and Haiti that would never have been contemplated by the founders of the UN in 1945 (Chesterman 2001: 112–62). Nevertheless, neither exception encompasses humanitarian intervention, understood here to mean the threat or use of armed force in the absence of a Security Council authorization or an invitation from the recognized government, with the object of protecting a population at risk (Chesterman 2001: 1).

Leaving aside questionable attempts to reinterpret the Charter's clear provisions as allowing for an additional exception for humanitarian intervention in their own terms (Chesterman 2001: 45–87), it is sometimes argued that a new customary norm has created an additional exception to the prohibition. Customary international law allows for the creation of such norms through the evolution of consistent and widespread state practice (*Nicaragua (Merits)* [1986] ICJ Reports 14, 98) when accompanied by the necessary *opinio juris*— the belief that a practice is legally obligatory.[24] Some writers have argued that there is evidence of such state practice and *opinio juris*, most frequently pointing to the Indian action to stop the slaughter in East Pakistan in 1971, Tanzania's actions against Idi Amin in neighbouring Uganda in 1978–9, and Vietnam's intervention in Kampuchea in 1978–9. In none of these cases, however, were humanitarian concerns invoked as a justification for the use of force. Rather, as in the case of US operations in Afghanistan, self-defence was the primary justification offered in each case, with humanitarian (and other) justifications being at best secondary considerations.[25] The fact that states continued to rely on traditional justifications—most notably self-defence—thus, undermines arguments that the law has changed.[26]

Post-cold war examples of allegedly humanitarian intervention without explicit Security Council authorization, such as the no-fly zones in protection of the Kurds in northern Iraq and NATO's intervention in Kosovo, raise slightly different questions.[27] Acting states have often claimed that their actions have been 'in support of' Security Council resolutions, though in each case it is clear that the Council did not decide to authorize the use of force.[28] Indeed, it is ironic that states began to claim the need to act when the Security Council faltered in precisely the same decade that the Council's activities expanded so greatly. At a time when there was a far stronger argument that paralysis of the UN system demanded self-help, the International Court of Justice considered and rejected arguments that 'present defects in international organization' could justify an independent right of intervention (*Corfu Channel Case* [1949] ICJ Reports 4, 35). In Afghanistan, the United States appears to have made a considered decision not to seek even an implicit Security Council authorization, relying instead on the inherent right of self-defence and encouraging the reiteration of this right in the relevant Council resolutions.[29]

Interestingly, despite the efforts by some legal scholars to argue for the existence of a right of humanitarian intervention, states themselves have continued to prove very reluctant to embrace such a right—even in defence of their own actions.[30] This was particularly true in the case of NATO's intervention in Kosovo. This reluctance appears to have stemmed in part from a recognition of the dubiousness of such a legal argument, but also from a recognition that if any such right were embraced it might well be used by other states in other situations. Military action in support of the Palestinian people against Israel is the most commonly invoked scenario; in fact, it was the US action against Afghanistan that appeared to embolden Israel to escalate its military response to terrorist activities that, it argued, were sponsored or condoned by the Palestinian authority. Similarly, criticism of Russian policies in Chechnya diminished substantially after Russia demonstrated its support for the USA.

In addition, there appears to be some concern that the assertion of a right of humanitarian intervention might lead to the not-unreasonable demand that states asserting such a right ought to act with some degree of consistency. This was evident during the Rwandan crisis in 1994, when the United States and other governments resisted use of the term 'genocide' to describe the ethnically based mass murder as it would have made their policies of inaction untenable (Gourevitch 1999: 152–4). Such allegations of hypocrisy were levelled against Western states because of their inaction during East Timor's post-referendum violence in 1999—mere months after the Kosovo intervention. The charge of hypocrisy might have played some role in Australia's decision to intervene, but was less important than concerns about refugees, the stability of Indonesia, and domestic pressure groups (Chesterman 2001: 219–20).

It seems probable that, in the absence of the 11 September attacks, little would have been done by outsiders to change the situation of the Afghan people. The Taliban regime had been widely condemned for some years and it had been subject to Security Council-imposed sanctions since 1999 (SC Res 1267, 15 October 1999). Humanitarian agencies had been operating since the departure of Soviet forces and considerable assistance had been provided to the population—much of which went to the independent north-east of the country.[31] The Taliban government was recognized only by Pakistan, Saudi Arabia, and the United Arab Emirates, but there was no prospect of forceful regime change. The Council and various of its members had repeatedly expressed deep concern at the continuing discrimination against girls and women and at other violations of human rights and of international humanitarian law (see, for example, SC Res 1193, 28 August 1998 preamble), but UN and US policy on Afghanistan had fallen into a holding pattern. The nature of the Taliban regime and its near complete lack of allies meant that there was no challenge to the imposition of sanctions—but nor was there sufficient interest on the part of acting states to do anything more creative than impose a sanctions regime that bore little relation to the political situation on the ground (Cortright and Lopez 2002: 47–60).

What caused the shift in US (and, therefore, UN) policy on Afghanistan was a radical redefinition of its national interest. As indicated above, self-defence was the primary legal justification for the US response, though this became tempered by more humanitarian concerns as the operation continued. Within the United States the action was frequently presented as an armed reprisal—measures widely regarded as illegal in international law.[32]

The question to be examined in the next section is whether these shifting goals might lead to a more lasting transformation in the debates over humanitarian intervention. In particular, a recognition that disintegrating state institutions in countries like Afghanistan can provide a haven for terrorists might prompt a shift in the primary barrier to action to protect populations at risk in troubled countries. Far from being the legal prohibition of the use of force, this barrier is the perceived lack of interest in getting involved at all.

9.3   The national interest, state failure, and humanitarian intervention

Three months after NATO concluded its 78-day campaign over Kosovo, Secretary-General Kofi Annan presented his annual report to the United Nations General Assembly. In it, he presented in stark terms the dilemma confronting those who privileged international law over the need to respond to gross and systematic violations of human rights:

To those for whom the greatest threat to the future of international order is the use of force in the absence of a Security Council mandate, one might ask—not in the context of Kosovo—but in the context of Rwanda: If, in those dark days and hours leading up to the genocide, a coalition of States had been prepared to act in defence of the Tutsi population, but did not receive prompt Council authorization, should such a coalition have stood aside and allowed the horror to unfold?[33]

The hypothetical neatly captured the ethical dilemma as many of the acting states sought to present it. Could international law truly prevent such 'humanitarian' intervention?

The problem, however, is that this was not the dilemma faced in the context of Rwanda. Rather than international law restraining a state from acting in defence of the Tutsi population, the problem in 1994, as James Mayall demonstrates in his chapter in this volume, was that no state wanted to intervene. When France—hardly a disinterested actor—decided to intervene, this was swiftly approved in a Council resolution (though reference to 'impartiality', a two-month time-limit and five abstentions suggested wariness about France's motivation) (see Chesterman 2001: 144–7). As we have seen, the capriciousness of state interest is a theme that runs through the history of humanitarian intervention.[34] Following 11 September, military action purely to prevent humanitarian crises may seem unlikely: on the contrary, there has been far greater defence of state power even where that power may be used against civilians.[35] But there also appears to be some recognition that more might have been done earlier to prevent Afghanistan deteriorating to the point where it became a safe haven for terrorists. The main evidence of this new approach can be seen in the work of the Counter-Terrorism Committee established by the UN Security Council.[36]

This shift from military intervention to preventive action mirrors the move made in the ICISS report. Entitled 'The Responsibility to Protect', the report turns on its head the policy dilemma that had long paralysed debate on humanitarian intervention. Rather than examining at length the right to intervene, it focuses on the responsibility of states to protect vulnerable populations at risk from civil wars, insurgencies, state repression, and state collapse (ICISS 2001a). Discussing the report in February 2002, UN Secretary-General Kofi Annan observed that this was indeed a constructive development:

I admire your diplomatic skill in redirecting the debate, and—believe me—I wish I had thought of this myself. It would have saved me quite a few explanations of just what I was proposing in my [September 1999] speech. I say this because your title really describes what I was talking about: the fact that sovereignty implies responsibilities as well as powers; and that among those responsibilities, none is more important than protecting citizens from violence and war   (UN Doc SG/SM/8125, 15 February 2002).

As the ICISS report notes, action to protect a civilian population in another state is distinct from action in response to terrorist attacks against one's own. But the move from a right of intervention to a responsibility to protect applies to both situations. If more had been done to induce or compel the Taliban regime to protect the Afghan population, Afghanistan might have proved a less inviting haven for Al-Qaeda.[37] And, once the United States successfully removed that regime from power, it imposed a special responsibility (with the assistance of the UN and other countries) to leave Afghanistan a better place than they found it. Indeed, one of the central contradictions in the ongoing US activities in Afghanistan is that its nation-building efforts there are typically justified by reference to the war on terror; this partly explains why the USA is frequently criticized for having a military strategy in Afghanistan but not a political one.

Secretary-General Annan emphasized in 1999, and again at a speech at the International Peace Academy in November 2000, that discussion of 'intervention' for humanitarian purposes should be defined as broadly as possible. Focusing solely on military action both distracts attention from the real issue—helping people in need—and risks compromising the work of the true humanitarians, whose relief work is essential to assisting Afghans (or other populations) take back control of their lives.[38] As the ICISS report makes clear, any military action should be regarded primarily as a failure—of the state that bears primary responsibility to protect the people under its care, and of the international community for failing to help it or to help them.

It remains to be seen, of course, whether the response to this insight will be to pursue greater engagement with the many states whose institutions are on the point of collapse, or to pick and choose those states seen as harbours for terrorists and enforce regime change. One major lesson that should be taken from Afghanistan—evidenced by the changing US statements on the topic—is that regime change requires far more than a short, sharp military strike. This tempered the initial shopping list of countries for military action (including open talk of targeting Somalia and Yemen; see, for example, Peter Slevin and Alan Sipress, 'Tests Ahead for cooperation on Terrorism; Several Countries on Blacklist Have Helped US, but Only Marginally So Far', *Washington Post*, 31 December 2001), and led to a greater focus on intelligence and military cooperation. This is a far cry from the sort of institution-building that might help prevent states falling into lawlessness—indeed, there are concerns that the new doctrine will amount to a reversion to cold war us-and-them politics, propping up cooperative regimes regardless of their human rights records. But it is a start.

Nevertheless, the September 2002 publication of the National Security Strategy of the United States suggests that unilateral action for subjectively determined reasons remains firmly on the agenda. The document asserts that the USA will defend itself and its citizens against terrorism by identifying and destroying the threat 'before it reaches our borders':

While the United States will constantly strive to enlist the support of the international community, we will not hesitate to act alone, if necessary, to exercise our right of self-defense by acting preemptively against such terrorists, to prevent them from doing harm against our people and our country.[39]

The possibility that such a doctrine might be invoked by other states for less noble causes is implicitly recognized in the injunction that others should not 'use pre-emption as a pretext for aggression' (www.whitehouse.gov/nsc/nss.html, 15).

The Strategy is said to be based on 'a distinctly American internationalism that reflects the union of our values and our national interests' (www.white house.gov/nsc/nss.html, 1). This mix of values and interests was apparent in the changing articulation of the war aims in Afghanistan; it also permeated the debate over military action against Iraq throughout 2002 and early 2003, as the plight of the Kurds and the Shia Muslims was invoked as proof of the awfulness of Saddam Hussein's regime, but with clear opposition to the possibility that they might secede from a post-conflict Iraq. This bore disturbing similarities to the ambiguous signals sent to the same groups in the immediate aftermath of the Gulf War in 1991.

9.4   Conclusion

Until the end of the cold war, the code names of military operations tended to be chosen randomly in order to preserve operational security. Though some leaders (notably Winston Churchill) liked to override these random choices, a revolution in military packaging occurred when the United States prepared to invade Panama in 1989. Immediately prior to the invasion commencing, General James Lindsay, Commander-in-chief of Special Operations Command, called the operations officer on the joint staff to complain about the mission's code name. 'Do you want your grandchildren to say you were in Blue Spoon?' he is reported to have asked. The operation was swiftly renamed 'Just Cause' (Richard Tomkins, 'Military Branding', *Financial Times* (London), 14 February 2002; see further Chesterman 1999).

The US military operations in Afghanistan also underwent a name change, for slightly different reasons. They were initially referred to as 'Infinite Justice'—a title that captured the rhetoric of President Bush and the national sentiment in the weeks after 11 September. This was swiftly changed, however, when the Council on American–Islamic Relations and other Muslim groups complained that only God could dispense such justice (Jonathan Weisman, 'Mobilization Name Changes', *USA Today*, 26 September 2001). The rhetorical shift was consistent with the more general transformation in the packaging of the US military action, from reprisal, to self-defence, to a war on terror, and finally to a more general war against evil itself. This change was at least partly strategic, but operated largely at the level of propaganda.

Following the terrorist attacks, the Bush Administration swiftly sought and received Security Council endorsement of its position that this was an attack on the United States and that action taken in self-defence was justified against 'those responsible for aiding, supporting or harbouring the perpetrators, organizers and sponsors of these acts' (SC Res 1368, 2001). Self-defence does not require any form of authorization (though measures taken should be 'immediately reported' to the Council, UN Charter, Article 51), but the fact that the UN was involved so quickly in a crisis was widely seen as a welcome counterpoint to the unilateralist impulses of George W. Bush's Administration (see, for example, Gerard Baker and James Kynge, 'APEC Meeting: Leaders Condemn Terrorist Attacks', *Financial Times*, 22 October 2001).

Nevertheless, the decision to seek Security Council approval also reflected a troubling trend through the 1990s. Military action under its auspices has taken place only when circumstances coincided with the national interests of a state that was prepared to act, with the Council in danger of becoming what

Richard Falk has described as a 'law-laundering service' (1994: 628). Such an approach downgrades the importance of authorization to the point where it may be seen as a policy justification rather than a matter of legal significance. A consequence of this approach is that, when authorization is not forthcoming, a state or group of states will feel less restrained from acting unilaterally.[40]

In the context of humanitarian intervention, it was widely hoped by human rights activists that such a departure from 'traditional' conceptions of sovereignty and international law would privilege individual well-being over states' rights. In fact, as we have seen, humanitarian intervention has long had a troubled relationship to the question of national interest. Many attempts by scholars to formulate a doctrine of humanitarian intervention require that an acting state be disinterested (or 'relatively disinterested') (see, for example, Fonteyne 1974: 261; Scheffer 1992: 291; Chesterman 2001: 229). By contrast, in one of the few articulations of such a doctrine by a political leader, Prime Minister Blair proposed his own criteria during the course of NATO's Kosovo campaign, one of which was whether 'we' had national interests involved (Evans 1999).[41] It is not only the United States that sees its values being intimately bound up with its interests.

The US military action in Afghanistan is, therefore, distinct from the traditional conception of humanitarian intervention, but the politics bear suggestive similarities. Operation Enduring Freedom, like most of the incidents claimed as humanitarian intervention, in fact displayed a range of intentions—some clearly genuine, some asserted, others claimed after the fact. At the same time, however, it showed a recognition on the part of the acting state that, to be effective, such interventions cannot be purely military in character. Ultimately, this latter insight into the complex nature of intervention may come to be more important than legal arguments proposed in the hope that states will undertake interventions for altruistic purposes.

10

Conclusion: Humanitarian Intervention after 11 September

Jennifer M. Welsh

'Is it possible to resist evil without succumbing to the dangers of righteousness?'

Tzvetan Todorov, Amnesty Lectures, 1 February 2001

The above question, posed by one of Europe's greatest thinkers on morality, has been a driving force behind this study of humanitarian intervention. Since the end of the cold war—and arguably well before—scholars and policymakers have struggled to balance two seemingly conflicting sets of norms in international society: those committed to state autonomy and the self-determination of peoples, and those committed to the protection of individual human rights. When interventions for human protection purposes have occurred, such as in Kosovo, they have been condemned by some as dangerous breaches of an international order based on sovereignty and non-intervention. On the other hand, failures to intervene to prevent mass slaughter, as in Rwanda, have raised questions about the international community's commitment to upholding universal human rights. As Secretary-General Kofi Annan proclaimed in September of 1999: 'if humanitarian intervention is, indeed, an unacceptable assault on sovereignty, how should we respond to a Rwanda, to a Srebrenica—to gross and systematic violations of human rights that affect every precept of our common humanity?' (Annan 2000: 48).

The controversy does not end here. What makes the policy of humanitarian intervention particularly divisive is its reliance on highly destructive and unpredictable means: military might. Thus, in addition to shining the spotlight on an uncomfortable tension between state sovereignty and individual rights, interventions for humanitarian purposes lead us into the more contentious terrain of the legitimate use of violence in international society. The trauma of the Second World War generated one answer to this question of legitimacy—and for many scholars and statesmen it remains *the* answer: force can be used only in self-defence or as part of an enforcement action authorized by the United Nations Security Council. Any attempt to qualify this general prohibition is consequently viewed as a dangerous erosion of the body of norms that have underpinned international peace and security for over fifty years. To give in to one exception—humanitarian intervention—is to open the floodgates to many others, including rescue of nationals or pre-emptive self-defence.

Though mindful of this controversy, the contributors to Part One of this book argued in favour of an exceptional right of military intervention in cases of supreme humanitarian emergency. For Henry Shue, such intervention is a critical 'default duty' that the international community must exercise when individual sovereign states fail to fulfil their responsibilities to their citizens. In other words, the members of international society should view the relationship between sovereignty and intervention as complementary rather than contradictory, by conceiving sovereignty as conditional upon respect for a minimum standard of human rights. It was precisely this strategy of reconciliation that was employed by ICISS, the body established to generate a new consensus on the principles involved in the humanitarian intervention debate. The Commission's basic principles are worth reiterating in full:

State sovereignty implies responsibility, and the primary responsibility for the protection of its people lies with the state itself. Where a population is suffering serious harm, as a result of internal war, insurgency, repression or state failure, and the state in question is unwilling or unable to halt or avert it, the principle of non-intervention yields to the international responsibility to protect   (ICISS 2001*a*: p. xi).

In Chapter 3, Nicholas Wheeler charted the impact of this notion of 'sovereignty as responsibility' in the language and behaviour of states and international organizations. In contrast to the cold war, when humanitarian claims were rejected by international society as a legitimate basis for the use of force, the years following the fall of the Berlin Wall have seen a new activism by the UN in matters that had previously been treated as locked within the domestic jurisdiction of states. However, as I note in my own chapter, there are substantial limits on this new norm that stem from two sources; just war arguments about last resort and proper authority; and objections from non-Western states about the erosion of the norm of non-intervention. Consequently, while the Security Council has become more willing to authorize the use of force for humanitarian purposes, its members have been reluctant to base their rationale on human rights considerations alone; instead, the Council has invoked more traditional conceptions of threats to international peace and security.

Part Two of this book examined in more detail the cases in which force has been used in the name of civilians in peril. In Chapter 5, Adam Roberts discussed the implications of this trend for the UN. As he argues, humanitarian intervention has affected the UN deeply not just because of the normative controversy it has sparked, but also because it has proved problematic in practice for the organization and its individual member states. In reviewing the key examples of intervention from the 1990s, Roberts reveals that the situations prompting military action varied greatly in nature in scope—from situations of complete state failure to the brutality of a particular regime—and involved differing degrees of host-state consent. Such diversity of experience makes it difficult for the UN to learn any general lessons about when and how it should engage in intervention to protect civilians. What is clear, however, is that timely and effective action to prevent mass suffering requires a particular state with the capability, interest, and will to lead the military effort. This 'lead-nation'[1] requirement was met in the cases of East Timor (Australia), Bosnia (the United States), and Sierra Leone (the United Kingdom), but was notably lacking in the critical phase of the Rwandan crisis. As a result of this track record, the UN is left defending itself on two fronts: from those who attack it for selectivity and politicization; and from those who insist that humanitarian intervention must be 'disinterested' if it is to be perceived as legitimate.

Chapters 6 and 8, by Nicholas Morris and Ian Martin, provided invaluable perspectives on humanitarian intervention from those on the 'inside'. In the case of Morris, the story is about the delicate and complex role that humanitarian organizations play in situations of conflict, and how their effectiveness can—ironically—dissuade powerful states from taking the necessary steps to counter the root causes of human suffering. What Morris also shows is that if the international community does choose to act, its intentions must be clear, credible, and consistently communicated if it is to be effective in ending human right violations. In the case of Bosnia, the UN failed on these dimensions, issuing ambiguous resolutions and authorizing action that was incommensurate with the resources available. Such ambiguity had the disastrous consequence of raising false expectations on the part of suffering civilians, and emboldening those who were committing the atrocities.

Ian Martin's discussion of the East Timor crisis demonstrates how a long-standing case of 'non-intervention' was rapidly transformed into a successful instance of unified action by the international community to address massive human rights abuses by the Indonesian security forces. It was the political changes in Indonesia itself—rather than a new concern for East Timor expressed by the UN—that launched the chain of events leading to the independence vote and the subsequent violence. It was also Indonesia that prevented the UN from sending in an international security force to maintain stability during the referendum and its aftermath. As Martin shows, this deference to Indonesian promises to maintain order, coupled with weak contingency planning by the UN, left the international community unprepared to undertake military action once the post-ballot chaos began. Yet, only eleven days after the announcement of the referendum, INTERFET was mandated by the Security Council to 'use all necessary means' to restore peace and security and facilitate humanitarian assistance.

What made a speedy intervention possible in East Timor was an extraordinary diplomatic effort by the Secretary-General, and the leadership of a country with a clear national interest and a significant military force on standby. Martin argues that the East Timor case is so particular that its lessons are hard to generalize and transfer to other situations. In contrast to Kosovo, where international law and sovereignty were compromised, international action in East Timor was undertaken with Security Council authorization and the consent of the Indonesian government. These two factors made the action acceptable to the traditionally reluctant interventionists in the Council, such as China and Russia. They also suggest caution about proclaiming a new and general right of humanitarian intervention to rescue civilians in danger.

This cautious approach was adopted by James Mayall in his overview of international involvement in Africa. As Mayall demonstrates, a series of African conflicts (such as Namibia, Mozambique, and Ethiopia) have been addressed with international assistance under the relatively uncontroversial banner of peacekeeping—that is, with the conditions of host-state consent and UN impartiality. Those actions that have gone beyond the chapter VI context, and posed more fundamental challenges to notions of sovereignty and order, have had tragic consequences, leading Western states to be wary about interventions for humanitarian purposes on the African continent. In addition, the international community has been confronted in Africa with the spectre of complete state breakdown—something that offends what Mayall calls international society's 'middle class morality'. While this squeamishness was ultimately overcome in the decision in 2003 to send an EU-led force to the Democratic Republic of Congo, it has played a significant role in delaying international action in Liberia. In particular, memories of Somalia haunted the Bush Administration as it debated whether or not to contribute to an international force in July 2003. In the words of US Senator John Warner, head of the US Armed Services committee: "Is it in our vital national security interests? What are the details of that mission? And what is the exit strategy?" A successful humanitarian intervention in the context of state failure requires not just short-term relief and support for a new political authority, but a prolonged effort in state-building. The imperial implications of such a task have not been lost on Western policymakers, who must now consider an entirely new range of consequences when debating the age-old question of whether to intervene.

10.1   The search for criteria

Given the wide variety in the practice of humanitarian intervention since the end of the cold war, does it make sense to search for general rules or guidelines for policymakers? In the period since the NATO bombing of Kosovo, a number of scholars, practitioners, and international bodies have attempted to devise criteria that could be used by the Security Council to assist its decision-making in situations of humanitarian crises.[2] Many believe such a checklist would make the Council more effective and less likely to equivocate, as it did so tragically in the case of Rwanda. Furthermore, codification of criteria would reduce the perceived gap between law and morality with respect to interventions for humanitarian purposes, thereby increasing the legitimacy of international law. ICISS has devoted much energy to this task, and proposed two concrete steps for moving the debate forward: a General Assembly resolution embodying the notion of the 'responsibility to protect', and new Security Council guidelines for responding to military interventions with a humanitarian purpose—including agreement to suspend use of the veto in such situations (ICISS 2001a: 74–5).

But while attractive on the surface, there are a series of challenges associated with codifying such criteria. As the 'restrictionist' international lawyers would argue, any exercise that attempts to articulate legitimate instances of intervention could reverse the progress made by the UN to outlaw the use of force in international society.[3] Indeed, by creating a new right of humanitarian intervention in certain cases, there is a risk of more frequent resort to intervention in less compelling circumstances. As Jane Stromseth argues, the current system reduces this probability because 'states engaging in humanitarian intervention know that they have an extraordinarily high burden of justification' (Stromseth 2003: 257).

The second problem facing codification is that the current hegemon in the international system, the United States, is strongly opposed to establishing criteria that might tie its hands in the future. At the Security Council retreat of May 2002, where the ICISS recommendations were discussed, the USA was noticeably unenthusiastic about the debate.[4] US reluctance to support any written guidelines for humanitarian intervention derives from two different sets of concerns: its desire to avoid entanglements that do not directly affect its national interests, and its insistence that in cases where US military action is necessary it must be free to interpret notions such as 'last resort' and 'proper authority' on its own terms. The inability to solve the 2003 Iraq crisis through diplomacy, or to obtain an additional Security Council resolution explicitly authorizing force, will only strengthen US opposition to those proposing codification.

Finally, by putting our energies into establishing firm criteria, we divert our attention from the heart of the problem: how states and organizations operationalize them. Even supposedly clear guidelines such as 'large scale' or 'extreme emergency' are not foolproof; they are ultimately subject to political judgement. In 1999, Kosovo certainly constituted 'extreme' for some in the international community, though not for others (notably China, India, and Russia). Chechnya has not crossed the threshold for anyone, despite the fact that the level of abuse of civilians was and is substantially higher here than it was in Kosovo prior to intervention. In the end, checklists can only represent necessary, and not sufficient, conditions for a decision to intervene.[5] Despite the wish of academics and civil servants to establish ideal scenarios, the unruly processes of argument and discussion within the Security Council, and within the military councils of individual states, remain the key factors determining the future incidences of interventions for humanitarian purposes.[6]

10.2   The aftermath of 11 September

In the midst of the debate on humanitarian intervention among lawyers, international relations scholars, and policymakers, the world's attention was captured by the horrific attacks on New York and Washington on 11 September 2001. For many, those events and their aftermath have superseded the international community's concern about the plight of individuals in situations of humanitarian emergency, and placed more fundamental concerns about survival at the top of the policy agenda.[7] As Canadian Ambassador to the UN Paul Heinbecker has put it, while the interventions in Kosovo and East Timor were all about protecting the vulnerable 'other', in Afghanistan and Iraq, the motivation was protecting 'self'.[8] This fact helps to explain, for example, why the international community failed to extend the security coverage offered by the international stabilization force beyond Kabul after the fall of the Taliban; the suffering of civilians elsewhere in the country was clearly a lower priority for the interveners.[9]

As Nick Wheeler suggested in Chapter 3, one reading of 11 September also appears to reverse the momentum behind the norm of sovereignty as responsibility. Indeed, in the course of waging war on terrorism, the powers of sovereign states within their jurisdictions have been increased. In the United States, the new Patriot Act allows the government to detain aliens without charge for seven days, and members of identified terrorist organizations can be deported or barred from entering the country without judicial review. In the UK, the Anti-Terrorism Crime and Security Act allows the secretary of state to reject asylum claims of people deemed to be a threat to national security, broadens the state's authority to detain suspected terrorists, and curtails appeals by asylum seekers.

In addition, the experience of 11 September and the requirements of the war on terror may have dampened Western states' enthusiasm for criticizing the treatment of civilians within other sovereign jurisdictions. Interestingly, states that were previously subject to international criticism for internal repression have skilfully deflected attention by labelling their actions as 'counter-terrorist'. Before 11 September, Western states largely rejected Russia's depiction of its war in Chechnya as a counter-terrorist operation. Yet, Russia's rapid closing of ranks with the United States in the struggle against Al-Qaeda quickly resulted in a marked diminution in official criticism from Western governments. China also has sought to deploy the discourse of anti-terrorism to deflect criticism of its campaign of repression in Xinjiang. And Israel has effectively associated its campaign against Palestinian groups in the Occupied Territories with the global campaign against terror.

Nonetheless, I would argue that the issues surrounding humanitarian intervention that we have discussed in this volume will continue to preoccupy scholars and statesmen engaged with the broader war on terrorism. First, it is clear that post-cold war changes in the conception of sovereignty remain relevant in a post-11 September world. As Simon Chesterman observed in the last chapter, the terrorist acts of 2001 brought home to Western states the reality that instability within or collapse of a state anywhere in the world can have implications that reach far wider than that particular region. This is true not only for failed states such as Somalia or Afghanistan, but also for a country such as Pakistan, which accepted the assistance of outside powers that had a stake in its ability to control rebel and terrorist forces. Addressing the challenges posed by failed states has become a crucial plank in Western states' strategies for combating new security threats (Rotberg 2002: 127–40).

Second, the debate over humanitarian intervention has revived the just war discussion about what constraints—if any—should be placed on the use of force in international society. These just war principles, which pertain to both just cause and just conduct, animated much of the commentary on the use of force in Afghanistan and Iraq. Hence, while George W. Bush proclaimed that 'there are no rules'[10] in the war against the perpetrators of 11 September, concerns were expressed within the certain segments of the international community about proportionality and protection of civilians in the military campaign against Al-Qaeda and the Taliban.[11] Similarly, much of the opposition to the so-called second resolution on Iraq stemmed from the belief that diplomacy had not been exhausted fully and that the USA and UK were, therefore, contravening the just war principle of 'last resort'.[12]

Questions about 'proper authority', which were so central to the post mortem discussions on Kosovo, continue their prominence in discussions about the role of the Security Council in authorizing the use of force by states. As Inis Claude observed almost four decades ago, one of the major functions of the UN in international society is its role as a 'collective legitimiser' (Claude 1966: 367–79). Yet, the failure to obtain Council authority in recent cases of military action (most notably Kosovo and Iraq), coupled with the ineffectiveness of the UN in the face of genocide in Rwanda, has led critics to investigate alternative mechanisms and institutions for ensuring peace and security in the twenty-first century. The full implications of the breakdown of the Security Council consensus on Iraq are only starting to become clear. But according to many American commentators, this episode could spell the end of US willingness to work within the multilateral constraints of the UN system for a generation.[13] Historians may come to view the Kosovo intervention as the first step on the road to a post-Security Council era.

More fundamentally, the crisis over Iraq highlighted growing concerns about the implications of the new 'Bush Doctrine'[14] and the potential erosion of the normative framework on the use of force established by the UN Charter. While virtually all states accepted the invocation of Article 51 by the United States as the rationale for its military action in Afghanistan,[15] the UN was torn apart on the question of whether war against Iraq in March 2003 was justified under the rules of the Charter. What is noteworthy about this debate on 'just cause', however, is the degree to which humanitarian rationales were voiced by American and British officials to bolster public support for an attack against Saddam Hussein[16]—even though the primary *casus belli* was Iraq's possession of weapons of mass destruction in contravention of UN resolutions. Initially, the depiction of the crisis over Iraq gave very little prominence to the suffering of civilians; instead, it focused on the threat to potential interveners. Yet, as opposition to military action continued, and the weakness of the link between Saddam Hussein and Al-Qaeda was exposed, figures such as Tony Blair began to trumpet the moral case for war to a population desperate for a compelling reason to put Western soldiers at risk. When the military campaign concluded, and the mass graves containing Saddam's opponents were unearthed, pro-war Western commentators pointed to further evidence that regime change had been warranted. Others were quick to jump on this practice as a cynical manipulation of Western publics, and there is a strong case to be made against viewing the Iraqi campaign as a humanitarian intervention. But the practices of Blair and Bush can also be viewed as evidence of the powerful sway that humanitarian claims have in contemporary international society. In fact, David Rieff has contended that in the post-cold war era it has become virtually impossible for a Western democracy to wage war 'without describing it to some extent in humanitarian terms' (Rieff 2002: 240).

Finally, the experience of the international community in reconstruction efforts after humanitarian interventions could yield valuable lessons for the casualties of the war on terror—namely, Afghanistan and Iraq. In fact, the Bush Administration's thinking on nation-building has gone through a significant evolution, from expressly eschewing any interest in nation-building at the outset of the Afghanistan campaign[17] to actively planning for a post-war Iraq well before the massive bombing campaign of March 2003. The pressure from European allies (particularly the UK) and representatives of humanitarian organizations, combined with a greater public interest in 'winning the peace', help to explain the transformation. Thus, while the experience of intervention in Somalia had spurred the United States into a frantic search for exit strategies, the discussion over the shape of military action in Iraq incorporated—not without controversy—a significant element of follow-through and rebuilding. This metamorphosis suggests that the responsibilities of intervening states—whether for humanitarian purposes or as part of the war on terror—have expanded beyond just cause and just conduct to include an ambitious programme of social and political reconstruction. Although this enlarged sense of duty carries significant costs and implications for the states and organizations engaged in reviving failed states, it also shifts our perspective to that of victims rather than interveners. As the ICISS report persuasively argues, such a perspective 'refocuses the international searchlight back where it should always be: on the duty to protect communities from mass killing, women from systematic rape and children from starvation' (ICISS 2001a: 17). Perhaps, by taking on the viewpoint of the victim, those with the power and capability to intervene can finally balance the desire to resist evil against the dangers of succumbing to righteousness.

NOTES

1   Introduction

1. There are a series of publications that address different aspects of the debate: Hoffmann (1996); Mayall (ed.) (1996); Ramsbotham and Woodhouse (1996); Wheeler (2000); and Holzgrefe and Keohane (2003).
2. For the relationship between humanitarian intervention and international law, see Tesón (1997); Gray (2000); Independent International Commission on Kosovo (2000); Chesterman (2001).
3. The standard legal definition is *the use of armed force by one or more states or international bodies in another state without the consent of its authorities with the purpose of preventing widespread suffering or death among the inhabitants.* See Abiew (1999: 18).
4. Holzgrefe and Keohane, for example, restrict their focus to unauthorized humanitarian interventions. See Holzgrefe and Keohane (2003: 1).
5. One of the strongest criticisms can be found in Rieff (2002).

2   Limiting Sovereignty

1. By 'military intervention' I refer to one of the two types of coercive humanitarian intervention in the useful revised typology in Ramsbotham and Woodhouse (1996: 115), namely, forcible military humanitarian intervention. Their other type of coercive humanitarian intervention, coercive non-military, consists of sanctions.
2. For a classic statement, see Waldron (1981: 21–39).
3. Some would characterize the NATO bombing of Serbia in 1999 as behaviour change first, rule change later.
4. Bull (1984a: 3, 1984b: 195). The important difference between 'carried out by' and 'expresses the collective will of', that is, process and substance, is briefly discussed in Shue (1998a: 60–84).
5. Ramsbotham and Woodhouse (1996: 35). They have just indicated that they are using 'international society of states' in the sense of the 'English school' to contrast with an anarchical 'international system of states'.
6. It is, of course, not the case that where there are duty-imposing rules, there are rights. See Campbell (1975: 285–94).
7. Nothing follows about equality. Clearly there can be—I think, is—a system with unequal rights. That only means that there must be unequal duties. What there cannot be is a system with some rights and no duties.
8. Miller (1995: 108). Some other theorists reject the idea of universal basic rights altogether. Although that position can make for other interesting philosophical

debates up to a point, the debates are purely academic because, in practice, no serious policymaker ever proceeds on the assumption that some people have no rights at all, or that their most fundamental rights are totally alien to our own understandings. (In the latter case, we would be more likely to think we were mistranslating their language.) Miller's more nuanced and moderate position is much more valuable to consider.

9. For valuable reflections on how default duties might be spelt out, see ICISS (2001*a*) and Chapter 4, this volume by Jennifer Welsh.

10. For a deep exploration of these matters in terms of 'pathological homogenization' in the course of state-building, see Rae (2002).

11. The first of the 'core principles' formulated by the ICISS is 'State sovereignty implies responsibility, and the primary responsibility for the protection of its people lies with the state itself' (ICISS 2001*a*: p. XI).

12. For the many weaknesses of the Convention, see Damrosch (1998: 256–79). On 2 September 1998, the International Criminal Tribunal for Rwanda, meeting in Arusha, Tanzania, handed down the first convictions for genocide, which were against a former Rwandan district mayor, Jean-Paul Akayesu. On 1 May 1998, a former Rwandan government minister, Jean Kambanda, had accepted culpability for genocide; and he became on 4 September 1998 the first person to be sentenced for genocide (www.ictr.org).

13. I would be delighted to learn that this is not true. The text is readily available in, for example, Brownlie (ed.) (1992: 31–4).

14. A valuable collection of documents is in United Nations (1996). See S/1994/470 (20 April 1994) [Document 48, pp. 262–5] and SC Res 912 (21 April 1994) [Document 52, pp. 268–9].

15. See Rome Statute of the International Criminal Court, part 2, Article 6 (United Nations, A/Conf. 183/9 (17 July 1998), available at www.un.org/icc/romestat.htm and Wippman (2000: 85–104).

16. One revealing recent study is Barnett (2002).

17. It may, indeed, be that the current international norms were, in effect, projected outward by the dominant states—for a rich and fascinating argument for such a thesis, see Reus-Smit (1999).

18. France, of course, sent Opération Turquoise into Rwanda, but, intentionally or unintentionally, it did much more to rescue the killers than their victims. See Adelman and Suhrke (1996); Prunier (1997: chapter 8).

19. Also consider the UN abandonment of officially designated and partially disarmed 'safe area' Srebrenica a little over a year later, in July 1995; or, the hasty US pull-out from Somalia a few months before the pull-out from Kigali. A tradition seems to be forming: deserting defenceless people whenever as many as ten US or European peacekeepers are killed or in danger. (Ten Belgian peacekeepers were tortured to death and mutilated during the first night of the Rwandan genocide, evidently with the intention of precipitating the pull-out promptly voted by the Security Council. Planning documents leaked months earlier to the UN [the 'Black File'] had included the murder of European peacekeepers as part of the strategy, in accord with the Mogadishu precedent. See Adelman and Suhrke 1996.)

20. One is tempted to maintain that if among outside states Belgium and France have the most to answer for historically, any reasonable assignment of default duties to protect would move next to them. However, precisely because of their previous involvements, they also seem in many respects the least appropriate parties to be counted upon to do the right things—consider, for instance, Opération Turquoise. These are questions I will not pursue here. For the role of France (and others) in supplying arms, see 'Arming Rwanda: The Arms Trade and Human Rights Abuses in the Rwandan War', *Human Rights Watch Arms Project*, 6/1 (January 1994); 'Rwanda/Zaire—Rearming with Impunity: International Support for the Perpetrators of the Rwandan Genocide', *Human Rights Watch Arms Project*, 7/4 (May 1995) and Melvern (2000).
21. I repeat myself—see Shue (2003).
22. Compare the complementary argument in Buchanan (1993: 241).

3   The Humanitarian Responsibilities of Sovereignty

1. Prominent works include Fierke (1998); Finnemore and Sikkink (1998); Kratochwil (1989); and Wendt (1999).
2. There are important ontological differences between realist and Marxist theories, with the former emphasizing how states are guided by their interests, and the latter explaining such interests as a product of the power exercised by one social class within the state over subordinate classes. It is a crude Marxism that reduces the agency of the state solely to the machinations of class interests, but all variants on Marxism share a commitment to the idea that dominant economic classes have a pivotal influence on the foreign and defence policies of the state. See Linklater (1990).
3. Wendt (1999: 286). He gives the example of the UN-authorized US-led coalition that evicted Iraq from Kuwait for its violation of the sovereignty norm in 1991.
4. This conception of legitimacy refers to the moral understandings of the actors. The problem with this conception of legitimacy is that it tells us nothing about the normative value of the norm, or why it should be adhered to. As Ian Hurd puts it, 'saying a rule is accepted as legitimate by some actor says nothing about its justice in the eyes of an outside observer'. See Hurd (1999: 381).
5. Habermas accepts that it is impossible to eliminate differences of power and privilege in dialogical encounters. But he argues that the more these can be removed from the process, the freer the communication process can be. See Habermas (1993: 163).
6. See Chapter 5 in this volume for further discussion.
7. For a detailed discussion of this case, see Wheeler (2000: 55–78).
8. Author's interview with Sir David Hannay, March 1999. For a fuller discussion see Wheeler (2000: 141–6).
9. Sir David Hannay considers that the African states supported this action because they felt terrible 'shame. . . at what was happening in Somalia. A feeling that Africa was being found wanting and that every African solution that had been tried had failed'. Interview with Sir David Hannay, March 1999.

10. The Chinese Foreign Minister, Tang Jixuan, speaking at the United Nations in September 1999, stated that 'respect for sovereignty and non-interference are the basic principles governing international relations and any deviation from them would lead to a gunboat diplomacy that would wreak havoc in the world' (quoted in Barbara Crossette, 'General Assembly Opens Debate', *New York Times*, 23 September 1999).

11. Chomsky (1999: 11). Chomsky's position should be distinguished from the one espoused by Carr since Chomsky's argument relies on the notion that state elites are consciously abusing humanitarian values for their own ends. By contrast, Carr's critique of internationalism does not rest on the assumption that actors deliberately abuse such claims.

12. For a fuller discussion see Wheeler (2000: 147–52, 164–6).

13. I am grateful to Christian Reus-Smit for suggesting these tests.

14. I am excluding Cuba because it was already subject to crippling economic sanctions by the US.

15. This is the term used by Stephen Krasner to describe how states can always find a convenient pretext to justify action. See Krasner (1999: 63–5).

16. The Independent International Commission on Kosovo concluded that NATO's action 'was illegal but legitimate'. See Independent International Commission on Kosovo (2000: 4).

17. This was especially the case given the views of Russia and China that both the Serbs and the Kosovo Liberation Army (KLA) were responsible for the violence, and that all non-violent means had not been exhausted.

18. As Michael J. Matheson, the Acting Legal Advisor to the State Department later recalled, the rationale for intervention in Kosovo was a 'pragmatic basis for moving forward without establishing new doctrines or precedents that might trouble individual NATO members or later haunt the alliance if misused by others' (quoted in Johnstone, forthcoming).

19. The only NATO state to offer an explicit legal defence of NATO's intervention was the UK. For a discussion of the British position see Stromseth (2003).

20. Sofaer (2000: 16). This point is echoed by Roberts who argues that 'States engaging in interventions on humanitarian grounds, especially in the absence of Security Council authorization, act in a situation of legal and political precariousness, and it may be right that they should have that burden on their shoulders' (Roberts 2002).

21. The idea of applying the concept of mitigation to cases of humanitarian intervention was suggested in the early 1970s by Ian Brownlie. See Brownlie (1973: 146).

22. As Jane Stromseth puts it, 'NATO states did not argue "we are breaking the law but should be excused for doing so". Instead, NATO states, in sometimes differing ways, explained why they viewed their military action as "lawful"— as having a legal basis within the normative framework of international law' (Stromseth 2003: 244).

23. Speech by the Foreign Secretary, Robin Cook, to the American Bar Association lunch, QE II Conference Centre, London, 19 July 2000. (Available at http://www.ukun.org)

24. As Michael Byers and Simon Chesterman put it, 'States are not champing at the bit to intervene in support of human rights around the globe, prevented only by an intransigent Security Council and the absence of clear criteria to intervene without its authority. The problem, instead, is the absence of the will to act at all.' Byers and Chesterman (2003: 202).
25. Tony Blair, speech to the Labour Party Conference (2 October 2001), available at www.cnn.com/2001/WORLD/europe/10/02/ret.blair.address.
26. In launching 'Operation Enduring Freedom' on 7 October 2001, Bush declared: 'The oppressed people of Afghanistan will know the generosity of America and its allies. As we strike military targets, we'll also drop food, medicine and supplies to the starving and suffering men and women and children of Afghanistan.' See 'President Bush announces military strikes in Afghanistan' (7 October 2001), US Department of State International Information Programmes, available at www.usinfo.state.gov/regional/eur/terrorism/bush1007.htm.

4 Taking Consequences Seriously: Objections to Humanitarian Intervention

1. See also his treatment of the history of humanitarian intervention in Wheeler (2000).
2. Solidarism (and its counterpart Pluralism) was originally coined by Hedley Bull in Bull (1966).
3. As Wheeler notes in Chapter 3, one of the earliest articulations of 'sovereignty as responsibility' can be found in Deng et al. (eds.) (1996). Samuel Barkin adopts a similar approach in arguing that the meaning of sovereignty has shifted from control over territory (the cold war understanding) to the ability to guarantee the human rights of citizens. See Barkin (1998).
4. Henry Shue, Chapter 2, this volume.
5. Tzevtan Todorov, 'Right to Intervene or Duty to Assist?', The Oxford Amnesty Lectures: Human Rights, Human Wrongs, 1 February 2001.
6. A discussion of the legal positions can be found in the Independent International Commission on Kosovo (2000).
7. For a useful summary of contending legal approaches, see Holzgrefe (2003: 36–49).
8. I am referring here to Article 2(4) of the Charter, which requires members of the UN to 'refrain in their international relations from the threat or use of force against the territorial integrity or political independence of any State'.
9. See Schachter (1984: 646). The Charter prohibition on the use of force is also supported by subsequent UN declarations, such as the 1965 General Assembly Declaration on the Inadmissibility of Intervention and the 1970 General Assembly Declaration on Friendly Relations and Cooperation among States. The latter states plainly: 'No State of group of States has the right to intervene, directly or indirectly, for any reason whatever, in the internal or external affairs of any other State.' These declarations are viewed by many international lawyers as

authoritative interpretations of the Charter that contribute to the development of customary law. See, for example, Gray (2000: 5); Cassese (2001: 292).

10. Article VI of the Convention states that persons charged with genocide 'shall be tried by a competent tribunal of the State in the territory of which the act was committed, or by such international penal tribunal as may have jurisdiction with respect to those Contracting Parties which shall have accepted its jurisdiction'. As from 1 July 2002 the International Criminal Court could constitute such a tribunal.

11. Schabas (2000: 498). Schabas argues that several members of the Security Council, and in particular the Permanent Members, were extremely reluctant to use the word 'genocide' in a resolution concerning the Rwandan crisis, for fear that it 'would impose an obligation to act to prevent the crime'. Schabas (2000: 495).

12. There was a high level of debate around Article VIII during the drafting process of the Genocide Convention, including the argument that the Article should be deleted since its concerns were already dealt with under the collective security provisions of the UN Charter. See Schabas (2000: 502).

13. Legal realism posits a process of interaction between original texts and state behaviour that can lead to changes in the law. The 'classical view' of international law, by contrast, adopts a close textual analysis and contends that laws can change only through expiration or state consent. See Holzgrefe (2003: 38).

14. An example of this argument can be found in Reisman (1985).

15. The restrictionists would include Brownlie (1991); Gray (2000); Hilpold (2001); Byers and Chesterman (2003).

16. See, for example, Tesón (1997); Cassesse (1999); Greenwood (2000).

17. As Byers and Chesterman argue, 'Since clear treaty provisions prevail over customary international law, an ordinary customary rule allowing intervention is not sufficient to override Article 2(4). The only way intervention for purposes beyond those of self-defence of collective security could be considered legal is if such interventions had acquired the status of *jus cogens*' (Byers and Chesterman 2003).

18. See, for example, GA Res 2131 (1965); GA Res 2625 (1970); and GA Res 46/182 (1991).

19. The objective of the ECOWAS force (launched in August 1990) was not only to establish a ceasefire, but also to 'stop the senseless killing of innocent civilian nationals and foreigners, and to help the Liberian people to restore their democratic institutions'. See UN Doc. S/21485. In November of 1992, when fighting broke out between ECOWAS troops and forces loyal to Charles Taylor (and spilled over into neighbouring Sierra Leone), the Security Council adopted Resolution 788 under chapter VII.

20. This reasoning convinced China to refrain from the use of its veto with respect to Northern Iraq.

21. As Adam Roberts demonstrates in Chapter 5, there are two possible substitutes for Security Council authority: the General Assembly (articulated in Articles 10 and 11 of the Charter, and implemented through the 'Uniting for Peace' Resolution of 1950); and regional organizations (as laid out in chapter VIII of

the Charter). As Roberts shows, both of these alternatives to the Security Council have drawbacks and are of questionable legal status. See Chapter 5, pp. 85–6.

22. Adam Roberts, Chapter 5, p. 91. I have addressed the legitimacy of the Security Council in more detail elsewhere. See 'Authorising Humanitarian Intervention', in Price and Zacher (2004).

23. There is a burgeoning literature on the topic of international administrations. See, for example, Shain and Linz (1995); Chopra (1999); Caplan (2002); Chesterman (2002b).

24. For a further discussion of 'prescriptive realism' see Mason and Wheeler (1996).

25. 'The immediate existence of the state as the ethical substance, that is, its right, is directly embodied not in abstract but in concrete existence, and only this concrete existence, rather than any of those many universal thoughts which are held to be moral commandments, can be the principle of its action and behaviour' (Hegel 1991: 370). For a critique of the 'Hegelian Myth', see Tesón (1997: chapter 3).

26. Buchanan (1999). See also Nardin (2001: 64–5).

27. John Rawls, *A Theory of Justice*, cited in Buchanan (1999: 83). 'Natural duty' refers to a duty that individuals have independently of any special arrangement or institutional role.

28. The Constructivist account of interest formation can be found in Finnemore (1996); Wendt (1999).

29. For an analysis of Mill's position, see Vincent (1974).

30. The following arguments from Walzer can be found in Walzer (1980).

31. See, especially, the arguments by David Luban in Beitz (ed.) (1985: 195–216).

32. Walzer (2000: 101–8). The first of these exceptions was also advocated by Mill.

33. It should be noted that the consequentialism being put forth here is 'rule consequentialism'—a policy is right if it accords with a moral code which, if generally accepted, would produce the best consequences—versus 'act consequentialism'—the right policy is that which produces the best consequences. See the discussion of realist consequentialism in Mason and Wheeler (1996).

34. I have elaborated on this distinction between a procedural and substantive conception of legitimacy in Welsh (1995: 3–4).

35. For further discussion of Pluralism's limited notion of consensus, see Mayall (2000).

36. Michael Akehurst's chapter in *Intervention in World Politics* discusses four cases where the right to use force to protect nationals abroad was asserted: Belgium and United States in the Congo (1960 and 1964), the United States in the Dominican Republic (1965), the Israeli raid on Entebbe in Uganda (1976), and US action against Iran (1980). Akehurst (1984).

37. See Barkin (1998). China, for example, has signed on to the Covenant for Civil and Political Rights.

38. A history of this concept is provided by Gerrit W. Gong (1984).

39. For a discussion of developing countries' views on non-intervention, see Thakur (2002).

40. See the comments of Ambassador Shen Guofang (China's Deputy Permanent Representative to the United Nations) on China's decision to abstain on a vote supporting the arms embargo against Serbia. UN Doc. S/PV/3868 (31 March 1998) and SC Res 1160 (31 March 1998). The Chinese response to the NATO bombing of Serbia is summarized by Zhang Yunling (Zhang 2000). In contrast, China supported intervention in East Timor, due to the presence of two key factors: Security Council authorization and host state consent.
41. Zhang (2000: 122). For more on the roots of China's strong adherence to the principle of non-intervention, see Mitter (2003).
42. This distinction between conceptions of justice can be found in Bull (2000: 206–45).
43. Ayoob argues that today's state-builders in Africa and Asia should be allowed to use violence to battle against 'recalcitrant elements' in the same way that Europe or the United States did in past centuries.
44. I am grateful to Ngaire Woods, who helped me to formulate this response.
45. One notable example is China's use of the veto in February 1999 to block a continued UN peacekeeping presence in Macedonia. Commentators believe the veto was due to Macedonia's establishment of diplomatic relations with Taiwan.

5 The United Nations and Humanitarian Intervention

1. I have explored that international legal question more fully in Roberts (2002). Parts of the present survey draw on material in that article.
2. The first public use of the term 'United Nations' was in the title of the 'Declaration of United Nations' issued in Washington DC on 1 January 1942. Text in *Foreign Relations of the United States 1942* (Washington DC: US Government Printing Office), vol. 1: 25–6 (1960). (This series is referred to henceforth as *FRUS*.)
3. President Franklin D. Roosevelt, Statement to the Press, 15 June 1944. *FRUS 1944, General*, vol. 1: 643 (1966).
4. Chapter VIII(A)(7) of the document entitled 'Proposals for the Establishment of a General International Organisation', released on 9 October 1944 and published in *The Dumbarton Oaks Conversations on World Organisation, 21st August–7th October, 1944: Statement of Tentative Proposals* (London: HMSO, Cmd. 6560) (1944: 6); also in Russell (1958: 1019–28).
5. See, for example, Woodward (1971: 212, 217); Reynolds and Hughes (1976: 166–7); *FRUS 1942*, vol. I (1960: 21, 23).
6. Prof Karl Doehring, section on self-determination, in Simma (ed.) (2002: 63).
7. Prof Albrecht Randelzhofer, section on Article 2(4) of UN Charter, in Simma (ed.) (2002: 131). However, he goes on to suggest (p. 132) that if in the future there is a pattern of interventions to stop violations of humanitarian law, as in the Kosovo case, then 'eventually, a rule of customary international law might develop, making humanitarian intervention lawful'.

8. 1948 Genocide Convention, Article VIII. For a critical view of the provisions and working of the Convention see Kuper (1982: 36–9, 174–85).

9. In the ICTY/ICTR/ICC statutes, genocide is addressed in Articles 4/2/6, respectively; and crimes against humanity in Articles 5/3/7.

10. 'Universal Declaration of Human Rights', GA Res 217A (III) (10 December 1948), adopted with forty-eight in favour, none against, eight abstaining (Byelorussian SSR, Czechoslovakia, Poland, Saudi Arabia, South Africa, USSR, Ukrainian SSR, and Yugoslavia) and two absent (Honduras and Yemen).

11. The main agreements in the field are usefully collected in Brownlie (ed.) (1992).

12. 'Declaration on the Inadmissibility of Intervention in the Domestic Affairs of States and the Protection of Their Independence and Sovereignty', annexed to GA Res 2131 (XX) (21 December 1965).

13. For a judicious interpretation of these provisions of international humanitarian law, surveying the ways in which they can provide a basis for enforcement action by states and the UN, see Boisson de Chazournes and Condorelli (2000: 67–87).

14. For an authoritative account of the origins and meanings of common Article 1 see Kalshoven (2000: 3–61). This presents conclusive evidence that the negotiators at Geneva in 1949, in drawing up Article 1, did not have in mind anything approaching a legal right of parties to take action regarding violations in conflicts in which they were not involved. However, the author does accept that a moral if not legal right along the lines indicated has emerged.

15. The four 1949 Geneva Conventions on the Protection of Victims of War, Articles 49/50/129/146.

16. On the limits of the so-called 'universal jurisdiction' see the judgment of the International Court of Justice in the case of *Democratic Republic of the Congo* v. *Belgium*, 14 February 2002, available at www.icj-cij.org.

17. For an indication of just how extensive the use of vetoes was to stop Security Council resolutions that would have condemned particular interventions during the cold war, see Patil (1992: pp. viii–ix).

18. These three resolutions were vetoed on 4, 5, and 13 December 1971, respectively. Patil (1992: 207–14).

19. GA Res 2793 (7 December 1971), on Question considered by the Security Council at its 1606th, 1607th and 1608th meetings on 4, 5, and 6 December 1971. Despite this diplomatic defeat, New Delhi continued its military operations in East Pakistan until the Pakistani Army surrendered. On 'Uniting for Peace', see the discussion of authorization below, pp. 85–6.

20. SC Res 232 (16 December 1966), imposing sanctions on Southern Rhodesia; and SC Res 418 (4 November 1977), imposing an arms embargo on South Africa.

21. GA Res 43/131 (8 December 1988). See also the virtually identical terms of GA Res 45/100 (14 December 1990). A further resolution, GA Res 46/182 (19 December 1991) on 'Strengthening of the Co-ordination of Humanitarian Emergency Assistance of the United Nations', sometimes cited in discussions of a right of humanitarian assistance, contains as Guiding Principle 3 of its Annex an exceptionally strong and clear recognition of the sovereignty and territorial integrity of states.

22. See, for example, the report of the XVIIth Round Table of the Institute of Humanitarian Law, San Remo, on 'The evolution of the right to assistance' (1992) and Guicherd (1999: 22). In both these sources there is also reference to the practice of the UN Security Council, for example, in demanding that parties to a particular conflict should cooperate with international bodies in the delivery of humanitarian aid, as evidence of a right to assistance.

23. See Brownlie (1963), esp. at pp. 341–2 and 345. Also Ronzitti (1985: pp. xviii–xix, 108). Ronzitti explicitly excludes from his study the question of whether humanitarian intervention authorized by the UN Security Council is admissible.

24. Works published in the 1970s and 1980s reflecting a broadly favourable view of humanitarian intervention include Lillich (ed.) (1973), which contains as an appendix (pp. 197–221) an impressive paper by Jean-Pierre L. Fonteyne on 'Forcible Self-Help by States to Protect Human Rights: Recent Views from the United Nations'; Rufin (1986); Verwey (1986); and Tesón (1988).

25. The intervention in Albania was carried out by the Italian-led multinational protection force (MPF) in April–August 1997, having been authorized by SC Res 1101 (28 March 1997). The resolution defined the purpose of the mission as 'to facilitate the prompt delivery of humanitarian assistance, and to help create a secure environment for the missions of international organizations in Albania, including those providing humanitarian assistance'.

26. *Report of the Secretary-General pursuant to General Assembly resolution 53/35: The Fall of Srebrenica*, UN Doc A/54/549, New York (15 November 1999); and *Report of the Independent Inquiry into the Actions of the United Nations during the 1994 Genocide in Rwanda*, attached to UN Doc S/1999/1257, New York (16 December 1999). The report on Srebrenica is the more detailed and impressive of the two.

27. Barnett (2002: x, 4). The author, an academic, was on a year's secondment as a political officer of the US Mission to the UN, starting in late summer 1993.

28. SC Res 794 (3 December 1992) on Somalia; and SC Res 940 (31 July 1994) on Haiti.

29. See, for example, the hesitant conclusions on the international legal basis of non-Security Council based military action in two post-Kosovo War reports: the October 1999 Danish report on *Humanitarian Intervention: Legal and Political Aspects* (Danish Institute of International Affairs, 1999: 121–30); and UK House of Commons Foreign Affairs Committee (2000: para 132).

30. On 3 November 1950 the Western powers, needing continued support for their military action in Korea, secured the passage of GA Res 377 (V), known as the Uniting for Peace resolution, which stated that 'if the Security Council, because of lack of unanimity of the permanent members, fails to exercise its primary responsibility for the maintenance of international peace and security in any case where there appears to be a threat to peace, breach of the peace, or act of aggression, the General Assembly shall consider the matter immediately with a view to making appropriate recommendations to Members for collective measures, including in the case of a breach of the peace or act of aggression the use of armed force when necessary...'

31. Rule 83 of the Rules of Procedure of the General Assembly. Text in Von Mangoldt and Rittberger (eds.) (1997: 91).

32. The texts of Kofi Annan's major speeches on the subject were reprinted in pamphlet form in Annan (1999*a*).
33. Angela Kane (Director, Americas and Europe Division, UN Department of Political Affairs), address at Marshall Center, Garmisch, 16 May 2000.
34. Boutros-Ghali (1992: para 17). The report did not discuss humanitarian intervention directly, and its discussion of peace enforcement assumes that such action is in response to 'outright aggression, imminent or actual' (Boutros-Ghali 1992: para 44).
35. See, for example, GA Res 53/144 (9 December 1998), 'Declaration on the Right and Responsibility of Individuals, Groups and Organs of Society to Promote and Protect Universally Recognized Human Rights and Fundamental Freedoms', which emphasizes individual human rights, but at the same time stresses that 'the prime responsibility and duty to promote and protect human rights and fundamental freedoms lie with the state'.
36. On the complex range of considerations that led to the intervention in Haiti in 1994 see Malone (1998).
37. ICISS (2001*a:* 11–18). The report also refers more generally to a 'responsibility to react' (ICISS 2001*a:* 29).
38. Glennon (2001). This is a sustained and serious critique of the *jus ad bellum* as it developed in the course of the twentieth century. See also Glennon (2002).
39. *The National Security Strategy of the United States of America*, Washington DC, the White House, September 2002, covering letter of 17 September 2002 and p. 7, available at www.whitehouse.gov/nsc/nss.pdf.
40. For details of these two reports see above, n. 26.
41. *Report of the Panel on United Nations Peace Operations*, contained in UN Doc A/55/305 (21 August 2000), p. x. Lakhdar Brahimi is the former foreign minister of Algeria.
42. See esp. Caplan (2002). Caplan concentrates on operations in Eastern Slavonia, Bosnia, Kosovo, and East Timor. See also the useful discussions of international administration in *Report of the Panel on United Nations Peace Operations* (2000: para 76–83) and ICISS (2001*a:* 43–5).
43. For evidence of a sober approach, see Mayall (ed.) (1996), esp. pp. 18–24.

6   Humanitarian Intervention in the Balkans

1. The use of 'humanitarian' to describe a military intervention, whatever its motives and justification, raises a number of problems for humanitarian organizations. Recognizing this, ICISS uses 'military intervention for human protection purposes' instead of 'humanitarian intervention' and the concept of a responsibility to protect rather than a right of humanitarian intervention. See ICISS (2001*a*).
2. Article 70 of Protocol I additional to the Geneva Conventions of 12 August 1949 sets out the key principles, albeit in a specific not general context. The Protocol was adopted on 8 June 1977.
3. There are different views as to whether humanitarian organizations should be neutral. Neutrality, in the sense of not taking sides or engaging in controversy

of a political, religious, or ideological nature, is one of the core principles of the International Red Cross Movement. Throughout the conflicts covered in this chapter, UNHCR publicly denounced actions that caused human suffering and blocked relief, identifying the side or group responsible when this was known from first-hand observation, and urging that these be prevented or halted. The common reaction to the frequent direct interventions with a political leadership so implicated was either to challenge UNHCR's facts or to blame 'uncontrolled elements' (but not to question UNHCR's competence to make such interventions). UNHCR sought to avoid statements that could be taken to suggest what type of political or military action was an appropriate response by the international community.

4. Formally, the General Framework Agreement for Peace, initialled in Dayton and signed in Paris on 14 December 1995.

5. An important addition, Magaš and Žanić (eds.) (2001), makes the views of some key participants from within the region available in English. It sheds new light on matters relevant to the role of the international community, and convincingly places this less centrally than is generally the case in the accounts of outsiders.

6. The distinction is largely one of cultural identity and religion: the majority of the inhabitants of the former Yugoslavia are of the same Slav origin.

7. Initially a description of those in favour of a multi-ethnic Bosnia, who identified themselves as Bosnians, but with time increasingly used to describe Bosnian Muslims.

8. The report of the Secretary-General to the General Assembly on the fall of Srebrenica (A/54/549, 15 November 1999) also provides a chronological account of events leading up to the NATO air strikes.

9. The UN Transitional Administration for Eastern Slavonia, Baranja, and Western Sirmium (UNTAES) was established by SC Res 1037 (1996) of 15 January and disbanded 2 years later.

10. From SC Res 713 (1991) to SC Res 1021 (1995) at the conclusion of the Dayton peace agreement, the Security Council adopted 83 resolutions on the former Yugoslavia. From 1993, the majority invoked chapter VII of the UN Charter, which covers action with respect to threats to and breaches of the peace, and acts of aggression.

11. The Contact Group of representatives of France, Germany, the Russian Federation, the UK, and the USA was established in April 1994, initially with responsibility for negotiating a peace agreement for Bosnia. Italy became the sixth member during the Kosovo crisis.

12. In *Peacemonger*, Marrack Goulding's account of his experiences as the UN Under-Secretary-General responsible for peacekeeping, he writes that Sarajevo was favoured in the belief that its choice might have a stabilizing effect in Bosnia and on the grounds of impartiality (Goulding 2002: 309). However, the fact that Sarajevo was at that time a safer location than any in or nearer UNPROFOR's then operational area, the Croatian-Serb-controlled UN Protected Areas in Croatia, must also have been a consideration.

13. The case that this is not just arguable but demonstrable, and that the humanitarian action was a tool, is forcefully put by Simms (2001).

14. The first UNHCR Special Envoy, José-María Mendiluce, was asked in a Newsweek interview (7 June 1993) how he came to terms with the fact that UNHCR was an unwilling participant in ethnic cleansing by evacuating civilians from areas that the Serbs were attempting to purge of Muslims. He replied, 'I prefer to have 50,000 more refugees than 50,000 more bodies... when you are confronted with terrified people who are knocking on your door and say, "Please, help us to leave," this debate is finished'.

15. Responsibilities that he combined with those of Co-chairman of the International Conference until the end of 1993. Yasushi Akashi replaced him as SRSG in January 1994.

16. The UNHCR Special Envoy was based in the region and responsible for the humanitarian operation.

17. SC Res 819 of 16 April 1993 had established Srebrenica as a 'safe area'; in SC Res 824 of 6 May the Council declared that 'Sarajevo, and other such threatened areas, in particular the towns of Tuzla, Zepa, Gorazde, Bihac, as well as Srebrencia, and their surroundings should be treated as safe areas by all the parties concerned and should be free from armed attacks and from any other hostile act'. Both resolutions recalled the mandate of UNPROFOR and 'in that context' invoked chapter VII. SC Res 836 was adopted acting under chapter VII with no qualifications as to context.

18. In a report requested by the Security Council (S/1994/555 (9 May 1994)), the Secretary-General provided a detailed analysis of these contradictions and described their practical consequences for UNPROFOR. The report recommended specific approaches ('improvements in the short term'), and requested approval and authorization from the Council. It was not acted on by the Council.

19. This question is often accompanied by questions about the use of outside military forces to provide protection for humanitarian workers. UNPROFOR provided area protection where it could and close protection for convoys in some of the more dangerous locations. The risks run by humanitarian workers are great, and action to increase their protection is vital. However, it seems unlikely that outside governments would agree to deploy their forces into conflict zones, even with the (also unlikely) consent of the parties to the conflict, solely for the purpose of protecting humanitarian workers. And if they did, the concerns outlined in this paragraph might become relevant.

20. From an early stage in the war in Bosnia, there were powerful voices in the USA advocating the 'lift and strike' option. In late July and early August 1995 clear majorities in both Houses of the US Congress voted in favour of unilaterally lifting the arms embargo, an action that was vetoed by President Clinton. For a detailed account of the evolution of US policy on the Balkans during the 1990s, see Halberstam (2001). For a detailed rebuttal of the European, and especially British, arguments in favour of the embargo, see Simms (2001).

21. UNHCR published regular statistics on asylum seekers as reported by governments and on its estimates of numbers displaced within Kosovo and elsewhere in the FRY. These figures were used in the UN Secretary-General's reports to the Security Council.

22. Although the joint statement was initially partly successful in this aim, demands for respect of President Milošević's commitments therein, which included 'not to carry out any repressive action against the peaceful population', increasingly became a formal requirement and condition for a negotiated settlement. For example, SC Res 1199 of 23 September 1998 reproduced the text of the commitments in the joint statement and called for their full implementation.

23. For example, in its 8 August 1998 edition, *The Economist* noted, 'Unless he is restrained by some outside force—and NATO is the only available candidate— the likelihood is that Mr Milošević will offer the Kosovars neither a ceasefire nor partition. He will simply bulldoze his way through all of Kosovo, whatever the cost in human lives and regional peace.'

24. In *Waging Modern War*, General Wesley Clark writes 'Resolution 1199 was adopted under Chapter VII of the U.N. Charter, authorizing member nations to use "all available means" to enforce it. While not explicit, this was U.N. code for the use of force if necessary' (2001: 134). Chapter VII sets out the circumstances in which the Security Council may authorize the use of force, but the text of the resolution does not even imply such authority. General Clark goes on to describe the informal meeting of NATO defence ministers held the day the resolution was adopted, which led to the threat of air strikes.

25. In his UN press conference on 30 September, the outgoing President of the Security Council (the Swedish Permanent Representative) said that the 10 September UNHCR briefing had made starkly clear that the international community was facing a humanitarian disaster in Kosovo; following that briefing, the majority of Council members had underlined the need to take action. He went on to describe the adoption of SC Res 1199. (It may be noted that in Security Council discussion on Kosovo the representatives of China and the Russian Federation at times appeared to take the position that humanitarian reports should be limited to the problem and not address its causes.)

26. At that time, UNHCR estimated there were more than 200,000 persons displaced by the conflict within Kosovo, including over 10,000 still in the open. Directly after visiting some 3,000 of the latter on 26 September, the High Commissioner expressed her deep concern at what she herself had seen in a letter addressed to President Milošević and handed for delivery to one of his senior ministers.

27. In the 1991 census, the ethnic Albanian population of Kosovo (most of whom boycotted it) had been estimated at 1.6 million, out of a total of 1.9 million.

28. From 1993 to 1995 the UNSRSG had overall responsibility for all UN activities in the Balkans. He respected UNHCR's role and did not seek to influence its conduct of the humanitarian operation. This is, however, an issue that can create problems, sometimes compounded by the presence of non-governmental humanitarian organizations concerned to preserve their own independence.

29. After the FRY was denied automatic continuation of the SFRY's UN membership, the HIWG was the only UN-related forum to which it was invited and

which it continued to attend, even during the NATO action against the FRY over Kosovo.

30. ICISS (2001*a*). A synopsis of the principles is given on pages xi–xiii.

7   Humanitarian Intervention and International Society: Lessons from Africa

1. Jackson defined juridical sovereignty as the recognition of independence by other states and international institutions. He contrasted the new states whose sovereignty in many cases was juridical only with the empirical sovereignty enjoyed by established states where external recognition reflected a government's effective control of the state's territory and its population. See Jackson (1990).
2. For accounts of this process see Zartman (1966); Mayall (1971).
3. At a meeting held in Maputo by the International Commission on Intervention and State Sovereignty (ICISS), many participants argued that Africa had been marginalized by the Security Council, citing the contrast between the level of resources devoted to the Balkans with the failure to raise $150 million to support sub-regional peacekeeping efforts in Liberia. On the other hand Africa is the only continent whose general security problems have twice been the subject of Ministerial meetings of the Security Council, in 1997 and 1998. See ICISS (2001*b*: 362–5).
4. The OAU is the only international organization that not only required its members to oppose all forms of colonialism and neo-colonialism but also required them to be non-aligned in the cold war. Two events triggered the reconciliation of inter-African differences that preceded the signing of the OAU Charter in May 1963. The first was the Evian Agreements, which brought the Algerian rebellion to an end, with the result that West African troops were no longer involved in fighting a colonial war. The second was the decision of the United Nations Operation in the Congo (ONUC), engineered by the United States, to end Katanga's secession by enforcing its reintegration into the Congolese state.
5. This was the fate of Alaba Ogunswano, later Professor of Politics at the University of Lagos and Nigerian High Commissioner to Botswana, but then a PhD student at the London School of Economics. Ogunswano was arrested while conducting research in Tanzania on Chinese assistance to Tanzania and Zambia in the construction of the Tanzam railway. His release, some three weeks later, followed the personal intervention of the President.
6. For text see Kirk-Greene (ed.) (1971: 429–39).
7. For an example of this view, see Ayoob (2002).
8. For an analysis of some of their reactions, see Schnabel and Thakur (eds.) (2000: 213–70).
9. Non-Aligned Movement, XIII Ministerial Conference, Cartage, Columbia (8–9 April 2000), para 263. See also para 11 in which NAM member states reiterated their 'firm condemnation of all unilateral military actions including

those made without proper authorisation of the United Nations Security Council'. For text, see, www.nam.gov.za.

10. For the full text of the report of the Secretary-General on the establishment within the OAU of a Mechanism for Conflict Prevention, Management, and Resolution, see OAU Information Services Publication, Series II, *Resolving Conflicts in Africa* (1993). The Report was adopted in Cairo by the 29th Assembly of Heads of State and Government on 29 June 1993.

11. Examples would include Namibia, Mozambique, and the dispute between Ethiopia and Eritrea.

12. The reason is that the centralized state is a recent and exotic import in a largely nomadic society that was—and to a considerable extent still is—structured in terms of a shifting pattern of inter-clan competition and conflict. The ideological principle is identical to that expressed in the Bedouin Arab maxim: 'Myself against my brother; my brother and I against my cousins; my cousins and I against the world.' For more detailed accounts, see Lewis (1982; 1993).

13. Report of the Secretary-General to the Security Council (18 October 2002), S2002/1180.

14. For the text of these reports, see S/2001 (7 September 2001) and S/2001. Add.1. (10 September 2002); S/2002/267 (14 March 2002) and S/2002/987 (5 September 2002).

15. For an account of these events, see Hirsch (2001).

16. See Mayall (ed.) (1996: 23–4). A similar argument, in relation to the British Empire alone, is developed by Niall Ferguson (2003: 258–70).

8   International Intervention in East Timor

1. See Chapter 4, this volume, p. 56.

2. Department of Foreign Affairs and Trade (2000); National Security Archive, East Timor Revisited: Ford, Kissinger and the Indonesian Invasion, 1975–6, available at www.gwu.edu/%7Ensarchiv/NSAEBB/NSAEBB62.

3. My own account is in Martin (2001). See also Greenlees and Garran (2002); Marker (2003).

4. The official account of the development of Australian policy is in Department of Foreign Affairs and Trade (2001). See also Downer (2000); Greenless and Garran (2002).

5. The letter is quoted in full and its context is described by Tim Fischer, Deputy Prime Minister of Australia at the time it was written, in his *Seven Days in East Timor* (2000: 9–18).

6. Quoted in Greenlees and Garran (2002: 93), where there is a detailed account of the internal discussions within the Indonesian government.

7. This was the position consistently expressed by the then Australian Labour Party Shadow Minister of Foreign Affairs, Laurie Brereton. See also Maley (2000). The Australian debate is most fully reflected in the hearings and *Final Report on the Inquiry into East Timor* of the Senate Foreign Affairs, Defence and

Trade References Committee, available at www.aph.gov.au/senate/committee/ fadt_ctte/East%20Timor.
8. The full text of the Agreements is in *Report of the Secretary-General*, UN document A/53/951-S/1999/513 (5 May 1999). They consist of Annex I, 'Agreement between the Republic of Indonesia and the Portuguese Republic on the question of East Timor' (the main Agreement), to which is appended 'A constitutional framework for a special autonomy for East Timor' (the autonomy proposal); Annex II, 'Agreement regarding the modalities for the popular consultation of the East Timorese through a direct ballot' (the modalities Agreement); and Annex III, 'East Timor popular consultation' (the security Agreement). They are reproduced without the text of the autonomy proposal in Martin (2001: appendix 3). On the security issue in the negotiations, see Marker (2003: 150–5); Samuel (2003: 211–13).
9. The United Nations Mission in East Timor, mandated on 11 June 1999 by SC Res 1236 (1999).
10. The official UN account of this is in *Report of the Secretary-General regarding the Act of Self-Determination in West Irian*, A/7723 (6 November 1969). For a devastating critique, see Saltford (2002).
11. On the role of the Core Group, see Martin (2001: 129–30). Its functioning is more fully described and its significance assessed in Penny Wensley, Ambassador and Permanent Representative of Australia to the UN, New York, Speech, East Timor and the United Nations, Sydney (23 February 2000).
12. *Report of the Panel on United Nations Peace Operations*, A/55/305-S/2000/809 (21 August 2000), para 51, p. 9.
13. For an account of the Secretary-General's telephone diplomacy over this period, see Shawcross (2000: 390–7).
14. The mission's meetings are summarized in *Report of the Security Council Mission to Jakarta and Dili, 8 to 12 September 1999*, S/1999/976 (14 September 1999). More atmospheric accounts of the meetings can be found in a series of articles in the London *Independent*, 9–13 September 1999, by David Usborne, a journalist who accompanied the mission.
15. Ministers from Australia, Canada, Chile, Japan, Korea, Mexico, New Zealand, Peru, Philippines, Singapore, Thailand, United Kingdom, and United States; senior officials from Papua New Guinea, Vietnam, People's Republic of China, Russia, Malaysia, Brunei Darusalam, and Indonesia itself: Media Briefing, Auckland, 9 September.
16. Indonesia's senior representative present was Ginandjar Kartasasmita, Coordinating Minister for Economy, Finance and Industry.
17. On Australia's objectives and diplomacy during this period, see Department of Foreign Affairs and Trade (2001). See also Downer (2000); Wensley, Speech 'East Timor and the United Nations', 23 February 2000; Greenlees and Garran (2002).
18. Twenty-two countries ultimately participated in INTERFET: Australia (5,592 troops), Brazil (51), Canada (736), Denmark (2), Egypt (71), France (643), Fiji (189), Germany (81), Ireland (43), Italy (560), Jordan (707), Kenya (240), Malaysia (30), New Zealand (1,190), Norway (6), the Philippines (604), Portugal (285), the Republic of Korea (436), Singapore (275), Thailand (1,748), the United Kingdom (335), and the United States (639).

9 Humanitarian Intervention and Afghanistan

1. For an exhaustive defence of this position, see Franck (2001). See now Franck (2002).
2. See Chapter 1, this volume, p. 3.
3. For a discussion of the reconstruction role being played by the UN, see Chesterman (2002*a*).
4. President George W. Bush, Remarks by the President Upon Arrival at Barksdale Air Force Base (11 September 2001), available at www.whitehouse.gov/news/releases/2001/09/20010911-1.html.
5. President George W. Bush, Remarks by the President to Employees at the Pentagon (17 September 2001), available at www.whitehouse.gov/news/releases/2001/09/20010917-3.html.
6. The General Assembly condemned the 'heinous acts of terrorism' but did not refer to them as attacks. It also implicitly urged a judicial rather than military response: GA Res 56/1 (18 September 2001).
7. NATO Secretary-General Lord Robertson, Statement at NATO Headquarters (2 October 2001), available at www.nato.int/docu/speech/2001/s011002a.htm.
8. Proclamation 7463, 66 Fed. Reg. 48, 201 (18 September 2001).
9. Authorization for Use of Military Force, Pub. L. No. 107-40, 115 Stat. 224 (2001).
10. President George W. Bush, Address Before a Joint Session of the Congress on the United States Response to the Terrorist Attacks of September 11, 37 Weekly Comp. Pres. Doc. 1347, 1348 (20 September 2001) [Bush, Joint Address].
11. Bush, Joint Address, 1349.
12. Letter dated 7 October 2001 from the Permanent Representative of the United States to the United Nations Addressed to the President of the Security Council, UN Doc S/2001/946 (7 October 2001).
13. The term 'state-building' is often preferred in this context. For present purposes, 'nation-building' will be used as this was the term invoked during the US Presidential campaign and in the operations being discussed. See Chesterman (2002*b*: 46–7).
14. President George W. Bush, Remarks by the President in Roundtable Interview with Foreign Press (17 July 2001), available at www.whitehouse.gov/news/releases/2001/07/20010718.html.
15. George W. Bush, Remarks by President Bush and Prime Minister Koizumi of Japan in Photo Opportunity (25 September 2001), available at www.whitehouse.gov/news/releases/2001/09/20010925-1.html.
16. Press Briefing by Ari Fleischer (4 October 2001), available at www.whitehouse.gov/news/releases/2001/10/20011004-12.html.
17. George W. Bush, President Holds Prime Time News Conference (11 October 2001), available at www.whitehouse.gov/news/releases/2001/10/20011011-7.html. In the course of the US military action, there was considerable discussion about the role that the UN would play in post-conflict Afghanistan. Some feared that the UN would be handed a poisoned chalice once the United States had completed its military objectives; others eagerly looked forward to the 'next big mission' and a dominant role for the UN in rebuilding Afghanistan on the model of Kosovo and East Timor. These expectations were

tempered by the challenging security environment and the decision by major states contributing forces to the International Security Assistance Force (ISAF) to limit their presence to the capital city of Kabul and its immediate vicinity. Under the leadership of Lakhdar Brahimi, architect of the Bonn process, the UN mission adopted the guiding principle that it should first and foremost bolster Afghan capacity—both official and non-governmental—and rely on as limited an international presence and as many Afghan staff as possible. This has come to be referred to as the 'light footprint' approach: see Chesterman (2002a).

18. George W. Bush, Remarks by the President to United Nations General Assembly (10 November 2001), available at www.whitehouse.gov/news/releases/2001/11/20011110-3.html. Cf. Franck (2001).

19. George W. Bush, State of the Union Address (29 January 2002), available at www.whitehouse.gov/news/releases/2002/01/20020129-11.html.

20. UN Charter, Article 2(4). See, generally, Chesterman (2001).

21. In the *Corfu Channel Case*, for example, the United Kingdom claimed that an intervention in Albanian territorial waters was justified on the basis that no other state was prepared to deal with the threat of mines planted in an international strait. The International Court of Justice rejected this argument in unequivocal terms, but held that a declaration of illegality was itself a sufficient remedy for the wrong: [1949] ICJ Reports 4, 35–6. Similarly, after Israel abducted Adolf Eichmann from Argentina to face criminal charges, Argentina lodged a complaint with the Security Council, which passed a resolution stating that the sovereignty of Argentina had been infringed and requesting Israel to make 'appropriate reparation'. Nevertheless, 'mindful' of the concern that Eichmann be brought to justice, the Security Council clearly implied that 'appropriate reparation' would not involve his physical return to Argentina: S/4349 (1960); SC Res 138 (1960).

22. For a thorough discussion of these issues, see Chesterman (2001).

23. Although this latter species of military action is sometimes considered in the same breath as unilateral humanitarian intervention, Council authorization changes the legal questions to which such action gives rise. See, generally, Chesterman (2001: 112–218).

24. Chesterman (2001: 109): 'Either the States taking such action or other States in a position to react to it, must have behaved so that their conduct is "evidence of a belief that this practice is rendered obligatory by the existence of a rule of law requiring it"' (quoting *North Sea Continental Shelf Cases* [1969] ICJ Reports 3).

25. See generally Murphy (1996: 83–281). Other examples sometimes cited include Belgian intervention in the Congo (Léopoldville) (1960), Belgian and US intervention in the Congo (1964), US intervention in the Dominican Republic (1965), Israeli intervention in Uganda (the Entebbe Operation) (1976), Belgian and French intervention in Zaïre (1978), French intervention in the Central African Empire/Republic (1979), US intervention in Grenada (1983), and US intervention in Panama (1989–90).

26. Such justifications are important, as they may provide evidence of change in the law. As the International Court of Justice has observed: 'The significance

for the Court of cases of State conduct *prima facie* inconsistent with the principle of non-intervention lies in the nature of the ground offered as justification. Reliance by a State on a novel right or an unprecedented exception to the principle might, if shared in principle by other States, tend towards a modification of customary international law': *Nicaragua (Merits)* [1986] ICJ Reports 14, 109. Some authors reject this understanding of international law. On this approach, see Byers and Chesterman (2003).

27. For a discussion of the Nigeria-led ECOWAS actions in Liberia and Sierra Leone, see Chesterman (2001: 134–7, 155–6).

28. SC Res 688 (1991), which condemned the repression of the Iraqi civilian population in the wake of the Gulf War, was the first of the fourteen resolutions on Iraq *not* adopted under chapter VII of the UN Charter (enabling the Council to authorize the use of force). SC Res 1199 (1998), which demanded action to improve the humanitarian situation in Kosovo, explicitly stated that, 'should the concrete measures demanded in this resolution . . . not be taken, [the Council has decided to] consider further action and additional measures'.

29. See, for example, SC Res 1373 (2001), preamble: *'Reaffirming* the inherent right of individual or collective self-defence as recognized by the Charter of the United Nations as reiterated in resolution 1368 (2001)'.

30. But see Anthony Aust, Legal Counsellor, FCO, statement before HC Foreign Affairs Committee, 2 December 1992, *Parliamentary Papers*, 1992–3, HC, Paper 235-iii, p. 85, reprinted in *British YBIL* vol. 63: 827 (1992). This was one of a number of rationales given for the no-fly zones in Iraq. See Chesterman (2001: 196–206).

31. The strength of these agencies sometimes complicated the reconstruction effort under the Bonn Process, as agencies were asked to submit themselves to varying degrees of oversight by embryonic institutions: Chesterman (2002a: 41).

32. See Bowett (1972: 10); *Corfu Channel* case [1949] ICJ Rep 4, 35; *Nuclear Weapons* [1996] ICJ Rep 226, 246, para 46; Declaration on Friendly Relations, GA Res 2625(XXV) (1970) ('States have a duty to refrain from acts of reprisal involving the use of force.'). Cf. Levenfeld (1982: 40).

33. Secretary-General Presents His Annual Report to the General Assembly, UN Doc SG/SM/7136-GA/9596, 20 September 1999. This and other speeches on intervention have been collected in Annan (1999a).

34. For a discussion of earlier periods, Chesterman (2001: 7–44).

35. In addition to actions by Israel and Russia, cited above, see, for example, Human Rights Watch Press Release, 'Uzbekistan: US Cautioned on New Ally' (4 October 2001), available at www.hrw.org/press/2001/10/uzbek1004.htm.

36. SC Res 1373 (28 September 2001). See now www.un.org/terrorism.

37. In 1999, the Council had imposed sanctions against the Taliban regime for failing to hand over Osama bin Laden to face an indictment by the United States for, *inter alia*, the 7 August 1998 bombings of the United States embassies in Nairobi, Kenya, and Dar es Salaam, Tanzania: SC Res 1267 (1991).

38. Kofi A. Annan, 'Opening Remarks' (International Peace Academy: Humanitarian Action Symposium, New York, 20 November 2000), available at www.ipacademy.org.

39. The National Security Strategy of the United States of America (President of the United States, Washington, DC, September 2002), available at www.white-house.gov/nsc/nss.html, 6.

40. For a useful discussion on the responsibilities that a veto-wielding power bears, see ICISS (2001a) (pointing the way toward a 'code of conduct' for the use of the veto). On the question of Council authorization, see further Chesterman (2001: 112–218).

41. The five criteria were the following: Are we sure of our case? Have we exhausted all diplomatic options? Are there military options we can sensibly and prudently undertake? Are we prepared for the long term? And do we have national interests involved? Cf. Vaclav Havel's statements that NATO's intervention was 'probably the first war that has not been waged in the name of "national interests," but rather in the name of principles and values': Havel (1999: 4, 6).

10   Conclusion: Humanitarian Intervention after 11 September

1. For more on the so-called 'lead nation model', see Ryan (2002: 23–44).

2. Examples would include: Wheeler (2000), former British Foreign Minister Robin Cook, Guiding Humanitarian Intervention (19 July 2000), available at www.fco.gov.uk and the ICISS (2001a). The six ICISS criteria are (1) *just cause*: Military intervention is an exceptional measure, only to be undertaken in extreme humanitarian emergencies; (2) *right intention*: The primary motive of the military action must be humanitarian; (3) *last resort*: All non-military options must be explored before force is used; (4) *proportional means*: The nature of the force used must be proportionate to the humanitarian objective, and limited in scale and intensity; (5) *reasonable prospects*: The operation must have a reasonable chance of success, and negative consequences of force must not outweigh the consequences of inaction; and (6) *right authority*: Military action should be authorized by the UN Security Council.

3. Chesterman is representative of this view that establishing further exceptions to Article 2(4), and designing criteria to regulate them, would be detrimental to larger efforts to develop an international rule of law. See Chesterman (2001: 229–32).

4. It should be noted that other Security Council members were also concerned about committing to criteria. According to the British and French ambassadors, there was widespread opinion in the meeting that if new situations emerged—for example, in Burundi or the Congo—the five permanent members and broader Council would lack the political will to deliver troops and would restrict themselves to condemnatory resolutions. Similarly, Russia expressed strong reservations about any codified guidelines that would limit its use of the veto. 'La Russie s'oppose a un "usage raisonne" du droit du veto', *Le Monde*, 3 June 2002.

5. Adam Roberts, 'Intervention: Suggestions for Moving the Debate Forward', Submission to the International Commission on Intervention and State Sovereignty, Roundtable, London, 3 February 2001.

6. As this book went to press, the proponents of ICISS were conceding that any formal kind of codification—whether a legally binding convention or amendment to the UN Charter—are both unlikely and unwise. Instead of pushing for the issue to be placed on the UN agenda, the Canadian government has attempted to gain support for the ICISS recommendations on a regional basis—particularly, in Africa and Asia. In the former case, the inclusion by the African Union and SADC in their organizational charters of explicit provisions for intervention to curb genocide, war crimes, and crimes against humanity is potentially very significant.

7. See, for example, Gaddis (2001: 14).

8. The Responsibility to Protect: Galvanizing Support for Responsible International Action, Notes for Remarks by Ambassador Paul Heinbecker, Wilton Park, 11 February 2003.

9. I am grateful to Nicholas Morris for emphasizing this point.

10. George W. Bush, Press Conference, 17 September 2001.

11. Conservative estimates are that several thousand Afghan civilians died as a consequence of the US military campaign. This has led critics such as Noam Chomsky to question the inhibiting effects of humanitarian norms. See Chomsky (2001). For a critical assessment of how far the United States lived up to its humanitarian claims in Afghanistan, see Nicholas J. Wheeler (2003).

12. For more on the applicability of the just war framework to the war on terror, see Rengger (2002: 360–1).

13. See, for example, William Safire, 'No, the UN is paralysed, as usual', *International Herald Tribune*, 11 March 2003.

14. The elements of the doctrine were expressed in an early form by President Bush in his January 2002 State of the Union Address. They were later codified in the *The National Security Strategy of the United States of America*, available at www.whitehouse.gov/nsc/nss.pdf. For more on the implications of the doctrine, see Farer (2003: 53–89).

15. The support for US action was exemplified by Security Council Resolution 1368, which recognized the right of states to individual and collective self-defence, and Resolution 1373 (taken under chapter VII) which made it obligatory for states to cooperate in the fight against terrorism.

16. See, for example, Remarks By the President in Address to the Nation, 17 March 2003, available at www.whitehouse.gov/news/releases/2003/03/20030317-7.html. In his address, President Bush declares: 'Many Iraqis can hear me tonight in a translated radio broadcast, and I have a message for them. If we must begin a military campaign, it will be directed against the lawless men who rule your country and not against you. As our coalition takes away their power, we will deliver the food and medicine you need. We will tear down the apparatus of terror and we will help you to build a new Iraq that is prosperous and free.'

17. See Simon Chesterman, Chapter 9.

BIBLIOGRAPHY

Abiew, Francis Kofi (1999). *The Evolution of the Doctrine and Practice of Humanitarian Intervention*. The Hague: Kluwer Law International.

Adelman, Howard and Suhrke, Astri (1996). *Early Warning and Conflict Management. Volume 2. The International Response to Conflict and Genocide: Lessons from the Rwanda Experience*. Copenhagen: DANIDA.

Akehurst, Michael (1984). 'Humanitarian Intervention', in Hedley Bull (ed.), *Intervention in World Politics*. Oxford: Oxford University Press, 95–118.

Annan, Kofi A. (1999a). *The Question of Intervention: Statements by the Secretary-General*. New York: United Nations Department of Public Information.

——(1999b). *Preventing War and Disaster: A Growing Global Challenge*. New York: United Nations Department of Public Information.

——(2000). *We the Peoples: The Role of the United Nations in the 21st century*. New York: United Nations.

Ayoob, Mohammed (2002). 'Humanitarian Intervention and State Sovereignty'. *International Journal of Human Rights*, 6/1: 81–102.

Barkin, Samuel (1998). 'The Evolution of the Constitution of Sovereignty and the Emergence of Human Rights Norms'. *Millennium*, 27/2: 229–52.

Barnett, Michael (2002). *Eyewitness to a Genocide: The United Nations and Rwanda*. Ithaca: Cornell University Press.

Beitz, Charles (ed.) (1985). *International Ethics: A Philosophy and Public Affairs Reader*. Princeton: Princeton University Press.

Boisson de Chazournes, Laurence and Condorelli, Luigi (2000). 'Common Article 1 of the Geneva Conventions Revisited: Protecting Collective Interests'. *International Review of the Red Cross*, 82/837: 67–88.

Boutros-Ghali, Boutros (1992). *An Agenda for Peace: Preventive Diplomacy, Peacemaking and Peace-keeping*. New York: United Nations.

Bowden, Mark (1999). *Black Hawk Down: A Story of Modern War*. New York: Atlantic Monthly Press.

Bowett, Derek W. (1972). 'Reprisals Involving Recourse to Armed Force'. *American Journal of International Law*, 66/1: 1–36.

Brownlie, Ian (1963). *International Law and the Use of Force by States*. Oxford: Clarendon Press.

——(1973). 'Thoughts on Kind-Hearted Gunmen', in Lillich (ed.), 139–48.

——(1991). *International Law and the Use of Force by States*. Oxford: Clarendon Press.

——(ed.) (1992). *Basic Documents on Human Rights*, 3rd edn. Oxford: Clarendon Press.

Buchanan, Allen (1993). 'The Morality of Inclusion', *Social Philosophy & Policy*, 10/2: 233–57.

——(1999). 'The Internal Legitimacy of Humanitarian Intervention'. *Journal of Political Philosophy*, 7/1: 71–87.

Bull, Hedley (1966). 'The Grotian Conception of International Society', in Herbert Butterfield and Martin Wight. (eds.), *Diplomatic Investigations: Essays in the Theory of International Politics*. Cambridge, MA: Harvard University Press, 51–74.

——(1984*a*). 'Introduction', in Hedley Bull (ed.), *Intervention in World Politics*. Oxford: Oxford University Press, 1–5.

——(1984*b*). 'Conclusion', in Hedley Bull (ed.), *Intervention in World Politics*. Oxford, Oxford University Press, 181–95.

——(2000). 'Justice in International Relations: The 1983 Hagey Lectures, in Kai Alderson and Andrew Hurrell (eds.), *Hedley Bull on International Society*, Basingstoke: Macmillan, 206–45.

Burke, Edmund (1981). 'Reflections on the Revolution in France', in Paul Langford (ed.), *The Writings and Speeches of Edmund Burke*, vol. VIII. Oxford: Oxford University Press.

Byers, Michael (2002). 'Terrorism, the Use of Force and International Law After 11 September'. *International and Comparative Law Quarterly*, 51/2: 401–14.

——and Chesterman, Simon (2003). 'Changing the Rules About Rules? Unilateral Humanitarian Intervention and the Future of International Law', in J. L. Holzgrefe and Robert O. Keohane (eds.), 177–203.

Campbell, T. D. (1975). 'Perfect and Imperfect Obligations'. *The Modern Schoolman*, LII: 285–94.

Caplan, Richard (2002). *A New Trusteeship? The International Administration of War-torn Territories*. IISS Adelphi Paper 341. Oxford: Oxford University Press.

Carr, E. H. (1939). *The Twenty Years Crisis, 1919–1939: An Introduction to the Study of International Relations*. London: Macmillan.

Cassese, Antonio (1999). 'Ex Iniuria Ius Oritur: Are We Moving Towards International Legitimation of Forcible Humanitarian Countermeasures in the World Community?' *European Journal of International Law*, 10/1: 23–30.

——(2001). *International Law*. Oxford: Oxford University Press.

Chesterman, Simon (1999). 'Rethinking Panama: International Law and the US Invasion of Panama, 1989', in Guy S. Goodwin-Gill and Stefan A. Talmon (eds.), *The Reality of International Law: Essays in Honour of Ian Brownlie*. Oxford: Oxford University Press.

——(2001). *Just War or Just Peace? Humanitarian Intervention and International Law*. Oxford: Oxford University Press.

——(2002*a*). 'Walking Softly in Afghanistan: The Future of UN State-Building'. *Survival*, 44/3: 37–46.

——(2002*b*). 'East Timor in Transition: Self-Determination, State-Building and the United Nations'. *International Peacekeeping*, 9/1: 43–72.

Chomsky, Noam (1999). *The New Military Humanism: Lessons from Kosovo*. Monroe: Common Courage Press.

——(2001). *9–11*. New York: Seven Stories Press.

Chopra, Jarat (1999). *Peace Maintenance: The Evolution of International Political Authority*. London: Routledge.

Clark, Wesley K. (2001). *Waging Modern War: Bosnia, Kosovo, and the Future of Combat*. New York: Public Affairs.

Claude, Inis L. Jr. (1966). 'Collective Legitimization as a Political Function of the United Nations'. *International Organization*, 20/3: 367–79.

Cortright, David and Lopez, George A. (2002). *Sanctions and the Search for Security: Challenges to UN Action: A Project of the International Peace Academy*. Boulder: Lynne Rienner.

D'Amato, Anthony (1990). 'The Invasion of Panama was a Lawful Response to Tyranny'. *American Journal of International Law*, 84/2: 516–24.

Damrosch, Lori Fisler (1999). 'Genocide and Ethnic Conflict', in David Wippman (ed.), *International Law and Ethnic Conflict*. Ithaca: Cornell University Press, 256–79.

Danish Institute of International Affairs (1999). *Humanitarian Intervention: Legal and Political Aspects*. Copenhagen: Danish Institute of International Affairs.

Deng, Francis M. (1993). *Protecting the Dispossessed: A Challenge to the International Community*. Washington, DC: Brookings Institution.

—— (1995). 'Frontiers of Sovereignty'. *Leiden Journal of International Law*, 8/2: 249–86.

——, Sadikiel Kimaro, Terrence Lyons, Donald Rothchild, and I. William Zartman (eds.) (1996). *Sovereignty as Responsibility: Conflict Management in Africa*. Washington, DC: Brookings Institution.

Department of Foreign Affairs and Trade (2000). *Australia and the Indonesian Incorporation of Portuguese Timor 1974–1976*. Victoria: Melbourne University Press.

—— (2001). *East Timor in Transition 1998–2000: An Australian Policy Challenge*. Canberra: Department of Foreign Affairs and Trade.

Downer, Alexander (2000). 'East Timor—Looking Back on 1999'. *Australian Journal of International Affairs*, 54/1: 5–10.

Evans, Michael (1999) 'Conflict Opens "Way to New International Community"' Blair's Mission; *The Times* 23 April 1999.

Falk, Richard A. (1994). 'The United Nations and the Rule of Law'. *Transnational Law and Contemporary Problems*, 4/2: 611–42.

Farer, Tom (2003). 'Humanitarian Intervention Before and After 9/11', in J. L. Holzgrefe and Robert Keohane (eds.), 53–89.

Ferguson, Niall (2003). *Empire: How Britain Made the Modern World*. London: Allen Lane.

Fierke, Karin M. (1998). *Changing Games, Changing Strategies: Critical Investigations in Security*. Manchester: Manchester University Press.

Finnemore, Martha (1996). *National Interests in International Society*. Ithaca: Cornell University Press.

—— and Sikkink, Kathryn (1998). 'International Norm Dynamics and Political Change'. *International Organization*, 52/4: 887–917.

Fischer, Tim (2000). *Seven Days in East Timor: Ballot and Bullets*. St Leonards NSW: Allen and Unwin.

Fonteyne, Jean-Pierre L. (1974). 'The Customary International Law Doctrine of Humanitarian Intervention: Its Current Validity Under the UN Charter'. *California Western International Law Journal*, 4: 203–70.

Franck, Thomas M. (2001). 'Terrorism and the Rights of Self-Defense'. *American Journal of International Law*, 95/4: 839–43.

—— (2002). *Recourse to Force: State Action Against Threats and Armed Attacks*. Cambridge: Cambridge University Press.

—— (2003). 'Interpretation and Change in the Law of Humanitarian Intervention', in J. L. Holzgrefe and Robert O. Keohane (eds.), 204–31.

Freedman, Lawrence and Boren, David (1992). ' "Safe Havens" for Kurds', in Nigel S. Rodley (ed.), *To Loose the Bands of Wickedness: International Intervention in Defence of Human Rights*, London: Brassey's 43–92.

Gaddis, John Lewis (2001). 'And Now this: Lessons from the Old Era for the New One', in Strove Talbott (ed.), *The Age of Terror: America and the World After September 11*. New York: Basic Books.

Glennon, Michael J. (2001). *Limits of Law, Prerogatives of Power: Interventionism after Kosovo*. New York: Palgrave.

—— (2002). 'The Fog of Law: Self-Defense, Inherence, and Incoherence in Article 51 of the United Nations Charter'. *Harvard Journal of Law and Public Policy*, 25/2: 539–58.

Gong, Gerrit W. (1984). *The Standard of 'Civilisation' in International Society*. Oxford: Clarendon Press.

Goulding, Marrack (2002). *Peacemonger*. London: John Murray.

Gourevitch, Philip (1999). *We Wish to Inform You that Tomorrow We Will Be Killed with Our Families: Stories from Rwanda*. London: Picador.

Gowlland-Debbas, Vera (2000). 'The Functions of the United Nations Security Council in the International Legal System', in Michael Byers (ed.), *The Role of Law in International Politics: Essays in International Relations and International Law*. Oxford: Oxford University Press, 277–313.

Gray, Christine (2000). *International Law and the Use of Force*. Oxford: Oxford University Press.

Greenlees, Don and Garran, Robert (2002). *Deliverance: The Inside Story of East Timor's Fight for Freedom*. Sydney: Allen and Unwin.

Greenwood, Christopher (2000). 'International Law and the NATO Intervention in Kosovo'. *International and Comparative Law Quarterly*, 49/4: 926–34.

Guicherd, Catherine (1999). 'International Law and the War in Kosovo'. *Survival*, 41/2: 19–33.

Habermas, Jürgen (1984). *Theory of Communicative Action: Reason and the Rationalization of Society*. London: Heinemann.

—— (1993). *Justification and Application: Remarks on Discourse Ethics*. Cambridge: Polity Press.

Halberstam, David (2001). *War in a Time of Peace: Bush, Clinton, and the Generals*. New York: Scribner.

Hamilton, Keith (1995). 'Non-intervention Revisited: Great Britain, the United Nations and Franco's Spain in 1946', in *FCO Historians Occasional Papers*. No. 10, London: Foreign and Commonwealth Office, 46–63.

Havel, Vaclov (1999). 'Kosovo and the End of the Nation–State'. *New York Review*, 10 June 1999, 4–6.

Hegel, G. W. F. (1991). *Elements of the Philosophy of Right*. Cambridge: Cambridge University Press.

Hilpold, Peter (2001). 'Humanitarian Intervention: Is There a Need for Legal Reappraisal?' *European Journal of International Law*, 12/3: 437–67.

Hirsch, John L. (2001). *Sierra Leone, Diamonds and the Struggle for Democracy*. Boulder: Lynne Rienner.

Hoffmann, Stanley (1996). *The Ethics and Politics of Humanitarian Intervention.* Notre Dame: University of Notre Dame Press.

Holzgrefe, J. L. (2003). 'The Humanitarian Intervention Debate', in J. L. Holzgrefe and Robert O. Keohane (eds.), 15–52.

—— and Keohane, Robert O. (eds.) (2003). *Humanitarian Intervention: Ethical, Legal and Political Dilemmas.* Cambridge: Cambridge University Press.

Human Rights Watch (1999). *Human Rights Watch World Report 2000.* New York: Human Rights Watch.

Hurd, Ian (1999). 'Legitimacy and Authority in International Politics'. *International Organization,* 53/2: 379–408.

—— (2002). 'Legitimacy, Power, and the Symbolic Life of the UN Security Council'. *Global Governance,* 8: 35–51

ICISS (2001*a*). *The Responsibility to Protect: Report of the International Commission on Intervention and State Sovereignty.* Ottawa: International Development Research Centre.

—— (2001*b*). *The Responsibility to Protect: Research, Bibliography, Background: Supplementary Volume to the Report of the International Commission on Intervention and State Sovereignty.* Ottawa: International Development Research Centre.

Ignatieff, Michael (2003). 'State Failure and Nation-Building', in J. L. Holzgrefe and Robert O. Keohane (eds.), 299–321.

Independent International Commission on Kosovo (2000). *The Kosovo Report: Conflict, International Response, Lessons Learned.* Oxford: Oxford University Press.

Institute of Humanitarian Law, San Remo (1992). Report of the XVIIth Round Table, 'The Evolution fo the Right to Assistance'. *International Review of the Red Cross,* 291: 592–602.

Jackson, Robert (1990). *Quasi-States: Sovereignty, International Relations and the Third World.* Cambridge: Cambridge University Press.

—— (2000). *The Global Covenant, Human Conduct in a World of States.* Oxford: Oxford University Press.

Johnstone, Ian (2003). 'Security Council Deliberations: the Power of the Better Argument'. *European Journal of International Law,* 14/3: 437–80.

Jones, Bruce D. (2001). *Peacemaking in Rwanda: The Dynamics of Failure.* Boulder: Lynne Rienner.

Kalshoven, Frits (2000). 'The Undertaking to Respect and Ensure Respect in All Circumstances: From Tiny Seed to Ripening Fruit', in *Yearbook of International Humanitarian Law 1999,* vol. 2, The Hague: T. M. C. Asser Press, 3–61.

Keohane, Robert O. (2003). 'Political Authority after Intervention', in J. L. Holzgrefe and Robert O. Keohane (eds.), 275–98.

Kirk-Greene, Anthony H. M. (ed.) (1971). *Crisis and Conflict in Nigeria, A Documentary Source Book 1966–1970.* Oxford: Oxford University Press.

Kissinger, Henry (2001). *Does America Need a Foreign Policy? Toward a Diplomacy for the 21st Century.* New York: Simon and Schuster.

Krasner, Stephen D. (1999). *Sovereignty: Organized Hypocrisy.* Princeton: Princeton University Press.

Kratochwil, Friedrich (1989). *Rules, Norms and Decisions: On the Conditions of Practical and Legal Reasoning in International Relations and Domestic Affairs.* Cambridge: Cambridge University Press.

—— (1995). 'Sovereignty as *Dominium*: Is There a Right of Humanitarian Intervention?', in Gene M. Lyons and Michael Mastanduno (eds.), *Beyond Westphalia? State Sovereignty and International Intervention*. Baltimore: Johns Hopkins University Press, 21–42.

Kuper, Leo (1982). *Genocide: Its Political Use in the Twentieth Century*. New Haven: Yale University Press.

Levenfeld, Barry (1982). 'Israel's Counter-Fedayeen Tactics in Lebanon: Self-Defense and Reprisal Under Modern International Law'. *Columbia Journal of Transnational Law*, 21: 1–48.

Lewis, Ioan M. (1982). *A Pastoral Democracy: A Study of Pastoralism and Politics Among the Northern Somali of the Horn of Africa*. New York: Afrikana Press.

—— (1993). *Blood and Bone: The Call of Kinship in Somali Society*. Trenton: Red Sea Press.

Lillich, Richard B. (ed.) (1973). *Humanitarian Intervention and the United Nations*. Charlottesville: University Press of Virginia.

Linklater, Andrew (1990). *Beyond Realism and Marxism: Critical Theory and International Relations*. London: Macmillan.

Lynch, Marc (1999). *State Interests and Public Spheres*. New York: Columbia University Press.

Lyons, Terence and Samatar, Ahmed I. (1995). *Somalia: State Collapse, Multilateral Intervention, and Strategies for Political Reconstruction*. Brookings Occasional Papers. Washington: Brookings Institution.

Magaš, Branka and Žanić, Ivo (eds.) (2001). *The War in Croatia and Bosnia-Herzegovina 1991–1995*. London: Frank Cass.

Maley, William (2000). 'The UN and East Timor'. *Pacifica Review*, 12/1: 63–76.

Malone, David M. (1998). *Decision-Making in the UN Security Council: The Case of Haiti*. Oxford: Oxford University Press.

Marker, Jamsheed (2003). *East Timor: A Memoir of the Negotiations for Independence*. Jefferson: McFarland and Co.

Martin, Ian (2001). *Self-Determination in East Timor: The United Nations, the Ballot and International Intervention*. International Peace Academy Occasional Paper. Boulder: Lynne Rienner.

Mason, Andrew and Wheeler, Nicholas J. (1996). 'Realist Objections to Humanitarian Intervention', in Barry Holdern (ed.), *The Ethical Dimensions of Global Change*. Basingstoke: Macmillan, 94–110.

Mayall, James (1971). *Africa: The Cold War and After*. London: Elek Books.

—— (2000). *World Politics: Progress and Its Limits*. Cambridge: Polity.

—— (ed.) (1996). *The New Interventionism 1991–1994: United Nations Experience in Cambodia, Former Yugoslavia and Somalia*. Cambridge: Cambridge University Press.

Melvern, Linda R. (2000). *A People Betrayed: The Role of the West in Rwanda's Genocide*. Zed Books.

Mill, John Stuart (1875). 'A Few Words on Non-Intervention', in *Dissertations and Discussions: Political, Philosophical, and Historical*, vol. III, 2nd edn. London: Longmans, Green, Reader, and Dyer, 153–78.

Miller, David (1995). *On Nationality*. Oxford: Clarendon Press.

Mitter, Rana (2003). 'Order and Justice: China and the World in Historical Perspective', in Rosemary Foot, John Lewis Gaddis, and Andrew Hurrell (eds.),

Order and Justice in International Relations. Oxford: Oxford University Press, 207–35.

Morgenthau, Hans (1967). 'To Intervene or Not To Intervene'. *Foreign Affairs*, 45/3: 425–36.

Moynihan, Daniel Patrick (1975). *A Dangerous Place*. Boston: Little, Brown and Co.

Murphy, Sean D. (ed.) (2002). 'Contemporary Practice of the United States Relating to International Law'. *American Journal of International Law*, 96/3: 706–35.

—— (1996). *Humanitarian Intervention: The United Nations in an Evolving World Order*. Philadelphia: University of Pennsylvania Press.

Nardin, Terry (2002). 'The Moral Basis of Humanitarian Intervention'. *Ethics and International Affairs*, 16/1: 55–70.

Natsios, Andrew (1996). 'Illusions of Influence: The CNN Effect in Complex Emergencies', in Robert I. Rotberg and Thomas G. Weiss (eds.). *From Massacres to Genocide: The Media, Public Policy and Humanitarian Crises*. Washington DC: Brookings Institution.

Nolte, George (2000). 'The Limits of the Security Council's Powers and Functions in the International Legal System: Some Reflections', in Michael Byers (ed.). *The Role of Law in International Politics: Essays in International Relations and International Law*. Oxford: Oxford University Press, 315–26.

Onuf, Nicholas (1995). 'Intervention for the Common Good', in Gene M. Lyons and Michael Mastanduno (eds.). *Beyond Westphalia? State Sovereignty and International Intervention*. Baltimore: Johns Hopkins University Press, 43–58.

Patil, Anjali V. (1992). *The UN Veto in World Affairs, 1946–1990: A Complete Record and Case Histories of the Security Council's Veto*. Sarasota: UNIFO.

Philpott, Daniel (2001). *Revolutions in Sovereignty: How Ideas Shaped Modern International Relations*. Princeton: Princeton University Press.

Price, Richard and Mark Zacher (eds.). *The United Nations and Global Security*. Basingstoke: Palgrave (2004).

Prunier, Gérard (1997). *The Rwanda Crisis: History of a Genocide*. New York: Columbia University Press.

Rae, Heather (2002). *State Identities and the Homogenisation of Peoples*. Cambridge: Cambridge University Press.

Ramsbotham, Oliver P. and Woodhouse, Tom (1996). *Humanitarian Intervention in Contemporary Conflict: A Reconceptualization*. Cambridge: Polity Press.

Reisman, W. Michael (1984). 'Coercion and Self-Determination: Construing Charter Art 2(4)'. *American Journal of International Law*, 78/3: 642–5.

—— (1985).'Criteria for the Lawful Use of Force in International Law'. *Yale Journal of International Law*, 10: 279–85.

Rengger, Nicholas (2002). 'On the Just War Tradition in the Twenty-first Century'. *International Affairs*, 78/2: 353–63.

Report of the Panel on United Nations Peace Operations. UN Doc A/55/305 (August 2000).

Reus-Smit, Christian (1999). *The Moral Purpose of the State*. Princeton: Princeton University Press.

Reynolds, Philip Alan and Hughes, Emmet John (1976). *The Historian as Diplomat: Charles Kingsley Webster and the United Nations, 1939–1946*. London: Martin Robertson.

Rieff, David (2002). *A Bed for the Night: Humanitarianism in Crisis*. London: Vintage.

Roberts, Adam (1993). 'Humanitarian War: Military Intervention and Human Rights'. *International Affairs*, 69/3: 429–49.

—— (2002). 'The So-Called "Right" of Humanitarian Intervention'. *Yearbook of International Humanitarian Law 2000*, vol. 3, The Hague: T. M. C. Asser Press, 3–51.

Ronzitti, Natalino (1985). *Rescuing Nationals Abroad Through Military Coercion and Intervention on Grounds of Humanity*. Dordrecht: Martinus Nijhoff.

Rotberg, Robert I. (2002). 'Failed States in a World of Terror'. *Foreign Affairs*, 8: 127–40.

Rufin, Jean-Christophe (1986). *Le piège humanitaire*. Paris: Jean-Claude Lattès.

Rummel, Rudolph J. (1996). *Death by Government*. New Brunswick: Transaction Publishers.

Russell, Ruth B. (1958). *A History of the United Nations Charter: The Role of the United States 1940–1945*. Washington, DC: Brookings Institution.

Ryan, Alan (2002). 'The Strong Lead-Nation Model in an *ad hoc* Coalition of the Willing: Operation *Stabilise* in East Timor'. *International Peacekeeping*, 9/1: 23–44.

Saltford, John (2002). *The United Nations and the Indonesian Takeover of West Papua, 1962–1969*. London: Routledge Curzon.

Samuel, Tamrat (2003). 'East Timor: The Path to Self-Determination', in Chandra Lekha Sriram and Karin Wermester (eds.), *From Promise to Practice: Strengthening UN Capacities for the Prevention of Violent Conflict*. Boulder, CL: Lynne Reiner.

Schabas, William A. (2000). *Genocide in International Law: The Crime of Crimes*. Cambridge: Cambridge University Press.

Schachter, Oscar (1984). 'The Legality of Pro-Democratic Invasion'. *American Journal of International Law*, 78/3: 645–50.

Scheffer, David J. (1992). 'Toward a Modern Doctrine of Humanitarian Intervention'. *University of Toledo Law Review*, 23: 253–93.

Schnabel, Albrecht and Thakur, Ramesh (eds.) (2000). *Kosovo and the Challenge of Humanitarian Intervention: Selective Indignation, Collective Action, and International Citizenship*. Tokyo: United Nations University Press.

Shain, Yossi and Linz, Juan J. (1995). *Between States: Interim Governments and Democratic Transitions*. Cambridge: Cambridge University Press.

Shaw, Martin (1996). *Civil Society and Media in Global Crises*. London: Pinter.

Shawcross, William (2000). *Deliver Us From Evil: Peacekeepers, Warlords and a World of Endless Conflict*. New York: Simon and Schuster.

Shue, Henry (1996). *Basic Rights: Subsistence, Affluence, and U.S. Foreign Policy*, 2nd edn. Princeton: Princeton University Press.

—— (1998a). 'Let Whatever Is Smouldering Erupt? Conditional Sovereignty, Reviewable Intervention, and Rwanda 1994', in Albert J. Paolini, Anthony P. Jarvis, and Christian Reus-Smit (eds.), *Between Sovereignty and Global Governance: The United Nations, the State and Civil Society*. London: Macmillan, 60–84.

—— 'Thickening Convergence: Human Rights and Cultural Diversity', in Deen Chatterjee (ed.), *The Ethics of Assistance: Morality and the Distant Needy*. Cambridge: Cambridge University Press (2003).

Simma, Bruno (ed.) (2002). *Charter of the United Nations: A Commentary*, 2nd edn. Oxford: Oxford University Press.

Simms, Brendan (2001). *Unfinest Hour: Britain and the Destruction of Bosnia*. London: Penguin.

Skinner, Quentin (1988). 'Some problems in the Analysis of Political Thought and Action', in James Tully (ed.). Meaning and context: Quentin Skinner and his critics. Cambridge: Polity Press. 97–118.

Sofaer, Abraham (2000). 'International Law and Kosovo'. *Stanford Journal of International Law*, 36: 1–22.

Stromseth, Jane (2003). 'Rethinking Humanitarian Intervention: the Case for Incremental Change', in J. L. Holzgrefe and Robert Keohane (eds.). 232–72.

Tesón, Fernando R. (1988). *Humanitarian Intervention: An Inquiry into Law and Morality*. Dobbs Ferry, New York: Transnational Publishers.

—— (1997). *Humanitarian Intervention: An Inquiry into Law and Morality*, 2nd edn. Dobbs Ferry, New York: Transnational Publishers.

Thakur, Ramesh (2002). 'Intervention, Sovereignty and the Responsibility to Protect'. *Security Dialogue*, 33/2: 323–40.

UK House of Commons, Foreign Affairs Committee (2000). *Fourth Report: Kosovo: Vol. I: Report and Proceedings of the Committee*. London: Stationery Office.

United Nations (1996). *The United Nations and Rwanda, 1993–1996*. United Nations Blue Book Series, vol. X. New York: United Nations.

Verwey, Wil D. (1986). 'Humanitarian Intervention', in Antonio Cassese (ed.), *The Current Legal Regulation of the Use of Force*, Dordrecht: Martinus Nijhoff. 57–78.

Vincent, R. J. (1974). *Nonintervention and International Order*. Princeton: Princeton University Press.

Von Mangoldt, Hans and Rittberger, Volker (eds.) (1997). *The United Nations System and its Predecessors*, vol. I, *The United Nations System*. Oxford: Oxford University Press.

Waldron, Jeremy (1981). 'A Right to Do Wrong'. *Ethics*, 92/1: 21–39.

Walzer, Michael (1983). *Spheres of Justice: A Defense of Pluralism and Equality*. New York: Basic Books.

—— (1995). 'The Politics of Rescue'. *Dissent*, 42/1: 35–41.

—— (2000). *Just and Unjust Wars: A Moral Argument with Historical Illustrations*, 3rd edn. New York: Basic Books.

—— (2002). 'Arguing for Humanitarian Intervention', in Nicolaus Mills and Kira Brunner (eds.). *The New Killing Fields: Massacre and the Politics of Intervention*, New York: Basic Books, 19–35.

Welsh, Jennifer M. (1995). *Edmund Burke and International Relations*. New York: St. Martin's Press.

—— (2004). 'Authorising Humanitarian Intervention', in Richard Price and Mark Zacher (eds.). *The United Nations and Global Security*. Basingstoke: Palgrave.

Wendt, Alexander (1999). *Social Theory of International Politics*. Cambridge: Cambridge University Press.

Wheeler, Nicholas J. (2000). *Saving Strangers: Humanitarian Intervention in International Society*. Oxford: Oxford University Press.

—— 'Humanitarian Intervention after September 11', in Anthony Lang (ed.), *Humanitarian Intervention* (2003).

Wight, Martin (1966). 'Western Values in International Relations', in Martin Wight and Herbert Butterfield (eds.), *Diplomatic Investigations: Essays in the Theory of International Politics*. Cambridge, MA: Harvard University Press, 89–131.

Wippman, David (2000). 'Can an International Criminal Court Prevent and Punish Genocide?', in Neal Riemer (ed.), *Protection Against Genocide: Mission Impossible?* London: Praeger, 85–104.

Woodward, Llewellyn (1971). *British Foreign Policy in Second World War*, vol. II, London: HMSO.

Zhang, Yunling (2000). 'China: Whither the World Order after Kosovo?', in Albrecht Schnabel and Ramesh Thakur (eds.) 117–27.

Zartman, I. William (1966). *International Politics in the New Africa*. Englewood Cliffs: Prentice Hall Inc.

Index

Note: Bold page numbers indicate chapters